HIGH PERFORMANCE LEADERSHIP

HIGH PERFORMANCE LEADERSHIP

Creating, Leading and Living in a High Performance World

GRAHAM WINTER

John Wiley & Sons (Asia) Pte Ltd

This publication is designed to provide accurate and authoritative information in regard to the subject matter covered. It is sold with the understanding that the Publisher is not engaged in rendering professional services. If professional advice or other expert assistance is required, the services of a competent professional person should be sought.

Other Wiley Editorial Offices

John Wiley & Sons, Inc., 605 Third Avenue, New York, NY 10158-0012, USA
John Wiley & Sons Ltd, Baffins Lane, Chichester, West Sussex PO19 1UD, England
John Wiley & Sons (Canada) Ltd, 22 Worcester Road, Rexdale, Ontario M9W 1L1, Canada
John Wiley & Sons Australia Ltd, 33 Park Road (PO Box 1226), Milton, Queensland 4046, Australia
Wiley-VCH, Pappelallee 3, 69469 Weinheim, Germany

Library of Congress Cataloging-in-Publication Data:

ISBN 0-470-82081-0

Typeset in 11/14 point, Plantin by Linographic Services Pte Ltd
Printed in Singapore by Saik Wah Press Ltd
10 9 8 7 6 5 4 3 2 1

To my wife, Carol,
and sons, Mark and Ben

CONTENTS

ACKNOWLEDGMENTS

I could not have written this book without the guidance, help and support of many people who shared their wisdom and energy.

A very special thanks to Sara Taylor my indispensable assistant, not just for her countless hours of work on the manuscript but also her intelligence and insights that helped and challenged me to make this a more powerful book. Also, to Tim Dansie for his invaluable assistance in reviewing the drafts, and Kate Morefield for the research that got the whole project off to a great start.

Veronica White has been a persistent supporter of the whole concept of High Performance Leadership and I thank her along with her PwC Consulting colleagues Grace Chopard, Kevin McCaffrey, Christina Kirk and Chris Horsley for their support and counsel, and for kindly providing me the access to interviews from the PwC Consulting Executive Survey.

The team at Digi Artists have been a wonderful resource for my business, Strategize, with their work on the diagrams and in bringing the High Performance Leadership Programme to life. It has also been great to have advisors like Frank Prez and Debra Hassen who I can rely on for their counsel.

A book needs real events and experiences to bring it to life and I have been very fortunate in the calibre of people who generously gave their time and wisdom. Many thanks to Dr Bill Griggs for sharing his valuable and limited time to introduce me to the high performance world of emergency medicine; Duncan Chessell for his very personal insights into the unique challenges of climbing Everest, and Stuart Eliis for revealing the leadership challenges of Special Air Services. I also appreciated the help of Craig Kelly, Kate Renshaw and Nicole Beatson of Elite Sports Properties and their clients Shane Gould and Louise Sauvage whose insights added significantly to the book.

In the corporate world, Mike Heard, Jon Westover and John Cerini gave me the opportunity to work with the organizations that they lead and contributed their personal insights into making Australian businesses world class. I am also very grateful to each of the contributors who kindly agreed to interviews and/or to providing a testimonial: Darren Williams, James Strong, Allan

Moss, Professor Bill Ford, Catherine Livingstone, Christine Charles, Doug Stace, Gordon Cairns, Greg Bourne, Karl Sundstrom, Margaret Hansford, Mick Keelty, Philip Chambers, Shane Garland, Sue Vardon, Craig McLatchey, Herb Elliott Simon Edwards, Andrea Galloway and Teoh Eng Hong.

It has been my good fortune to find a publisher as professional as Wiley, and I thank the crew at the Singapore office, particularly Nick Wallwork, Malar Manoharan, Pauline Pek, John Owen, Chris Newson and Adeline Lim for their absolute professionalism at every stage of the process.

A particular thanks to Leigh Hodges, for his belief in High Performance Leadership and to Teoh Siew Hong and D'Arcy Walsh, for their persistence and vision that an Aussie could and should be writing this book. I am also grateful to Ron Steiner, for always being at the other end of the phone to tell me to think bigger and to Adrian Porter for giving me the chance to be here.

On a more personal level, to Carol, Mark and Ben: thank you so much for the love and support that encourages me to be myself, and to my parents, Bill and Muriel Winter who gave me the opportunities that took me into the world of high performance.

Finally, to my many clients and colleagues over the years, I hope that you see some of yourself amongst the ideas, experiences and learnings in this book. Thank you for your support and trust.

PREFACE

Introducing High-Performance Leadership

We live in a high-performance world and I have been very fortunate to work at close hand with many people who exemplify the qualities that are needed to succeed in these conditions.

In *High-Performance Leadership* you will find their wisdom and experiences, interwoven with a practical strategy for you as a leader to take yourself and your organization to a higher level in the fast, fluid and ever-changing business world of the 21st century.

That practical strategy — embodied in the High Performance Leadership Programme on which the book is based — has been designed and implemented successfully in numerous private- and public-sector organizations. Feedback reinforces that it is a practical approach, easy to apply across an organization and yet substantial enough to deal with the complexity of organizational life.

Using an array of examples of high-performance organizations from business, Olympic sport, special military forces, the arts, medical retrieval services and an Everest expedition, you will find that *High-Performance Leadership* comes to life in a mix of tools, techniques, models and ideas that you can immediately apply to your business.

High-Performance Leadership is about creating agile, adaptable and responsive organizations. Importantly, it is written and illustrated in a style that will make as much sense to your operational staff as to the CEO.

This means you will be able to implement the principles and practices in a single team or right across a large organization.

High-Performance Leadership introduces an array of concepts such as "Strategic Leaders", "High Performance Program", "performance models" and "Business Athletes". We explore the roles of Strategic Leaders/Coaches within the high-performance environment and guide you through the process of building the Performance Model for your own high-performance program (unit, team, organization). We also take a look at a number of projects that we have used successfully in organizations that have adopted the High Performance Leadership Programme as a development strategy.

I should emphasize that this is not an academic leadership approach or a panacea for all the business challenges of the 21st century. Neither is it one of those over-simplistic books that translate sports analogies into business.

High-Performance Leadership is outlined over four sections.

The Global Game

Section One begins with the performance challenges of the 21st century business world. For Performance Leaders this is *the* game and it truly is a "global game" in which speed, agility and world-class standards are crucial to success.

This global game challenges all leaders to create and sustain a high-performance culture in which people manage multiple stakeholders, respond to rapid shifts in markets and technologies, and still maintain service and product quality at the highest levels. And it is this global game for which *High-Performance Leadership* has been designed.

In this section you will learn from the performance strategies and experiences of one of the world's top Olympic teams and learn how these same strategies can be creatively applied in all high-performance environments.

You are a Business Athlete

In Section Two, you will be challenged to think of yourself as a Business Athlete and to follow the same principles of performance mastery as the Olympic athlete. You will hone your skills in areas that are essential to playing the global game of business, including building personal relationships, managing your energy, defining a clear direction and turning yourself into a high-performance brand.

By better understanding the psychology of your own performance and developing these skills, you will also be far better equipped to lead and coach others in the global game of business.

Performance Leadership: A Competitive Advantage

Competitive and performance advantage is underpinned by capabilities and there are few capabilities that are more difficult to copy than performance leadership. In Section Three, you will be challenged and coached in the three core roles of the Performance Leader:

- Strategic Leadership
- Performance Coaching
- Development Coaching.

Strategic Leaders create the umbrella strategy and culture, while Development Coaches protect and build the capabilities of the organization and Performance Coaches create the environment in which people deliver exceptional results. Each of these roles is essential to creating and sustaining agility and capability in high-performance environments.

Designing your High Performance Leadership Model

All Olympic coaches have their own performance model which acts like a template in which they build their program. In Section Four, you build your own Performance Model while learning from the experiences of Performance Leaders in fields of business, Olympic sport, special forces and beyond.

It is this dynamic Performance Model, supported by your personal performance and coaching skills, that is High-Performance Leadership.

Each chapter in this section deals with one element of the Performance Model and shares many of the projects and activities that are part of the High Performance Leadership Programmes that have been implemented in organizations around the world.

Link the book and website

The global game changes so fast that it is essential to continually upgrade the materials that form the High Performance Leadership Programme. Accordingly, we invite you to visit the accompanying website — www.highperformanceleadership.biz — to discuss implementation issues, to see programs that are available and share and update your knowledge.

I hope you enjoy the book and find it an essential companion in your journey through the global game of business.

FOREWORD

The journey of a thousand miles begins with a single step
– Confucius

Embarking on a journey invites innovations and challenges. We emerge stronger, wiser and enriched by the experience.

As in life, so too in business. Organizations worldwide are operating in an environment of increasing volatility. High Performance Companies today require High Performance Leadership more than ever before to bring the organization along on the journey.

The key to an organization's success will be the development of a culture that nurtures leadership at all levels. The leaders who succeed will be passionate about their undertaking. They will be able to win the hearts and minds of their people, and by their actions, inspire their fellow travelers.

Successful leadership will demand the ability to focus, not only on that first step, but also on the destination. It is about extracting performance in the short term while investing in the long-term viability of the organization. Results to shareholders and a long-term response to future stakeholders.

A company can take many paths to success. High organizational performance in the future will require agility - the ongoing flexibility of business strategies and the alignment of systems, technology and culture to enable a timely response to opportunities or threats. Yet, underpinning that agility, there must also be discipline, structure, processes and boundaries to keep everyone moving in the same direction.

Consistent high performance is the sum of the actions of a large number of individuals.

To drive performance, organizations must be purposeful about leadership. This book provides a pragmatic framework for nurturing High Performance Leaders.

Investment in flexible and resilient leaders will create the foundations for both present and future peak performance. High Performance Cultures will come to the fore, particularly in the times of volatility.

High Performance Leaders build cultures that can maintain the forward momentum. Strong cultures have demonstrable congruence between values, actions and results.

There is no silver bullet.

High Performance Leadership is about having the speed and the agility to act quickly, but with a very sound foundation of operational excellence.

Grace Chopard
Partner
Asia-Pacific Strategic Change Leader
PwC Consulting
6 September 2002

Section One

A High-Performance World

1

The Global Game

To paraphrase Richard Bach in *Illusions*, "What the caterpillar sees as the end, the butterfly sees as the beginning."[1]

An end and a beginning. Transformation.

As with the caterpillar, so with the world of business. The game has transformed itself, leaving behind the slow and predictable game of last century.

Driven by a potent mix of communications technology, consumerism, and social and political change, this is a totally different game: a global game of speed, opportunities, risks, innovation and relentless, often unpredictable, change. And not just in business, but in education, sport, the arts, science and medicine: in every area of human endeavor.

Personal and market niches have disappeared overnight, while industries, organizations, technologies, relationships and careers have all changed and are changing again. It is an environment in which we can take very little for granted, apart from the need to be agile, alert and high-performing.

As Richard Bach reminds us, we can see this as an end or a beginning.

If we see it as a beginning, then we do what successful organisms have done throughout the history of the planet: evolve and adapt to the changing conditions and, where possible, adapt the conditions to suit ourselves. If we see it as an end, then we resist. There may be niches where we can resist for some time but High-Performance Leadership is about engaging with the complexity and challenges of the global game. It is about creating an agile, high-performance outfit (team, unit, organization) that thrives in these conditions.

The caterpillar is dying. We must become the butterfly.

THE PERFORMANCE ENVIRONMENT

This is a book about performance and leadership, specifically about achieving high performance in business and the related fields of government, science, education and sport. To begin, we must therefore address the conditions in which the performance is to occur.

In other words, if you are going to hike across a mountain range, it would be foolish not to study the landscape; to understand the mountains, the valleys, the streams, the pathways and the plants and animals. In particular, you want to know about the attractions and the dangers, how the conditions might change over the day and night and how other hikers have tackled these, or similar, challenges.

In many ways, the global game of business is like a dynamic, volatile landscape of mountains and valleys that is being constantly reshaped by the business equivalents of earthquakes, volcanoes and erosion. It presents the challenge to create and sustain organizations that have the agility to adapt to the changing conditions and the power to shape some of the landscape to suit themselves. This has always been the way in performance environments.

The three "S's" of the performance environment

In the pre-global game, we had neat boundaries between countries and industries and the luxury of focusing on one major strategy for some time. Between 1984 and the present day, three things changed: **scale**, **speed** and **standards**. Through the challenges that they present, each has totally reshaped the performance landscape.

Scale: From national to global

The basic unit of landscape in the pre-global game was the "nation". Even the biggest corporations operated differently from one country to another, and the restrictions on flows of capital and trade ensured that performance was largely between players in a given country. The forces of democracy, trade deregulation and technology changed all that during the 1990s; now, the basic landscape unit is "global" and that means you are playing in a global game amongst the mega-merged organizations such as Exxon and Mobil, and BHP-Billiton, and small home-based enterprises with the reach of a multinational corporation.

Speed: From steady to fast

Have you noticed how things have become compressed? "Business at the speed of thought," as Bill Gates described it.[2] Organizations that once were designed for control and predictability are now being challenged to design and implement new strategies and technologies at literally the speed of light. Agility and responsiveness are the new capabilities of business because they deliver speed.

In a recent PricewaterhouseCoopers (PwC) Consulting Executive Survey,[3] Professor Bill Ford remarked, "In 1991, I asked a group of executives from a traditional finance company, how long it was taking them to match their competitors' product. The answer was — seven years. Now the response needs to be in weeks or even days."

Standards: From local to world-class

You don't have to go to Paris to buy Paris-quality anymore. Consumers expect and receive world-class service and products wherever they live. This combination of intense competition and customer demand ensures that, like elite athletes, we have to raise the bar and continue to excite and inspire ourselves and others to leap ever higher. "We have to measure ourselves globally and be genuinely world's best," says Mike Heard, CEO of Codan, an Australian-based designer and supplier of state-of-the-art radio communications and microwave telecommunications equipment.[4]

Figure 1.1 summarizes the changes in scale, speed and standards from the pre-global to the global game and some of the impacts they have had on organizations.

FIGURE 1.1 Changes in the performance landscape

Element	Pre-global game	Global game	Impact on organizations
Scale	Nation-based, with limited reach	Global reach	Increased competition
Speed	Steady and linear	Rapid and in many directions	Reduced timelines for all activities
Standards	National standard	World class	Everyone must have a world-class value-proposition

Leadership: More than a position on the landscape

Like most of your peers, you probably have little time left in your week to propose working harder or longer as an option. You face pressures and demands from business, from family and community and from your own personal needs and aspirations. These pressures will not subside and will, more likely, increase.

There is plenty written about leadership practices and tools for the global game. You've probably read *Harvard Business Review* and *Fast Company*, looked for gems from Covey,[5] Kotter[6] and Senge[7] and perhaps attended more leadership and team-building courses than you care to count. But reflect for a moment. Have you got a really practical Performance Model that can guide everyone in your organization to sustain performance in this complex performance landscape? And what about Performance Leadership? Can anyone in your outfit be a Performance Leader, or is leadership restricted to the executive table?

The global game demands Performance Leadership everywhere in organizations. It is not and cannot be limited to position or to the notion of career.

If you see yourself as a Performance Leader only when your business card says so, then you are blind to how your daily actions shape and influence the people with whom you interact. We are all leaders in so many different ways — of our families, professions, organizations, teams, communities and nations.

Individually and collectively we shape the world in which we live. Just as Nelson Mandela influenced a nation from a prison cell, so can each of us make a difference in our world, no matter where we fit into some organizational hierarchy or matrix.

You are very powerful. You lead. And yet there are few resources that speak to you as a Performance Leader and not just to your position. This book starts that dialogue, and I hope the models, strategies and tools presented here can help you to convert others to the cause of High-Performance Leadership.

WHAT IS RESHAPING THE PERFORMANCE LANDSCAPE?

Globalization, technology and social change continue to transform the business landscape. They are the drivers of change and they shape the agenda for Performance Leaders across the world.

Before moving on to explain the principles and strategies of High Performance Leadership, I must highlight a few points about each that are relevant to our purpose. Please scan these points before moving on to the next chapter.

FIGURE 1.2 Three forces that are reshaping the business landscape

THE GLOBALIZATION OF BUSINESS

Globalization is not new (witness colonization by England, Spain and others in centuries past) but the last three decades of the 20th-century gave birth to a new, more dynamic form that reshaped and redefined business and personal lives.

It began with the export pushes by Asian countries in the 1980s but really took off from the early 1990s, when governments reduced or removed many of the barriers to trade and opened their markets and state-run institutions to competitors and investors from all over the world. More recently, we have seen the mega-mergers (Daimler-Chrysler, for example) that continue to reduce the number of key players in industries as diverse as telecommunications, accounting and automotive. Internet and related technologies have further accelerated the rate of change and they continue to drive efficiencies in value chains (with the promise of much more to come).

The terrorist attacks of September 11, 2001 and the ensuing battles perhaps pushed globalization back towards a sort of nationalism, but the genie is out of the bottle and no amount of protectionism from the U.S. or anyone else is going to reverse the trend.

Globalization means that your business now competes with other businesses from all over the world. The performance landscape is the world and few of the old walls and fences have survived.

It is this factor more than any other that drives the frantic search for higher levels of performance. Customers no longer have one choice or a handful of choices: they are literally bombarded by global marketers with one aim in mind: to position their brand as a winner.

While your local grocery store is under siege from the boardrooms of multinationals, the global businesses themselves face possible extinction from virtual competitors with user-friendly websites and massive warehouses. For example, Evans and Wurster[8] point to the difference between Barnes and Noble bookstores, which carry an average inventory of 200,000 titles, and Amazon.com with its 4.5 million volumes. Located on millions of computer screens worldwide, Amazon.com gives people the power to navigate through a virtual bookstore without the company having to carry the inventory at the same place as customers navigate. It is a different paradigm and one that challenges traditional businesses to adapt and evolve, or die.

Competition breeds competition and no one, not even governments, is immune. And that is why we must question our paradigms, and challenge and change our strategies and operations in ways that we could not have envisaged just a few years ago.

Old paradigms are risky

In all of this there are risks and opportunities. Joel Barker[9] warned us that new paradigms put the people who practice the old paradigms at risk. And as the lifespan of our paradigms continues to shrink, corporations cannibalize their own operations and products in search of new and better ways. They outsource, right-size, refocus, repackage, merge, de-merge and do whatever is needed to find a profitable niche.

As with products, so with leadership practices. Traditional leadership practices ("male as boss", "command and control") have a limited lifespan in this era of globalization. They suit neither the complexity of the game nor the aspirations of people.

If old paradigms are risky then so are new ones. With risk comes reward and one of the characteristics of high-performance environments is that the separation of rewards increases. Whether changing organization design, making a career change, launching a totally new product or forming an alliance with a competitor, you can expect to win or lose — big.

Some 10 or 20 years ago, the "strategic-planning paradigm" was pretty straightforward. Basically you wrote the plan, then put it in the drawer and led (or, rather, "managed") the business along reasonably predictable lines. Contrast that to the Unilever view of globalization given by its chairman, Niall Fitzgerald: "The more we learn, the clearer it becomes that there are no rules, no magic bullets, no one-size-fits-all templates. The key thing is flexibility and adaptability."[10]

The new paradigm must allow for new, aggressive and unforeseen competitors, a leaner and more demanding workforce of employees, contractors and partners, multiple stakeholders and new technologies that offer (or threaten) to totally transform your businesses.

No one really knows where globalization will lead or even if it will collapse as governments begin to erect new barriers. Nevertheless, it challenges us to think and act outside the paradigms of our current industries and professions, even though those very industries and professions trained us to work and stay within the defined boundaries.

Of course, there are plenty of books, magazines and websites that happily encourage you to discard the old paradigm. Unfortunately, there aren't many that give you a new one! And when you know that the old paradigm has become obsolete, and not been replaced, you get stuck in a no-decision, no-action situation that is very dangerous in a fast-moving high-performance environment.

High-Performance Leadership is a paradigm that helps leaders to make sense of performance environments. It offers strategies for fast planning, capturing knowledge on the run, creating agile performance units and freeing up the potential of people. It can guide you and your colleagues to move beyond the pre-global game practices and to deal with the uncertainty that comes when your existing paradigms have become obsolete.

THE POWER OF TECHNOLOGY

Hand in hand with globalization has come the explosion in information processing and communication technologies that have reshaped the business landscape. Of all these technologies, it is the Internet that Harvard Business School Professor Clayton Christensen aptly describes as a "disruptive technology".[11]

The Internet has transformed the power of individuals and the dynamics of organizations and markets. It has dramatically changed the three "S's" by creating immediate global scale (reach) at what has become known as *net speed* and, in doing so, changed the standards that markets expect for time and location. As reported in the PwC book *Wisdom of the CEO*,[12] "The Internet makes the concept of time and place more or less meaningless for trading goods and services".

While most of us started by sending e-mails and building websites, most organizations now use the Internet to bring their staff, suppliers, partners and customers together. When giants like Ford and General Motors put their multi-billion-dollar purchasing operations on-line to create a virtual marketplace that analysts speculate might be worth more than the parent company, you know it's a whole new game.

The Internet has already changed our world and there are undoubtedly transformations to come in all manner of technologies. Thierry Breton, chairman and CEO of Thomson multimedia, one of the world's five largest consumer-electronics manufacturers, suggests that these changes "call for strengthened management" and require that "quick response is a strategic imperative".[13]

Know your game

Organizations that aspire to be high performing must stay in tune with technologies developed inside and outside their own industry because the speed and quantum of technology change is genuinely transformational. As we will discuss in Section Four, some build a Performance Model that equips them as fast *adapters*, while others aim to be *shapers* of the game. A prime example of the latter is EMC Corporation, a world leader in intelligent enterprise-storage systems, which has a philosophy described by CEO Michael Ruettgers as "Disrupt or be disrupted".[14]

Whether you plan to be a fast adapter, a shaper or both, it is essential that you understand the global game and that means knowing the difference between what James Carse[15] has described as "finite" and "infinite games". Finite games have clear rules and boundaries, known competitors, a well-defined playing field and the main objective is winning. Infinite games have no timelines, few, if any, rules or boundaries and survival is more important than winning single events. The global game has elements of both but, clearly, there has been a shift towards the infinite and in those conditions agility, alliances and acceleration replace stability, self-interest and sluggishness.

Most experts believe that the rate of global change is going to accelerate further over the next decade, which suggests that the real technological boom isn't here yet. In product life-cycle terms, this is probably just the initial uptake of a new product or technology, which precedes the really big wave of mass markets. For example, the uptake of computing and access to the Internet amongst the general population is a number of years from peaking, even in the U.S., Europe, Australia and other technology leaders.

Imagine what is going to happen to your business when the average consumer is on-line, confident with the security of transactions and facing a massive range of choices. Advanced Internet applications that act like brokers search through the Internet and bring them products, services and information tailored to their unique needs. The consumer as leader; corporate leaders at every level responsible for meeting those needs. Now that's a revolution!

FIGURE 1.3   Moving towards an infinite game

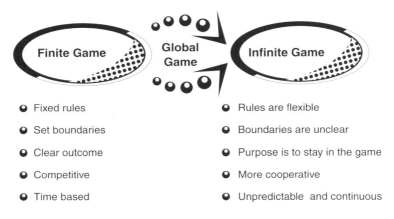

● Fixed rules	● Rules are flexible
● Set boundaries	● Boundaries are unclear
● Clear outcome	● Purpose is to stay in the game
● Competitive	● More cooperative
● Time based	● Unpredictable and continuous

Rarely, except in war, have leaders seen their organizations so at risk. It is a call to action for organizations to find, develop and retain Performance Leaders who can create the adaptable and responsive teams and organizations that thrive in this high-performance environment.

Capture the value of new technologies

Capturing the advantages of new technologies and turning them into real performance and real value is a core responsibility of all leaders, and yet the implementation of new technologies has been notoriously poor in delivering the promised results. This capability for rapid and effective strategy execution is fundamental to High-Performance Leadership.

In Chapters 15 and 18 we look at how the skills of the traditional "Boss" actually slow down the process of executing new strategies. The new Performance Leaders are much less like the Boss and more like Olympic coaches who create and foster a performance culture that makes strategy execution a winning feature of their program.

SOCIAL CHANGE

Woven amongst the forces of globalization and technology is a new, more complex dynamic between organizations and their customers, workforce and community. Power and information no longer reside just with institutions and, increasingly, the success of your organization will depend on your ability to form relationships with stakeholders, to understand their needs and to deliver in a way that adds value to all.

The new customer

Every client of our consulting business tells me that their customers are becoming more demanding and harder to satisfy. Is this your experience?

The global game is definitely changing behavior patterns so that 21st-century customers expect and demand more value; define that value in a more personal way; and, increasingly, research and buy on-line.

The expectations and behavior of customers are changing just through the sheer choice of products and services available in the global marketplace. We drive through to collect food, bank on-line and get home delivery, so it is not surprising that we walk out of a shop that makes us queue for five minutes. Researching on-line lets us find lower prices for books, computers and accommodation without the hassle of driving, parking and haggling. Cost comparison is now much easier, which makes it more difficult for businesses to set a high margin, or even to keep people loyal to their brand.

We define value in far more personal terms and even get offended when mass marketers trample over our personal space trying to sell us one-size-fits-all solutions. As consumers, we have come to expect and demand the best quality, lowest price and instant availability.

The Performance Leadership challenge is to get these three elements in synch with what your customers perceive as *value*, which, as Karl Sundstrom of Ericsson asserts, is about "having a winning culture, relationship skills and the right solution for the customer".[16] Getting a culture that consistently provides those solutions is central to High-Performance Leadership.

FIGURE 1.4   Demands of the global customer

The new workforce

Performance Leaders across business, sport, the arts, science and beyond all know that attracting and keeping core talent is one of the keys to competitive advantage

Traditional 20th-century organizations offered employees a parent–child relationship in which the organization (parent) provided security in return for the loyalty and compliance of the employee (child). It was an unstated emotional relationship: a form of co-dependency that wasn't necessarily good or bad but its days are all but finished.

Global-game organizations reward performance not tenure. They expect mobility and know that the best way to attract high-performing people is to be a high-performing organization.

They seek a diversity that strengthens them. They can handle the values of Generation X, of working mothers and fathers who want a lifestyle. They know that their culture has to attract people from the total pool of talent if they are to survive and prosper.

The new stakeholders

The days of serving just a single stakeholder, such as the shareholder, are coming to an end as organizations become more transparent. This infinite and complex global game demands that you manage the expectations of your multiple stakeholders, including staff, shareholders, suppliers, customers, the environment and the communities in which you operate. Delivering profits through destroying the environment or community is not an option, so you need the skills to build relationships with your stakeholders and, ultimately, to add value to the total system.

The New Powerbrokers

No commentary on the global game would be complete without arguably the most potent social force that impacts on business and our daily lives: the media.

A key effect of globalization has been the fall in the power of governments, but there is no doubt that it has been aided and, one might say, led by the media. Noted author and journalist Susan Mitchell, in reviewing a book by Susan Faludi,[17] agreed that "power has shifted from parliaments to those who own the media", as "by owning the public airwaves you are able to influence public opinion".[18]

You only need to watch the reactions of politicians to being excluded from interviews on the top-rating current affairs and talkback programs to gauge the impact of the media.

The media has the power to not just influence business performance but to define what it means. It can stir up shareholders, mobilize customers, spook the government and make or break any business on which it sets its sights. Evidence that this is so came when a small but rapidly growing home-mortgage provider featured recently on a top-rating Australian TV current affairs program. The story was positive and almost immediately the business was swamped with inquiries.

The media presents a dilemma. It does not always speak the truth but people believe it. You must factor the media into your thinking and planning both as a positive source that can boost performance but also as a potential threat to survival.

Who knows, perhaps tomorrow the media will expose your industry for its taxation practices, or parade a disgruntled customer all over the country. Alternatively, a competitor might create a joint venture with a media outlet and use the linkage to build a public profile, or collapse yours.

PERFORM OR PERISH

Whether you see the forces described in this chapter as positive, neutral, negative or all of these, there is no doubt that we are in a phase of massive transformation of markets, industries and societies.

It is a time when every organization needs a strategy to build the resilience and agility that the global game demands. That strategy is High-Performance Leadership and it begins in the next chapter.

2

A Strategy for the Global Game

The previous chapter demonstrated that the global game is a volatile performance environment in which opportunities and risks have been accelerated and expanded by the forces of globalization, technology and social change. This is a complex game that challenges leaders to think on a scale beyond geographic and industrial boundaries and to forge a new, more agile style of organization that suits the dynamic environment.

High-Performance Leadership is designed to equip you with the models, tools and techniques to create and sustain that style of organization under global-game conditions. It focuses particularly on creating what I call a "performance culture" and addresses the performance questions that leaders right across the world are asking. How, for example, do we ...

- ... accelerate and improve our strategy design and execution?
- ... create agile, fast, high-performing teams?
- ... foster a consistent performance ethic amongst everyone?
- ... make in-the-field learning and adaptation our advantage?
- ... build more-valuable networks and alliances?
- ... attract, grow and keep talented people?
- ... develop performance leadership in every part of the organization?

Ultimately these questions all lead towards one fundamental question: "How can we create and sustain a high-performance organization?"

To show you how the High Performance Leadership Programme addresses this core question, let me explain the foundations of the strategy that began with my involvement in one of the world's high-performance systems (the Australian Olympic sport system) and which subsequently has been tested and refined in many business organizations and through inputs from other high-performance programs and systems, including medical retrieval, an Everest expedition and special military forces. I will begin with the Olympic sport system because this vividly illustrates the principles that underpin High-Performance Leadership.

FOUNDATIONS OF THE HIGH-PERFORMANCE LEADERSHIP STRATEGY

Australia is a small country by world standards, with a total population of just 20 million people spread across a vast landscape, thousands of kilometers away from the U.S., Europe and Central Asia.

In the 1950s, the country was a world sporting power, finishing in the top five at the Melbourne Olympics (35 medals, including 13 gold) and being a dominant player in non-Olympic sports such as tennis, golf and cricket. The reasons for the dominance included ready access to sporting facilities, a climate conducive to sporting activity, a good and increasing standard of living and a national passion for sport in any form. Also, Australia did not face the same period of rebuilding infrastructure that challenged Europe and Asia following the Second World War.

Australia grew accustomed to its sons and daughters winning in the pool, on the track and in just about any sporting field. However, during the 20 years following the 1956 Melbourne Olympics, Australia's competitive position gradually declined before finally bottoming out in 1976, when the Australian team returned from the Montreal Olympics without a gold medal for the first time since the Berlin Games of 1936 and finished a distant 32nd on the medal count.

FIGURE 2.1 Australian Olympic Medals 1956–1976 (total of gold, silver, bronze)

Melbourne 1956	Rome 1960	Tokyo 1964	Mexico 1968	Munich 1972	Montreal 1976
35	22	18	17	17	5

None of the factors contributing to Australia's dominance in the previous era had changed. In fact, sporting facilities had improved, standards of living had continued to rise and, of course, nothing had altered the climate.

What had changed was the behavior of the rest of the world, and the European nations in particular. In simple business terms, Australia's competitive advantage was in areas that were not sustainable. While the country relied on talent and basic training, the leading nations started to take a scientific and strategic approach to sport. They saw performance opportunities, developed capabilities and capitalized on them.

Australia reacted quickly and strongly after Montreal, creating a sport system that, by 1996, had put Australia back in the top ten in the world (41 medals, nine gold) and, at the 2000 Sydney Olympics, in fourth place on the medal tally behind only U.S., Russia and China. In addition, Australia also boasted world champions in rugby, golf, cricket, netball and surfing.

Figure 2.2 shows the top six Olympic nations at the Sydney Games, including their approximate populations.

FIGURE 2.2 Ranking of nations by total medals at Sydney Olympic Games

Medal ranking	Nation	Total medals	Approx population (millions)
1	United States	97	278
2	Russia	88	145
3	China	59	1,200
4	**Australia**	**58**	**19**
5	Germany	57	83
6	France	38	59

The Australian Olympic sport system is, I believe, one of the great high-performance systems in the world. Per capita, this system produces the greatest results in the world, and it is this system and the turnaround principles that sit behind it that were the inspiration and the framework for High-Performance Leadership.

The Olympic sport system provides a visible, dynamic example of how to create an environment in which high-performing individuals, teams and organizations can thrive, grow and succeed in a global game. As you will see later, many of the principles also hold true in other high-performance programs in business, military special forces, the arts, medical retrieval and Everest expeditions.

START AT THE STRATEGIC END

Most attempts to apply sporting metaphors and approaches to business have been rather shallow and have not addressed the strategic and performance systems, focusing instead on athletes' attitudes and behaviors.

This is useful and interesting but the mindsets and practices of athletes and their coaches are the *product* of the system(s) in which they operate; so to ignore this is tantamount to ignoring the culture of an organization when trying to understand the behavior of its people.

The factor that most shaped my thinking about the design of High-Performance Leadership was my initial business experience before becoming involved with elite sport. Whereas most Olympic team psychologists train and specialize in sports psychology, my training and early work experiences were in organizational psychology (with Coopers & Lybrand). In fact, I only got to enter the sports psychology field because of my own experience as a representative athlete.

The effect of this corporate training and experience was an interest in *how to build organizational systems and cultures* that produce top-level athletes. This is a different mindset from the discipline of sports psychology, which tends to focus heavily on the psychology of the athlete.

Through working with PricewaterhouseCoopers and clients of my own business, I soon came to realize that there were huge benefits in synthesizing a very practical and powerful performance strategy for business that used the framework of the sport system, and combined it with organizational development and complexity principles.

I believed that the latter was important to help leaders to understand the link between the chaos and complexity of high-performance environments. It is a view that has been shared by many of the CEOs with whom I have worked. One of these was Christine Charles who, while leading a 25,000-person human-services organization, commented that "We need leaders and a culture that understands and can deal with complexity".[1]

THREE TIERS

The Australian sporting system is designed around three tiers:

- Strategic framework (total Australian sport system). This is the umbrella ideology developed and applied through the peak bodies that are the architects and guardians of the strategic framework (Australian Olympic Committee, Australian Sports Commission, Confederation of Australian Sport).
- High-performance programs (individual sporting programs i.e. swimming, rowing etc). Each program has a Performance Model that is designed and operated by coaches and managers.
- High-performance athletes. This tier refers to the principles and practices of talented individual athletes and teams at training and in world-class competition.

THE STRATEGIC FRAMEWORK

The huge turnaround in the performance of Australian Olympic sport, and the continued success, is based on a strategic framework of six core principles. The application of these principles has evolved over time but the fundamentals continue to guide the architects of the strategic system. These principles are:

1. Maintain a vivid and understood imperative (mission)
2. Aim for excellence (by world standards)
3. Pick "winners" — go where there is capability and/or opportunity
4. Design a dynamic performance model in each unit (sport)
5. Support those units in the toughest performance environments
6. Reward only for performance and ideals.

The disciplined application of these principles has created one of the world's most resilient and adaptable performance systems, as measured by results, in the global game of Olympic competition. Importantly, these principles have also been embedded in the second tier of the system (the high-performance programs).

Let's now examine these principles in more detail and use them to guide us in designing a strategy for High-Performance Leadership in the global game of business. As you consider each principle, take a few moments to examine whether you are currently applying the principle in your outfit (unit, team, organization) and, if not, what the impact might be if you did so.

FIGURE 2.3   The three tiers of the Australian sport system

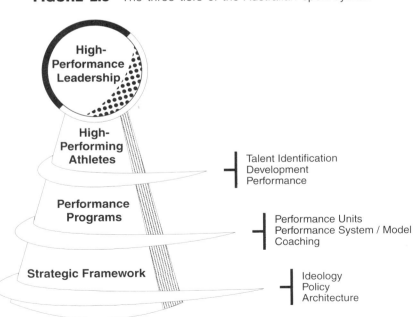

Principle One: Maintain a vivid and understood imperative (mission)

Australian sport has seen two vivid imperatives over the past 25 years. The first was the Montreal disaster. From the depth of that failure came the opportunity and appetite for new structures and processes that could establish a world-competitive system. We see the same impact of imperatives in the global game, as former Qantas CEO James Strong reflects, "The downturn in Asia did more to change staff attitudes in Qantas than anything else that we might have done in terms of cultural change".[2] Importantly, Montreal allowed all assumptions to be challenged: training processes, development programs, coaching styles, the use of sports science and organization design — nothing was sacred. Predictably, there was resistance and, inevitably, it came most from those who hankered for the halcyon days of the 1950s. They claimed that all that was needed was greater commitment to training by the athletes, but, fortunately, the architects of the new system understood that a new, intelligent performance system was needed.

FIGURE 2.4   Six umbrella principles of the Olympic sport system

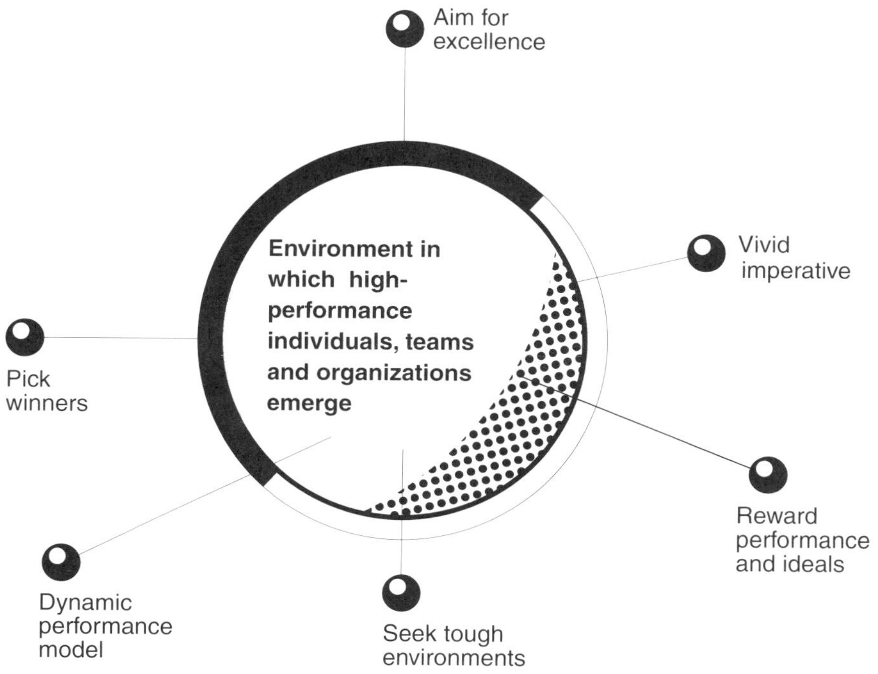

The second imperative was engineered by many of the architects of the system. This was the Sydney Olympic Games, which provided a major focal point and an imperative for Australia to showcase its capabilities, not just in staging the Games but in competition as well. Importantly, this imperative was shared not just by people inside the sporting community but also by other stakeholders, such as government, corporations and the general community. (This link between imperative and stakeholders is an important element in High-Performance Leadership: in other words, you usually have to convert more than just your close followers to the cause if it is going to be successful.)

I recall attending the Olympic Management briefing following the announcement of Sydney as the host of the 2000 Games. The speakers emphasized time and again that the success of the Games required two components: a well-staged event, and a top performance by the home nation. John Coates, President, Australian Olympic Committee and Chef de Mission 2000 Australian Olympic Team, linked the two in his message to athletes: "We are proud of this Team, and confident of the success of these Olympics."[3]

The importance of an imperative — whether it be unexpected, as in 1976, or engineered, as in 2000 — has been essential to mobilizing the resources needed to build and maintain the sports system. The challenge for Australia now is to find a third imperative.

An interesting aside: there are many who argue, and I am one, that the next imperative is not to go further in sport but, rather, to apply the principles of creating high-performing organizations to science and education — other niches where there are performance opportunities.

An imperative or cause or mission has long been understood as the key ingredient to creating high performance. Whether your imperative presents itself or it needs to be engineered, this is a central piece in the high-performance jigsaw.

Principle Two: Aim for excellence by world standards

The intention of the sport system was, and remains, unequivocal: to achieve excellence as measured by the highest standards.

For sports architects, that standard is medals at Olympic and World competition. The designers of the system knew that world sport is a global game, and while it is possible to aim for results in lower-level competition, such as the Commonwealth Games and regional competitions, these are false benchmarks that lead people to accept less than best.

Of course, sport has the advantage of Olympic Games and World Championships to give a very tangible performance standard. For other organizations, the challenge is also to aim for performance excellence and to define a standard by which that will be judged. That standard must be a part of the ideology and known to all in the system. As Alan Moss, CEO of the rapidly growing Macquarie Bank, advises, "If you've reached world's best practice you can be confident in taking your expertise off-shore".[4] In Macquarie Bank, the standard is world class: by what standard will your organization judge its performance?

Principle Three: Pick winners

The major focus of the Australian sport system in the early years was on seven sports (known derisively by those who were not included as the "super seven"). These were the sports (niches) in which the architects believed Australia had the potential to build a sustainable competitive position. Funds and resources were channelled in this direction. Not surprisingly, the vast majority of successes from Seoul, Barcelona, Atlanta and Sydney were in these sports, which included swimming, rowing, cycling, hockey and canoeing.

There is an extremely important principle here. That is, the decision was taken to pick and invest in winners based on potential capability to compete successfully at Olympic and World Championship standard.

Heading towards the Sydney Games, Australia continued its focus on the super seven but also used the leverage of the home Games to gain more government and corporate funding. This was directed, along with resources and expertise gathered from the super seven, towards the niche areas of women's and emerging sports. Once again the system architects "picked winners". Beach volleyball, women's hockey, women's water-polo, archery, sailing and women's *taekwondo* may not be mainstream sports but they were niches where results could be achieved. Gold medals in each of these sports rewarded the decision.

To put this in a business context, the "pick winners" concept means following the two criteria recommended by Dauphinais, Means and Price: "Participate in markets that offer high economic returns and/or in markets where the company can develop and sustain competitive advantages."[5]

FIGURE 2.5 Example of how Australia picked winners

High-return opportunities	Long-term competitive advantage
• *Taekwondo*	• Swimming
• Beach volleyball	• Rowing
• Women's water-polo	• Hockey
• Archery	• Canoeing
• Sailing	• Track cycling

Reflection: Where are the high-return opportunities and the areas of longer-term competitive advantage for your organization?

Principle Four: Design a dynamic Performance Model in each program

The architects (unlike senior leaders in many organizations) recognized that their expertise lay in putting together the umbrella strategy and environment, not in creating the high-performance sporting programs that were needed to achieve the overall mission. In each sport, something was needed to convert the broad strategy/ ideology into what worked for a particular sport. A common formula across sports would not work.

Accordingly, they recruited Strategic Leaders in each sport and gave them responsibility for building the Performance Model in that program. That model had to find, develop and capitalize on talent to achieve performance excellence at world standard while aligning itself with the guidelines of the major funding and support bodies.

An example of a Strategic Leader was Don Talbot, former head coach of Australian Swimming. Talbot rarely coached swimmers.

He built the Performance Model and coached the coaches in how to implement it. His success put Australia into the top two swimming nations, and included beating the U.S. at the 2001 World Championships.

Strategic Leaders were empowered to design their own Performance Models and to recruit coaches and support staff. However, the funding, program-evaluation and coach-development programs were coordinated at a central level, and then further refined over time in each sport. Coaching accreditation systems sorted out who could and could not coach, while athletes benefited from working with coaches who could develop their skills and lift their performance.

Principle Five: Support those units in the toughest performance environments

As the frequency of international competition increased and performance standards continued to rise, Australia had to deal with the disadvantage of distance from major competition sites. The risk was that the performance environment in Australia did not provide the challenges that athletes needed to inspire the development of physical, mental and technical skills. High performance is about adaptation and improvement and that requires interacting with the environment. As Tom Kelley of IDEO observes, "Whether it's art, science, technology or business, inspiration often comes from being close to the action".[6]

The strategy was simple: send squads of athletes overseas for extended periods of time, always looking for the best competition. This was particularly important for young athletes. It soon revealed those who couldn't cope at that level, and also showed the potential stars what was needed to be the best in the world.

This same strategy was applied to the 1996 Olympic team, when selection standards were actually lowered to ensure that the maximum number of younger athletes gained experience at an Olympics prior to Sydney. Performing in the tough environment reaped huge benefits because athletes prepared for Sydney knowing what to expect, rather than trying to visualize something that they had never done before.

The implication for organizations in this principle is that adaptation requires experience in various environments. By all means select niches where you can perform, but make sure that people learn and grow by exposure to different performance environments. This is supported by the study by McCall, Lombardo & Morrison from the Center for Creative Leadership which found that leaders attribute most of their success to experiences in the day-to-day business action.[7]

Principle Six: Reward only for performance and ideals

As you would expect, the sport system allocates funding and access to the best resources (including support personnel) based on performance excellence to agreed standards. In the mature sports, this is world-class standard (finals at World Championships and Olympics), while for developing sports it is a milestone along that pathway.

As in a natural ecosystem, those who adapt and/or evolve are the survivors and they get stronger, while those who have their opportunity and cannot perform face the consequences. High rewards and high consequences are a way of life in high-performance environments. Even the Olympics has left behind the world of amateurism because, as Olympic historian Harry Gordon writes, "It belonged to another age. Some moments of glory and glistening medals are not reward enough for a lifetime of dedication and discipline."[8]

Along with a strong focus on results, the Olympic ideals have also been used to shape Australian sport. In particular, the high level of funding received by the Sports Drug Agency is indicative of a commitment to producing results, but not at any cost. Teamwork is also a vital ingredient in the success of the Aussie team, as evidenced by the support of athletes for their teammates in other sports.

Combining a strong results-focus with a commitment to core values or principles is a common feature of high-performing organizations all over the world because, as Don Argus, former CEO of National Australia Bank (NAB), recounted of NAB's growth strategy, this provides "a powerful focused direction for all the employees".[9]

SUMMARIZING THE STRATEGIC FRAMEWORK (IDEOLOGY)

When it comes to high-performance sport, there is no country in the world that has been as successful on a per-capita basis as Australia. While some will argue that the country is obsessed with sport and spends too much money on it, we should remember that one of the criteria that defines high performance is shaping your environment. The sports architects have done this well: shaping the nature of government policy, securing major world sporting events and building the Australian Olympic Committee into a powerful corporation in its own right.

The ideology that is contained in the six principles has remained central to the *mission* since the 1980s.

Similarly, as I have developed, applied and evolved High Performance Leadership Programmes across business, government, sport and education, the six core principles have held true in diverse performance settings.

You will meet them again in later sections as they guide you to create your own High-Performance Program. Before that, though, we must explore the other two tiers of the system: the high-performance programs (each sport), and the mindset and practices of high-performance athletes.

HIGH-PERFORMANCE PROGRAMS

In high-performance environments, the organizational design that is emerging as highly effective at the operational level is what could be called a "High-Performance Program" (HPP). Examples of HPPs are the individual elite sports programs such as swimming and rowing, military squads and medical retrieval groups. We see them increasingly in business where they are the *building blocks* of design in most agile organizations. They can be as small as a single team, or made up of a number of teams or units. Essentially, they have a team focus and, as Katzenbach and Smith advise, they must be "the basic unit of performance for most organizations".[10]

It is also possible to consider the total system, such as the Australian sport system or a major corporation like IBM, as an HPP in its own right. As a leader, you will have a program for which you are responsible. Whether it is the whole organization, a division, a team or some other unit, the key is to develop this into a High-Performance Program.

There are four common elements in high-performance Olympic sport programs (and in HPPs in medicine, exploration and the military) that are directly relevant to developing a High-Performance Leadership strategy for business. These are:

- Performance Model
- Coaches implement and refine the Performance Model
- Support staff and processes
- Athlete-centricity.

These elements are shown in Figure 2.6 and explained below.

The Strategic Leader

As described earlier, one of the six core principles of the overall sport system was the appointment of a Strategic Leader to oversee the design and implementation of the program.

If you look at Australian Swimming, you will see a Performance Model that has been designed and shaped by Don Talbot in conjunction with his team of coaches and support staff. The two key elements here are the senior Strategic Leadership role (played

FIGURE 2.6   Four common elements in a High-Performance Program.

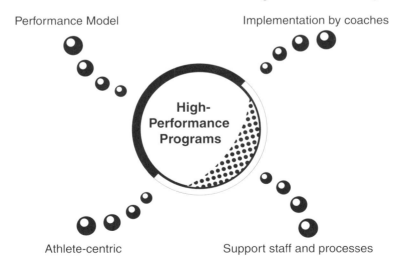

largely by Talbot) that focused strongly on securing future performance, and the notion of a Performance Model.

The concept and role of Strategic Leader challenges the common practice of business leaders, many of whom are heavily involved in the day-to-day activities of the business. Were that the case in Olympic sport, no one would be working on the model and refining it for the future. Sooner or later, performance would suffer.

In global-game conditions, it is essential that the leaders of HPPs work on future strategies — their interest must be sustainability and growth. If you lead an HPP, then one of your greatest responsibilities is to keep on developing a better Performance Model. Accordingly, I respectfully suggest that you and your colleagues take a major cut in pay if you are constantly operating at a micro level, unless the business is in a major state of turmoil and requires close attention for a short period of time.

If businesses are really going to capture the value of strategic leadership at the program level, and not just with the CEO, then the challenge is to find extra resources, or to re-prioritize so that all leaders spend time on building a better Performance Model.

The Performance Model

One of the key features of High-Performance Leadership is a Performance Model that you design and apply to your overall program (organization, division) and to the sub-programs (teams, units). All effective Performance Leaders have a basic model in mind and they work with their people to refine and implement it as the framework for their program.

A Performance Model includes elements such as strategic direction, goals, staffing, sourcing, measurement and learning, rewards and structures.

Creating a dynamic Performance Model is a core principle of High Performance Leadership and the whole of Section Four is devoted to guiding you through this process. To assist with this, it will provide insights from many High Performance Leadership Programmes from a range of activity areas.

Coaches implement and refine the Performance Model

The Performance Model for each Olympic program is implemented by coaches who play two interlinked roles. The Development Coach teaches and develops the athletes' skills and the capabilities of the program. The Performance Coach maximizes the performance of individuals and teams, bringing out the best in each.

By working together in these endeavors, coaches are the Performance Leaders who give the Olympic program a competitive advantage.

Coaches have a different mindset from most business managers: they are generally more active observers of behavior, and more proactive in giving feedback and in stretching people to think and act differently. Managers tend to come more from the position of Boss, which is less helpful to creating the sort of partnership that Louise Sauvage, Australia's world-champion wheelchair athlete, Olympic gold medallist and four-time winner of the Boston Marathon, calls the "coach–athlete partnership".[11]

From my observations of sports coaches and business managers throughout the world, I have formed the opinion that, by comparison with their sports counterparts, business managers are generally poor coaches. However, this is to be expected because they are not trained to coach and are given few practical coaching models and tools to guide them. Furthermore, many of the so-called coaching-skills programs in business are little more than counseling-skills courses. Having said all that, our experience with High Performance Leadership Programmes has demonstrated that most managers are coachable and become very effective Performance Leaders/Coaches once they are given the tools and environment.

As you begin to practice and apply the concepts of High-Performance Leadership, let the phrase "Be the Coach, not the Boss" remind you of your new role in the global game: a Performance Leader.

Support staff and processes

In the 1980s, the creation of a national network of Institutes of Sport put coaches in partnership with the best physiologists, bio-mechanists, doctors, physiotherapists, massage therapists, psychologists and program managers. These partnerships have led to significant increases in athlete performance. For example, the Australian Olympic Team in Seoul (my first experience) contained just two psychologists, while a third traveled specifically with the swim team (the total medical support team numbered less than 15). In Sydney, we had a team of 13 psychologists, and a total medical team of 87.

The importance accorded to having top-quality staff to support the coaches and athletes and the way they work together sets a great example of larger businesses and what they desperately need from their support functions. Yet you won't find service-level contracts in sporting teams. This would be absurd and confirmation that you'd got the wrong culture and probably the wrong people. The support staff and coaches work together for one reason: to get the best performance from the athletes.

Duncan Chessell, mountaineer and expedition leader, believes that this coordination between support staff is a core feature of all high-performance programs. He explained that, in putting together an expedition to climb Everest, "you have to get a support team who are motivated to carry out their role 100%, whether that role is summit sherpa, doctor, cook or website person".[12]

The roles and relationships between Strategic Leader, Performance/Development Coaches and support staff have honed the link between strategy development and execution. In programs such as rowing, track cycling and women's hockey, these roles have brought a world-class approach to developing high-potential athletes, to capturing learning, experimenting with and perfecting strategies and ultimately performing under pressure in the big events. By involving support staff and making them an integral part of the program, each of these sports has gone to a new level of performance.

As we look to the global game of business and the need for agility and high performance, there is much to learn from creating better integrated roles and broader capabilities for support staff. This is a key opportunity for businesses in the global game where new strategies must be designed and executed fast.

Athlete-centricity

Business organizations talk about people (employees) being the most important asset: but how often is this really the case? In sport, athletes and their performance is where it starts and ends. John Coates, President of the Australian Olympic Committee, has launched the past four Olympic campaigns by reminding the managers, coaches and support staff that they are there for one reason and one reason only — "to create the environment in which athletes can perform at their best".[13]

With this athlete-centric focus, an Olympic campaign has a much better chance of success than a business in which each group has its own agenda.

I believe that an essential element of High-Performance Leadership must be to encourage Performance Leaders to retain that emphasis on the importance of their Business Athletes (employees, teams, contractors and partners) because, as in the Olympic environment, these are the people who are ultimately responsible for performing and delivering results for customers, shareholders and other stakeholders.

Underneath the strategic umbrella of the Australian sport system each individual high-performance program has been given the resources and a mandate to take on the world.

High-Performance Leadership builds on the four common elements by providing a Performance Model for the global game, insights into the skills and practices of top-level Performance Leaders/Coaches and the practices that can lift the performance of Business Athletes.

THE ATHLETE MINDSET

The differences in ability between leading international athletes are so slight that success is more often determined by mindset than by sporting skill or physical fitness. On their best day, any number of athletes can win. However, the champions train and perform consistently at, or close to, their best and build a mental toughness or resilience.

Triple Olympic swimming gold medallist Shane Gould told me that the key is to get a balance between the demands of the task and your own perceived capabilities. The resilient athlete simply believes that they can withstand more pressure and still perform: so they do.[14]

As corporations implement new strategies and constantly search for growth, the real differences in performance also come increasingly from the mindset of the people involved. It is this mindset — a combination of empowering beliefs and resilient attitudes — that helps them to choose effective strategies and to implement them with quality and speed. In business it can be argued that everyone needs to have the mindset and skills of the athlete if they are to perform under the conditions of the global game. Business Athletes are central to success in the business game.

Performance psychology

The science and art of performance psychology has added enormously to our understanding of the high-performance attitudes and practices that lead to success. Sports, military and aviation psychologists have been influential in changing the nature of training and the preparation of performers to include a much greater emphasis on mental-skills development which, in turn, has created a more agile and resilient performer.

In the Australian sport system, psychologists have adopted two approaches. Popular amongst the clinically trained and longer-serving sports psychologists is what I call the "clinical model". These practitioners operate in a similar manner to a medical model, providing personal counseling services to athletes, mainly on a one-on-one basis.

The second model, popular amongst those psychologists with a background as athletes and coaches or in the corporate world, has focused on shaping the practices of coaches (including the performance system), while providing the one-on-one and group work with athletes only when needed. I call this the "system model".

From the clinical model we have learned about the personal psychology of the elite athlete, while the system model has helped to develop ways to transfer knowledge and skills to the coaches and athletes and to build successful programs. Action-learning techniques such as simulations and in-competition learning have resulted in tougher and more self-reliant athletes and teams.

Also important has been the focus on life-skills development and experiences which Shane Gould describes as essential to creating well-rounded athletes who have "a balanced perspective of themselves and their performance".[15]

But let's not be naïve

It is important, however, not to simply throw a blanket over the top Olympic and professional athletes and coaches in the naïve belief that if you do what they do you will be successful.

To do so would be to ignore three crucial factors:

* Translating successful approaches from one field to another is not straightforward and simple. Accordingly, while we draw much from Olympic and professional sport, High Performance Leadership Programmes has been built by looking not just at sport, but also other areas of high performance such as medicine, business, the military and the performing arts.
* High performers such as Olympic and professional athletes experience at least the same percentage of psychological disorders as the rest of the population. Amongst the household names are athletes whose outward success conceals personal traumas, ranging from depression, anxiety and obsessive disorders to substance abuse and interpersonal dysfunction.
* Success must be defined. There are many people with gold medals in their cupboards who have paid dearly for this success, while others have been strengthened by the journey. Success is not just the gold medal; there is clearly more to it than that.

CONSOLIDATING HIGH-PERFORMANCE LEADERSHIP

The global game certainly places great demands on you and others in your organization. Accordingly, my aim has been to weave the lessons from sport, business and other areas of high performance into a practical and coherent performance strategy without falling into the trap of making too literal an application of one field to the other.

Over the past five years, I have continued to refine the High Performance Leadership Programme to provide organizations and individuals with a practical ideology and process to take themselves and their program(s) to a new level.

The models and practices of High-Performance Leadership are laid out for you in the coming chapters. Underpinning the approach are the principles employed by the architects of the Australian sport framework and the concepts of Performance Model, Performance Leader/Coach and Athlete Mindset.

In Section Two you will learn how to develop the mindset and practices of the Olympic athlete. Section Three then introduces and explains the roles and practices of the Performance Leader/Coach and the framework of the Performance Model. In Section Four, you will be guided to build your own Performance Model in the same fashion as Olympic coaches build their high-performance programs.

Section Two

The Business Athlete

The Psychology of
Dynamic Performance

Like their Olympic counterparts, Business Athletes understand and capture the power of the most potent concept in performance psychology: the *dynamic performance zone*.

In the 1980s, Stuart Kauffman[1] and other students of high-performance environments discovered through research, what high performers already knew intuitively: that the best performances come in the dynamic physical and psychological zone between order and chaos known to complexity theorists as "the edge of chaos".

Olympic and professional athletes call this "the zone", while psychologists have labeled it "flow"[2] and the "Ideal Performance State".[3] It is not the neat mechanical state of mind and action that Bosses prefer but it is clearly where organizations, teams and individuals create their best performances, and it offers breakthrough possibilities for Business Athletes.

Not surprisingly, much of the psychological preparation of Olympic athletes and teams is geared around creating an environment and mindset that brings people into this zone of dynamic performance. For example, when asked about the most important thing that Olympic coaches could do to assist athletes to perform at their best, Shane Gould replied that giving athletes the skills and environment for flow had to be the number-one priority.[4]

I also believe that the same principle applies to business. *High-Performance Leadership* will therefore help you to understand how the zone of dynamic performance applies to your personal performance.

"Just Imagine"

Your home city is bidding to host the next prestigious World Expo and, as a leader of the Bid Committee, you will give the final presentation to the international selection panel at its meeting in New York.

For over two years, your city has maintained a slight lead over rival cities but the latest intelligence suggests that the voting is so close that it could hinge on your presentation. You are confident in your city's Expo strategy and your skills to sell the message. It all comes down to being at your best on the day.

A few days before the presentation, you are invited to a High Performance Leadership Forum where business professionals and international athletes are discussing their experiences of performing in demanding conditions.

- A soccer player talks about the World Cup Final: about weaving at full speed through opposition defenses, making split-second decisions before scoring the winning goal.
- A neurosurgeon explains how a complex operation flowed almost effortlessly, exactly as she had planned and visualized hours before. She describes being almost in awe of herself, as if watching the performance instead of being a part of it.
- A golfer describes an inner calmness that helped to filter out the attempts by people in the gallery to psych him out in the final round of a tournament.
- A chief executive describes how 500 employees came together on one day and, with energy and passion, created a new vision for the business that has transformed the whole organization.
- Finally, the skipper of an America's Cup yacht recalls his crew's preparation leading up to the final and deciding race. "We knew we had the talent and the boat; we'd done the work; so, it just came down to entering our zone when we needed it."

The words stick in your mind: " ... entering our zone when we needed it". You chat with the presenters and ask about their strategies for entering and remaining in the zone. With these in mind you prepare for the Expo presentation and go on to deliver one of the best performances of your career.

WHAT IS THE ZONE?

The zone is "the ideal performance state" or "flow". It is the state of mind and body in which we perform at, or near to, our best. It is easily recognized in sport but it is relevant to all areas of performance such as business, the performing arts and medicine.

For Olympic athletes, golfers and tennis players, being in the zone means better concentration, more control over emotions, confidence, alertness, great decision-making and, ultimately, better performances. It is a dynamic state: one in which we are not totally in control but, as Mihaly Csikszentmihalyi explained, it gives us our best performances.[5]

Olympic athletes set themselves to be in the zone on the day of competition and during training sessions. They know from experience and practice how to trigger the ideal performance state in which they can access all of their abilities, without any self-imposed negative influences.

Everyone experiences the zone

The zone is not the exclusive property of sporting champions. It is available to everyone, from students facing exams to business people confronting daily business challenges.

In the dynamic business conditions of the global game, being in the zone offers you better decision-making, more creativity and greater resistance to stress and burn-out. For your business, it opens possibilities to increase the productivity of meetings, to lift the performance of individuals and teams, to enhance strategic planning and problem-solving, and even to give your customers some in-the-zone experiences. The zone is unquestionably the central concept in performance psychology.

We have all, probably unknowingly, experienced being in the zone, sometimes vividly and sometimes just as great clarity of thinking and a feeling of flow or enjoyment. Experiencing the zone is like entering another dimension. Occasionally, you might penetrate to the very center of the zone to find a performance of such exquisite quality as might be experienced on just a few occasions in a lifetime. This is like the one-off peak performance sought by the Olympic champion or the opera singer. You may now be recalling a personal experience of being in the zone.

More often, though, the demands of business are like those faced by the distance runner, or by professional baseball and basketball players. These are demands to maintain consistency over months and years, to handle tiredness and fatigue, to peak many times and to always be able to "put in" when something important emerges. Under these (endurance) conditions it is performance quality and self-mastery over the longer term that is important — with the occasional big moment. In this sense, it really is a "zone" and not just a peak.

Reflection: Are you under pressure to shorten the time from idea to market launch, to find a creative edge in strategy, to meet the multiple demands of stakeholders and to create the fast and flexible culture that can capture that first-mover advantage? How can you do this and not spin out or burn out? Adopt the practices used by athletes as they seek ways to trigger their zone!

Whether playing a final at Wimbledon, or finalizing the corporate plan, you will do it better when you are in your zone.

GET TO KNOW YOUR ZONE

Can you recall some of your in-the-zone experiences in business? Perhaps it was an important presentation that just flowed, a project in which everything fell smoothly into place, or just a day when you stayed above the turmoil and saw everything from a strategic view.

The first step in getting to know your zone is learning to recognize the experience and noting the changes in the way you *think*, *act* and *feel*. This means looking not just for the one-off peak experience but also for those times when your thoughts are clearer, your ideas flow better and even your least-favorite people cannot mess up your day! (A useful guide is to think of the "business zone" as your best 20% of time).

To identify your in-the-zone experiences, begin by looking at Figure 3.1, which records a Business Athlete's experiences of being in the zone. Look for similarities and differences in your experience of the zone.

FIGURE 3.1 Being in the zone: A Business Athlete's experience

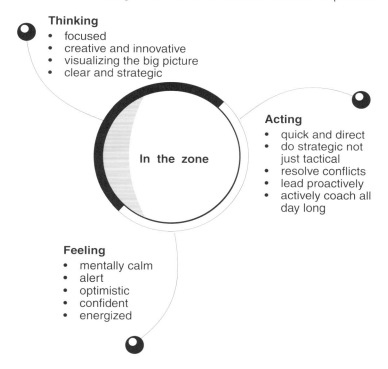

Organizations that implement High-Performance Leadership find that the productivity of leaders increases immediately they start to apply the principles of the zone. This is not surprising when you consider that the list above reads just like a model of capabilities or competencies for Performance Leaders in the global game. In so many cases, leaders do not need greater skills, ability and experience, but rather the capacity to bring out their best and use what they already have.

Know your zone: Questions from the coach

Consider the following questions or have your personal coach challenge you to explore these issues:

- What do you do better when you are in the zone?
- How would you describe your attitude when in the zone?
- How does being in the zone affect your relationships?
- How much more productive are you when in the zone?

MAXIMIZE YOUR IN-THE-ZONE TIME

You can learn to capture more in-the-zone time by tackling the following three steps that are a part of the psychological-skills training of most Olympic athletes:

1. Identify what triggers your in-the-zone experiences
2. Find what blocks the zone (creating out-of-zone experiences)
3. Actively manage the key triggers and blockers to zone performance.

HOW TO IDENTIFY THE TRIGGERS: IT IS YOUR OWN UNIQUE ZONE

Triggering your zone isn't as simple as the law of gravity! It doesn't always work, but with experience and planning you will gain an understanding of your own psychology. That self-knowledge will empower you to control those things that increase your in-the-zone time and, most importantly, you will learn how to trigger the zone when you most need it.

Be wary of undervaluing the search for self-understanding because, as Warren Bennis reminds us, "Technologically we are very advanced but psychologically we are babes in the wood. We don't know ourselves or anyone else very well."[6]

Triggering your zone requires more than just mimicking a checklist of habits or characteristics of successful people. Such lists can be helpful, but it is much more powerful to be alert to learning about your zone, and then deciding which of these practices really suit you. This is a key step in the self-mastery that characterizes the Business Athlete.

Athletes keep performance diaries to track their zone triggers and we have found success using this approach in projects during

High Performance Leadership Programmes. We have also found that people learn and gain insight from discussing others' experience of the zone.

Learn from other people's zone triggers

There are several zone triggers that are common amongst people who perform well in fast and dynamic environments. The following seem to be common amongst business clients we are working with:

- Know what you want
- Fit the challenge to your capabilities
- Create ... build things fast
- Start optimistic and stay optimistic
- Energize ... be fit for business
- Create your own "zone environment"
- Know your stuff.

Let's briefly explore these seven triggers to prompt your thinking about what triggers your in-the-zone experiences. As you consider each trigger, reflect also on how you could use this understanding as a Performance Leader to help others to enter their zone.

Know what you want

Business Athletes find and commit to a clear vision of what success means for them and they pursue it passionately via a virtual stairway of goals and deadlines. The message seems simple: "Know what you want *and* what you don't want". Cross the line between wishing and total commitment.

On a daily basis, however, the global game throws up all manner of distractions in the shape of new opportunities, crises and annoyances. The people who create more in-the-zone time are ruthless and realistic about their priorities. They delegate, delay or dump things, refer new issues back to their ultimate goal and accept that operating on the edge of chaos means shifting their goals from time to time. Nevertheless, they maintain a commitment to goals and deadlines because that gives the focus and the success that generates in-the-zone experiences. (In Chapter 4 we explore the challenges of setting goals in a global game.)

Fit the challenge to your (perceived) capabilities

One of the most common zone triggers is the balance between the challenge and the skills and capabilities of the Business Athlete. In simple terms, if you believe that climbing the mountain is too easy, then you'll be uninterested or distracted; and if you think it is too difficult, you'll be too fearful or overwhelmed. The zone is the space in between these two situations, where we see the challenge as fitting our capabilities at a stretch.

FIGURE 3.2 Relationship between challenge and performance

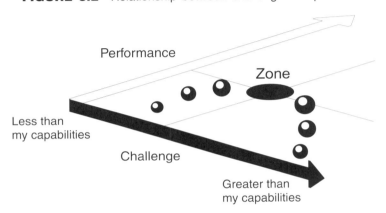

Duncan Chessell believes that one of the keys to climbing Everest is to know your physical and mental limits. In my discussions with him, he explained that some mountains are very physically demanding and others are more mentally demanding. Everest, he says, is both of these, and many climbers push past their physical limits because of the many mental pressures that go with climbing the world's highest peak. These pressures include the achievement itself, costs, time away from family and work, and the expectations of self and others. He strongly advocates learning about yourself and your capabilities and being mindful of pushing to the edge but without going over.

Developing the objective awareness of the extent of your capabilities and having a mindset and environment that encourages you to step (safely) a little beyond what you currently know to be those capabilities seems to be a key. Perhaps the words of Nelson

Mandela at his 1994 Inaugural Speech capture what you, as a Performance Leader, might do to stretch your thinking about your own capabilities: " … who am I to be brilliant, gorgeous, talented, fabulous? Actually, who are you not to be? You are a child of God. Your playing small does not serve the world."

Create … build things fast

Have you noticed how people involved in a new project seem energized and absorbed in what they are doing? The creative process acts as a natural trigger to the zone and, in return, the zone sparks greater creativity. This cycle of high performance fits a fast-moving, high-technology world in which intellect is wealth.

The creative process doesn't necessarily require sitting around trying to invent something. It is being involved in or approaching something as a "creating" activity instead of a business process, in the manner described in detail by Robert Fritz in his book aptly titled *Creating*.

Just this simple change in mindset increases the likelihood of better performance. Use this to your advantage by putting teams into a creative space (a new environment, a fresh new segment of a project), building brainstorming into your business activities and speaking the language of creating.

At a personal level, ensure that you have a regular infusion of fresh work and non-work projects that stimulate your creativity.

The great dancer Mikhail Baryshnikov adds another dimension when he speaks about creating for others: "The essence of all art is having pleasure giving pleasure."

Start optimistic and stay optimistic

Business Athletes trigger their zone when they take an optimistic view of the world and also when they connect with positive, creative people. I know from working closely with Olympic athletes that keeping them more optimistic assists them to handle the pressures of competition, sponsors and the media.

In business, if the projector fails before the presentation, the product is late for launch, a competitor wins a big account, or a PA resigns, the Business Athlete acts optimistically. They move forward, take the initiative and do their best while others are spectators.

Optimism is an underrated commodity in the workplace and it can be fostered by Performance Leaders and become a key to the culture.

Energize: Be fit for business

Winning athletes run faster and further, jump higher and lift heavier weights than their competitors. With more energy, power, flexibility and endurance they stay in their zone for longer and so make the most of their abilities.

Business Athletes are increasingly building "time buffers" around their work programs. These are short breaks to re-energize. Many use these breaks for walking, stretching or water-based exercises that are natural triggers to the zone.

Building or maintaining the physical energy and fitness of workers was seen as a health or wellness issue by 20th-century organizations. In the 21st century, we need to see it as a performance-enhancement and risk-mitigation issue, and so build strategies into corporate plans and daily work activities.

It is common sense that increased energy from better exercise and diet will trigger the zone and this provides even more energy in return. This is why Business Athletes will be better equipped to capture more of the myriad opportunities and challenges that emerge in the global game. There is a competitive advantage to be gained from fitness and smart businesses will move to secure that edge.

Create your own zone environment

The performance environment affects your mental state but there is often little that you can do about it. Technology, buildings, travel, company policies, resources and organization charts are all factors that can put you in or out of your zone.

While poor performers fret about having the best possible environment, high performers create a micro-environment around them in the midst of chaos. It works in the pressure-cooker of the Olympic Village and it works in business too, as we shall see in Chapter 5.

High performers create their own environment in even the most dynamic of conditions. They can be lobbed into a veritable sea of ambiguity and create a physical and/or mental space that works for them. Take, for example, the members of medical retrieval teams: highly trained, specialized and multi-skilled, self-reliant, adaptable, they perform in the toughest of conditions. Dr Bill Griggs, Director of Trauma Services at Royal Adelaide Hospital, says that being able to create a micro-environment in a hostile environment (at car wrecks, in the desert, under water) is essential to performance for his medical staff.[8]

Know your stuff

The seventh trigger is the most obvious.

To trigger in-the-zone performances requires competency. The higher the level of competency the greater the chances of experiencing the zone. Top golfers experience the zone more often and for longer than the average club golfer.

Duncan Chessell says that above all else he believed that he had the right capabilities (skills, fitness, experience) and the right support team to reach the summit of Everest and return.

Build competency as a key factor in creating high performance for yourself and others.

Reflection: Take a few moments now to reflect on what triggers your zone. Perhaps it will be some of the seven triggers that we have just covered, or others that are personal to you. Over the next week, be mindful of how your actions and mindset influence the zone. Experiment to see what works for you and then reap the benefits.

THE ZONE — MISSING IN ACTION

Understanding what triggers your zone is vital to being a high performer, but it is just as important to understand your "out-of-zone" experiences and to know what triggers them.

Out-of-zone experiences generally fall into two categories: overload (too hyped/stressed/excited) and underload (too bored/fatigued/unmotivated). Both are compounded by a negative or pessimistic mindset.

Overload: Going past the zone

Dynamic performance is about activity: an almost endless stream of important events and changes (in life and business). The challenge is to find the right level — at which you are stimulated but not overloaded.

Unquestionably, the global game has the potential to overwhelm us with its quantum of opportunities, rapid change, complexity and uncertainty. Even the most disciplined person can get too much stimulation, just as top athletes get overwhelmed by events such as the Olympic Games. This shows up in the way we think, act and feel. Some of the common signs that dynamic performance is faltering are outlined in Figure 3.3.

FIGURE 3.3   Experiences of being overwhelmed

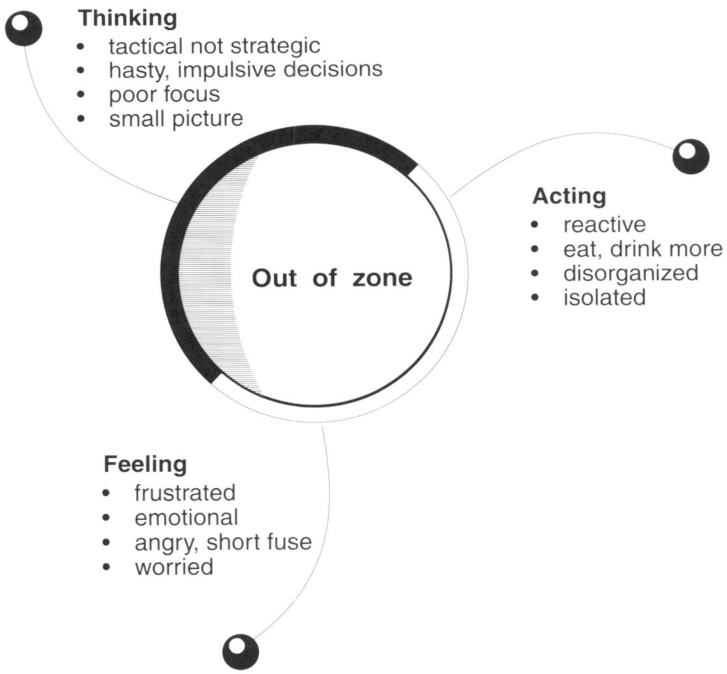

Thinking
- tactical not strategic
- hasty, impulsive decisions
- poor focus
- small picture

Out of zone

Acting
- reactive
- eat, drink more
- disorganized
- isolated

Feeling
- frustrated
- emotional
- angry, short fuse
- worried

Overload is a personal (subjective) experience, determined by our thinking and the pressure we put on ourselves. You see this in big sporting events, where the favorite under-performs because of too much pressure created by too many expectations (overload), while the "underdogs", free from such expectations, play in their zone. Jennifer Capriati's rise to the top of world tennis and the struggle for Martina Hingis to hold onto the number-one ranking may be examples of the effects of expectations. For Capriati there were few expectations in comparison with Hingis, who carried the burden of expectation.

In highly-charged environments, top performers are aware of the signs of overload and understand the triggers of those feelings, thoughts or behaviors. Many of the strategies that they employ are explained in the remaining chapters in this section.

Make time for recovery

Preventing chronic overload is a major issue in most performance environments. From battle fatigue in the military to the overload of air-traffic controllers and teachers, we recognize the dangers of being too hyped for too long. To minimize these effects Performance Leaders apply the physiological principle of recovery, scheduling their work programs to include periods of high intensity interspersed with recovery activities designed to regenerate physical and mental energy.

Choosing the best cycles of activity and recovery is mainstream practice in Olympic sport, through processes such as yoga and meditation, but remains a novelty in the business world. Its time is coming.

Underload: Falling short of the zone

Have you felt lethargic and uninterested when working on a project which is going particularly slowly, or perhaps hit a flat spot where nothing seems to spark your interest?

This is underload — simply, a lack of challenge — and it will almost certainly keep you out of your zone. The signs of being under-challenged include lack of motivation, sluggishness, negativity and lack of creative ideas.

Some of the most common causes of being under-challenged in the global game include:

- "Let-down" at the end of a project or major event
- Working without knowing the big picture (purpose)

- Repetitive tasks
- Activities which don't stimulate the intellect
- Familiarity.

Be alert to the signs that your energy level is too low, take note of what seems to trigger those feelings, thoughts or behaviors and structure your activities accordingly.

AVOID THE OUT-OF-ZONE TRIGGERS

Athletes and performers such as actors and singers are sometimes criticized for being too temperamental or finicky about their preparation. They want special low-fat food, quiet, and airline flights that arrive before the evening.

Why? Well, chances are that they have learned from bitter experience that fatty meals, noise and interruptions to their sleep patterns can knock them out of their zone. As professionals they can still perform in this state but not for too long, and that is something to be managed by the top performer.

It is easy to slip into poor habits and actually trigger failure through not understanding what creates your out-of-zone experiences.

The challenge, however, is to understand those factors that legitimately inhibit your zone, while not getting over-sensitive to things that are not as important. For example, the last thing that a professional tennis player wants is a list of conditions under which they can't perform. Top athletes are mentally tough, which means they can perform in a wide variety of conditions. Business Athletes must be able to do the same.

As a general rule, performers focus on managing what they can control or influence, while minimizing the impact of uncontrollable factors (such as the weather and the economy). If you travel long distances on business, you probably understand this principle and manage your food, drink and sleep patterns to arrive in better shape than inexperienced passengers, who typically eat all the food, consume alcohol and sleep haphazardly if at all.

MAKE THE ZONE A PRIORITY

The zone is custom-designed for the global game. Look at the following descriptions from leading Business Athletes of their in-the-zone experiences:

- "Thinking more clearly and strategically"
- "Solving complex problems quickly"
- "Visualizing the future with amazing clarity"
- "Communicating and coaching effectively with my team"
- "More productive: doing more in less time using less energy"
- "Teams getting to high performance really fast"
- "Staying positive even when things are not working".

The average business person sees the dynamic performance zone as a nice experience, the product, perhaps, of good luck; as not controllable and too vague to be useful. Business Athletes see it as a core element, a secret ingredient in performance. It is to be studied, created and captured for the benefit of individuals and teams.

For Performance Leaders, the zone offers insights into the psychology of their own performance and a foundation for developing a High-Performance Leadership strategy for their organizations.

As you learn and practice the skills of the Business Athlete covered in the remainder of this section you might become just as skilled as an Olympic athlete at entering and sustaining your zone. The global game requires nothing less.

4

A Sense of Direction

Conventional wisdom suggests that, almost universally, high performers have a constantly clear vision of where they are heading.

Books and motivational speakers pick up on this theme of clear vision and insist that we must clearly envisage the ideal future and then set about achieving it. To not do so is almost to show weakness or admit defeat.

The argument for clarity of vision is all the more compelling when business books give case study upon case study of successful organizations which were created by leaders with a strong and clear vision of success for their business. Those leaders foresaw the company, its people, products, size, market position and profitability in the future and then led themselves and their organization into that future.

But all of this was in a pre-global-game world that was more linear, slower and more predictable. Does it apply in the conditions of the global game? Can we be so sure that this belief about clear vision holds true in an environment that is uncertain, complex, dynamic and unlike previous conditions? And, if not, what strategy will you adopt to set your sights towards success?

THE CONCEPT OF VISION: YESTERDAY'S VISION?

After speaking recently at a conference in Sydney, I was asked by a promising young chief executive whether there was "really much value in taking the time and effort to create a detailed long-term vision for myself and my business when everything seems so unpredictable".

My answer was an absolute "Yes and No". "Yes" to envisioning ideal scenarios for the medium- to long-term future, and "No", it will probably not be in the specific "blueprint" form of past years. Thirty years ago the same person might have set a detailed 10-year vision for their career and business. It would have been a narrow, single-direction vision, carved out in a time when change was slow and orderly, and people were more inclined to follow a stereotyped career. Times have changed — a fact that Richard Branson took on board at Virgin: "My vision for Virgin," he wrote, "has never been rigid and changes constantly, like the company itself."[1]

More dynamic

A global-game vision will be more dynamic and could just as likely be a cause rather than an ideal "end-game". For example, I have a very successful private client whose business and personal vision is to create and sustain a fluid, fast-moving network of high-performing people capable of swooping on new opportunities as they emerge. She sees herself as being like a movie producer and each of her actors plays their part in making the total picture. Her view of life reflects the comment of management guru Charles Handy: "The world, or most of it, is an empty space waiting to be filled."[2] If you ask her to describe her vision for what will be happening three years from now, you will get a response such as, "I don't have a clue but it won't be boring, it will be profitable and it will be making a difference". Her actors design software, build franchise networks, renovate inner-city studios and package training courses. If you said they didn't have a vision, they'd just laugh and go looking for the next opportunity.

Our notions of vision and success have shifted in a generation. My father was an industrial chemist. He graduated from university, joined Unilever and remained there for over 30 years until he passed away. That was the vision of the times. It seems almost impossible now to plan a career with such certainty in a global game of mergers, acquisitions, downsizing, technology change and the like.

However, at any time in history a sense of direction has been fundamental to creating and sustaining high performance; which brings us to the basic question that is addressed in the remainder of this chapter: how do you find and maintain a sense of personal direction in what looks increasingly like an unpredictable and even directionless world?

FINDING DIRECTION IN A DIRECTIONLESS WORLD

One of the most powerful and consistent zone triggers for Olympic and Business Athletes is having a sense of purpose or direction. With a sense of direction we are more optimistic, proactive and prepared to seize the opportunities that the global game presents. Even more important is that you get your direction clear before you lead others in your program.

Your sense of direction will come from three core elements: passion for what you do, values that guide your decisions and actions, and goals and strategies to focus your efforts.

FIGURE 4.1 Three essentials in creating a sense of direction

These three factors blend together to provide the direction that shapes your performance and the quality of your life. I recommend using a personal coach to guide and challenge you in each area, so that you can keep them relevant in the shifting performance conditions.

Let's look at the strategies that you and your coach can employ in each of the three areas.

IT'S ALL ABOUT PASSION

I prefer "passion" to "vision". That's partly because "vision" has been overused, turned into a fad and often failed to deliver on its promise. It is also because I don't believe that vision is essential for creating and sustaining a high level of personal performance.

I've seen many Olympic athletes who did not have a vision; didn't have a clue, in fact, what their destination should be. And yet, a year or two later when they're interviewed by the press they tell how their success came from a clear, long-term vision! Did they have a vision? Perhaps there was a fuzzy view of what they wanted, but what made the difference wasn't vision; it was passion.

It was refreshing that one of Australia's greatest Olympians, rower Nick Green, explained in pre-Olympic briefings to athletes how he could never have envisaged winning two Olympic gold medals and four World Championships. His initial vision, he said, was simply to get a trip overseas. Perversely, he was first selected when the World Championships were held in Tasmania!

What motivated and directed Nick Green and his crew members to Olympic gold was a passion for finding out how good they could be: "Our ambition," he has said, "was to be the best we could be as athletes."[3]

Passion oozes from high-performing people and teams. Passion leads them back, time and again, to find or reaffirm a vision. Vision consolidates, passion initiates. Passion creates the power that then finds expression in the vision.

I venture to suggest that it was Da Vinci's passion for invention, Mandela's passion for freedom and Mozart's passion for music that led them to create and fulfill a vision. Passion first, then vision.

Passion with a purpose

Passion without purpose can be misdirected. The result: too much wasted energy. Passion with purpose makes things happen and that is why Performance Leaders will always try to link passion to a purpose through goals and strategies. We will explore this more fully shortly.

Passion helps to form and fuel the big picture. Business Athletes are passionate: sometimes about a vision; sometimes about a cause or an endeavor; but, most often, about what they do.

Sit with a good coach and tell them that you don't have a vision and they'll tell you that this is not unusual or a sign that disaster lies ahead. But tell them that you can't find your passion or unlock it in others, and you and they have a problem. Passion is more than enthusiasm. You and your business need your enthusiasm but passion also translates into will: the relentless intent to make something happen or to get somewhere. This is the key to Olympic mindsets: passion for the activity and a total passion for seeing how far you can go with your personal and team capabilities.

For too many people in the workforce, their current career and roles are a historical accident. They have drifted away from what they are truly passionate about and, instead, have settled for something less. Organizations that want to succeed in the global game cannot afford to employ people who are less than passionate about what they do.

Passion: Questions from the coach

Get your coach to use some of the questions below to challenge whether you are doing what you are passionate about.

- What are you passionate about? Have you turned it into your career?
- What are the people who work for you passionate about? Can you get them to do that more often?
- Do you recruit passionate people?

Help the people in your business who are not passionate to see that they are wasting their lives and encourage them to find their passion elsewhere. You don't go to the Olympics with people who are not passionate about the sport and taking it to the peak. Why do anything different in business?

From passion comes vision

The Olympics disappeared for 2000 years. It was not until Sunday, April 5, 1896, when Baron Pierre De Coubertin realized his vision to re-create the Olympics in the traditions of the ancient Greek Games, that the world regained what is now our largest peacetime event and the only place that the nations of the world truly come together.

De Coubertin saw the Games as a vehicle for, and a symbol of, the educational and personal development that can result from participating in sport. His vision was to use sport to develop the character and psychological skills needed by athletes to prosper in their careers.

The concept of the Business Athlete borrows from the vision of people like De Coubertin, who have seen sport as a model and training ground for life.

The power of a vision

For many athletes, sporting dreams remain exactly that: a dream. We've all met those people who tell us that they had the talent and could have made it "if only … ". For some, however, the dream becomes a passion to which they commit many years of their lives.

That passion might be to compete at Olympic level, to "make-it" on the professional tennis tour or to drive in Formula One. Vision is passion in pictures: the big picture. The Olympic mindset is always passionate and always seeking a clearer vision, although in times of injury, loss of form or after major events such as the Games, the vision can become clouded. (You need only look at Australian sport after Sydney 2000 or the airline industry after September 11 for examples of clouded vision.) The passion is there to be world-class; the challenge is to define a clear enough vision or big picture so that people will "sign up" for the cause.

Perhaps your vision as a Business Athlete is to lead a company, invent a product, specialize in a field of science, provide better service or be the best in your field. Whatever the vision, it begins with passion and is sustained by passion through the foggy patches.

Finding inspiration

Sport, the arts and business inspire us, and no more so than when we see people who overcome adversity to achieve great things.

Jennifer Capriati, the child superstar of tennis, reached the semi-finals of the French Open at 14 years of age and then literally crashed into years of personal trauma, which saw her police mug-shot flashed around the world. To see her triumph at the 2001 Australian and French Opens, and to become number one in the world, was to see passion and vision come together.

José Carreras fought leukemia and won. His appearances with Luciano Pavarotti and Placido Domingo in the Three Tenors concerts and at the opening of the Barcelona Olympics inspired millions. Lance Armstrong battled the spread of testicular cancer throughout his body to climb, only a few years later, onto the winner's dais of the Tour de France. Inspiring stuff!

In business there are always success stories to inspire us. From Jack Welch to Richard Branson, Steven Spielberg to Rupert Murdoch: there are visible and less-visible examples. There is no excuse for lack of inspiration. Get out and see what others are doing; read; go to conferences. Let the stories of others inspire you and unlock your passion to go for things that perhaps you have only dared to dream about. This is the Business Athlete mindset: to do exceptional things.

Breakthrough thinking

The global game demands stretch and more stretch: and that means breakthrough thinking and actions.

Athletes in sport and business refuse to accept the status quo and are never satisfied with mediocrity, never prepared to compromise. As Herb Elliott, undefeated over 1500 meters, gold medallist at the Rome Games and Head of Athlete Services for the 2000 Australian Olympic Team, reflected: "Over the years, I haven't found the top athletes any stronger than anyone else. But somewhere within them is that understanding that the little compromise that seems so negligible is in fact a huge compromise."[4]

Reflect on your goals and the big picture. Do you have exciting goals or have you settled for second best? What about your business? Is it really out there? Are these the goals you would expect if you and your business were planning to compete at the next Olympics?

It is a curious contradiction that performance environments can make us so busy and even so successful in our niche that we cannot see outside of it. As Robert Kyosaki[5] has noted, one of the hardest things for us to do is to change the patterns that become our daily routines. That is a dangerous place to be when all around is shifting.

Are you aiming for the top league?

Countries have passion and vision too. Take the example of Singapore, one of the economic success stories of the past two decades. In its quest for excellence, it used sporting images and language to express a part of its vision:

> "We compete in the race of nations, whether we like it or not. We have done quite well competing in the second league. The next step is to make it to the top league. Our competitors are already doing that. Unless we do the same we will be left behind."[6]

Singapore's next challenge in the global game is to become passionate about empowerment and dynamic performance; about building on the excellence in management and order that brought success and becoming a creative, adaptive nation living and working on the edge of chaos. It must find a balance between creativity and control so it can out-innovate and stay ahead of competitors such as Taiwan, China and Malaysia. Its future depends on that.

Performance Leadership is about finding what people are good at: starting with you. Former Olympic and World decathlon champion Daley Thompson said that he has "always thought that everybody can be good at something and it's just a matter of finding it. Most people don't find the thing that they're good at until it's too late. I happened to find it when I was sixteen."[7] Get in touch with your passion: find what you are good at, connect with it, use it to make your contribution.

Reflection: What are you passionate about and how does this fit with the various aspects of your life — career/business, family, personal, social and spiritual? What do you see for each of these aspects in the future?

VALUES

"Values" is another of those corporate words that has got a bad name through misuse. Every business and team seems to have its list of values — which (ironically) many then set about to violate on a daily basis. Cynicism prevails across the corporate world when leaders talk of respect and then downsize without respect. They speak of trust and give no power to make decisions.

Despite all of this, nothing is more essential in times of change than a core set of guiding values or principles. But if you do not act in accordance with these values, your leadership power is weakened.

Values provide exactly what is needed in a complex, dynamic performance environment: a basis for making decisions in accordance with global principles but local application. The mountaineer Jim Hayhurst Snr espoused the view that "understanding your core values makes decisions easy. When you know who you are, you can make confident decisions and never second-guess yourself."[8]

A colleague of mine once had leadership responsibility in a U.S.-headquartered organization for West Asia, including large portions of China and all of India and Pakistan. He was told from day one that he was trusted to make all decisions provided they were made in accordance with three values: customer service, utmost integrity, and respect for anyone affected by his decision. He says that he never found himself in a situation where those three values were insufficient to help him to make a decision.

The values-driven organization seems destined to be the model for the global game, particularly as organizations try to manage the demands of multiple stakeholders (government, community, customers, shareholders).

If values-driven organizations are the future, then they will be created and nurtured by values-driven leaders and they will attract people with like values. For a Business Athlete, this means being deeply aware of their own value-system, and of the emerging values in society, and then acting in accordance with those values. As Shane Gould reminds us, "You can make money and live your values at the same time".[9]

Coaching values

A good personal coach will assist you to understand your current values and to establish new ones that are better suited to your world. In High Performance Leadership Programmes, we coach leaders one-on-one and in small groups to explore their values through three methods: values checklists; reflection; and feedback.

Values checklists are, as the name suggests, lists of values and values-related behaviors, such as recognition, respect, power, security, teamwork, family, freedom and happiness. They are used to discuss the range of possible values and to help the person to establish those that are core.

Reflection comes through questioning and thinking. We ask people what inspires them, what they dislike or avoid, and we help them to explore some of their key life events and decisions. Values explorations can be life-changing events for business leaders because so many understand their world but not their inner motivations and blocks.

Feedback comes from other people and includes interviews and surveys designed to give the leader information on how others see them acting out values in the workplace. The advantage of feedback is that it gives you a view of the differences between the values that you espouse and those that others see you living. It can, however, be very challenging and confronting, and needs to be handled sensitively.

The values-coaching techniques and the benefits are summarized in Figure 4.2.

Values coaching has become an increasingly important part of my work with business people because clarity of values gives what athletes and martial artists call "centeredness": a sense of *groundedness* or certainty that is powerful and relevant in the high-performance environment.

FIGURE 4.2 Values-coaching techniques

Values-coaching technique	Activities	Benefits
Values checklist	Use or develop a checklist of values; rank them and discuss relative importance	Expands your understanding of values and their relative priorities in your life
Reflection	Questioning and reflection on life events and experiences to tease out the core values	Increases self-awareness and helps to clarify your core values
Feedback	Interviews and surveys, and direct feedback by the coach	Brings awareness of how others see your values: reveals gaps between values and actions

GOALS AND STRATEGIES

If you believed all the bunk written about speed in the Internet age, you would reject goal setting, prioritization and project planning as old school, too slow, a waste of time, something to be done when there is nothing else to do. Just as Gordon Gecko pronounced, in the 1980s movie *Wall Street*, that lunch was for wimps, somewhere in the late 1990s goal setting and prioritization drifted into the same lane.

Don't believe it for one second. The ready-fire-aim school of business leaders burn resources, get lucky sometimes but are not destined to stay on top. If you are too busy to set, fine tune and manage your aim, you are at risk. You will get swallowed by activity, chase every possibility and not choose and focus on the real priorities.

The global game rewards goal setting and prioritization skills because they are so difficult to do under these circumstances. You will not always have clear goals about your career or about a product strategy. Expect periods of uncertainty and ambiguity, during which you will have only the big picture and your values to guide you as you navigate through challenges.

As a general rule of performance psychology, the clearer the goal the better the performance over time. Be careful with this, however, because if you convince yourself that you cannot move forward without a clear goal, then paralysis is at hand. Obsessive goal setting ruins performance — and lives, for that matter.

Performance environments reward those who continually scan, plan, act and adapt. They move forward while learning and adapting to the world.

FIGURE 4.3 Continual goal setting and refinement

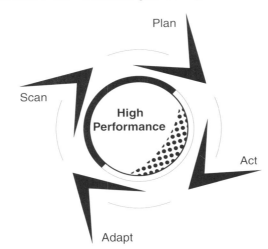

Motivational books preach goal setting as a commandment. "Begin with the end in mind," advises Stephen Covey.[10] Wise, yes, but not always possible. Sometimes in the journey we find the goal. It's a bit like putting on the running shoes and just doing it instead of waiting for motivation before jogging. Motivation follows action; goal clarity can also follow action. Climb the nearby hill, see the terrain and the goal is obvious. Sit and plan, and the goal might be set early but not with wisdom. There are no definite rules in the global game: just global principles to experiment with as conditions change.

In the global game the required capability is more than just setting goals; it is also the ability to move and navigate in the ambiguous spaces between goals, and to find the right goal.

Choose the right goals

Search for the most widely used and researched performance-enhancement technique and you will find goal setting. Hundreds of studies show that goal setting lifts performance and produces superior results. But it is not foolproof. Poor goal setting is also a major reason for under-performance.

When done well, your goals give you four key advantages:

Focus

Focus is essential to performance. Surgeon, student, salesperson, golfer: none can sustain performance without focus. Goals give the direction and purpose that set this focus. When an athlete says, "My goal is to make the national team to compete at the World Championships next year", this focuses their effort. Similarly, when an account executive says, "My goal is to win one major new account in the next two months", it gives focus to their efforts.

The global game is full of distractions. Focus implies mastery over distractions. Goals foster that mastery and boost confidence. When you master goal setting you expand your power as a Business Athlete. Research and practical experience also tell us that short-term goals are the most powerful in influencing behavior.

Motivation

High performers all over the world — whether climbing a mountain, passing an exam, winning new business or learning a new skill — use goals to motivate them. Selected and used wisely, our goals motivate us: done badly, they overwhelm and deceive us.

Discipline

Globalization has shrunk the space between local and world-class standards. Mostly they are one and the same thing. World-class performance requires discipline. It is rare to hear business organizations talk about discipline as a corporate value, and yet it is equally rare in many professions for it not to be included. Professionalism means discipline: goals instil a part of that discipline by encouraging persistence. Goals are an essential part of the Performance Model that you will build for your program and they are equally important for you as an individual.

Strategy

When an athlete commits to winning an Olympic medal the immediate next step is the strategy. A goal, no matter how big or small, leads us to devise strategies to achieve it. Whether it is to clean your desk or double the profitability of the business, a compelling goal leads directly to strategy. And Business Athletes are strategists and superb executors of strategy.

Set goals by performance cycle

The goal-setting cycle used by professional athletes and sporting teams is exactly the model to build into your Business Athlete practices. It features four time cycles: season; mid-season; monthly; and weekly.

I recommend the same structure for Business Athletes as a way to keep personal goals relevant. Figure 4.4 highlights how you might do this by working to a structure of 12 months, six months, one month and one week, and it also challenges you with an "acid test" for each cycle.

FIGURE 4.4 Goal-setting cycles

Cycle	Types of goals	Acid test
12-month	Set no more then six priority goals for the year, including one in each of the four key life areas: career/business, family, personal, social.	You have one specific goal in each life area for the next year.
Six-month	Set milestone targets at the six-month point (or half way for projects).	You have a specific six-month target or milestone for the social aspect of your life.
One-month	Set goals on a month-by-month basis.	You have two hours booked into your diary schedule for this month to review and set priority goals.
One-week	Use your diary scheduler to set priority targets for the week.	You have achieved most, if not all, of last week's goals

This is not rocket science; just a practical discipline that forms a framework to guide the rest of your performance activities. In a changeable world, knowing your priority goals is more important than in those times when you do have the luxury of time to plan. It is interesting to note the approach to goal setting adopted by Louise Sauvage: "My coach and I pause at the end of each year and outline my goals for the next year and then set the training and preparation goals."[11]

How to select your goals

Goal setting is so obvious and so easy that most people do it badly.

Be honest. Are you crystal clear about your priority goals for the next 30 days? The next three months? Could you benefit from tidying, tightening or targeting your goals? If so, read on for some coaching hints.

Balance your portfolio

Some years ago an argument was brewing in our community over a government regulation to ban competitive sport in schools. It had arisen mostly because of the pressure that parents were placing on children to win their tennis, basketball and football games. But, as Mike Turtur, Australia's Olympic cycling gold medallist in 1984, once said to me, if you lock six children in a squash court with a tennis ball and leave them there for 15 minutes, by the time you return they will have formed two teams and be having a competition.

Competition is not a problem of itself unless the focus on results consumes everything else. Balanced performers are not one-dimensional in their goals. Their goal portfolio includes multiple goals set in three broad areas: **results** (against self or others); **mastery** (development); and **passion** (enjoyment, satisfaction, fun).

FIGURE 4.5 Balanced goal portfolio

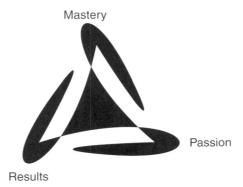

Mastery

Passion

Results

Beware of creating a toxic mindset that sees only results. If you are obsessed with constantly being "up for the game", your passion will quickly disappear. I see this regularly in all businesses and in sport. As Shane Gould advises, "When there is too much focus on winning, they [the coaches and athletes] forget about the importance of getting pleasure from what they are doing. Things become mechanical instead of [being] in flow".[12]

As an aside, there are a disturbing number of elite athletes for whom sport is socially acceptable self-abuse or "mutilation", to use the more emotive word. They strip away body fat and pound their muscles and joints into submission while the world encourages and parades them as role models. Chronic overwork is the work-site version of this affliction.

High and sustained performance can only be fuelled by the mix of improvement, passion and results. I have worked with many Olympic champions and business executives who, through maintaining a balanced portfolio of goals in the three areas, have achieved great things without the angst and destruction of self and others that often comes with the toxic mindset.

Select sharper and fewer goals

The speed and uncertainty of the global game often leads to setting too many goals and making them too vague. Instead of setting a vague goal, such as "I will improve my concentration during matches", a professional tennis player, for example, will sharpen it to "I will play three full sets, without losing focus on playing one point at a time".

Bypass vague wish lists, such as "I want to get more business from key customers", and go sharp with "I will increase my percentage of business from key customers by 10% over the next three months".

Sharp goals also help you to prioritize because you are not heading in a vague general direction. This is essential in a global-game environment where there is too much to do and even more coming.

As important as it is to have sharp goals, it is equally important to be able to say "No" to activities that divert resources from what is most important. Make it a habit to include a few points in your goal lists about what you will *not* do.

The advice to companies from marketing gurus Al Ries and Jack Trout is, "Whatever you are doing today, do fewer things tomorrow. But do them better."[13] This is great advice and equally applicable to companies and Business Athletes.

Stretch in private

While it is standard business practice to set "stretch goals" (because these are expected to lead to the best performance), I encourage you to consider a different approach that we discovered in sports psychology.

Some years ago, we asked athletes to state their base goals or targets publicly, and then to set stretch goals in private. In almost every case, this led to a lift in performance and/or motivation.

Aiming for the easier public goal gave the athlete a sense of progress (success), while the private stretch goal offered them something bigger to strive for without the pressure of public expectation. We've had similar success in business settings and suggest in Chapter 12 how to build this into your Performance Model.

Some companies now set sales quotas at (base) levels that a higher percentage of sales people can achieve. This makes sense, because more people will succeed and success then breeds further success. Try the base-goal and stretch-goal strategy for yourself and, if you like it, you can put it into the Performance Model for your program.

Let your goals serve you

The days of setting goals and leaving them untouched across some artificial time-frame (for example, a budget cycle) are gone. A changeable environment demands review and realignment of goals. Goals must serve you. They are a performance tool to assist focus and, if they focus you on the wrong things, why not change them?

Challenge your beliefs that changing a goal is an evasion or a weakness. If your team sets a goal to complete a project in six months and then, through objective measurement, finds that the project will take much longer or shorter, show common sense and re-schedule the goal, or allocate additional resources. This was exactly the approach adopted by Duncan Chessell: "I planned for up to three attempts at the Everest summit," he said, "and if that didn't happen I knew I would come back and try again. You have to be flexible in those conditions."[14]

The principle is clear. Use as much data as possible to set your targets. Engage the guidance of your coach to help you to set and keep those goals at the right level. Goal setting is a far more dynamic process than in the old game.

Hit the fairway

When professional golfers are in their zone, they think, "Hit the fairway"; when they are out of their zone, they are more likely to choose the negative, such as "Stay out of the trees".

The global game creates its share of crises that can easily have us looking at the trees instead of the fairway. The Olympic-athlete mindset is to bounce back very quickly from setbacks and look to turn things to their advantage. This same mindset can begin with you and become embedded into the culture of your program through the goal statements that you use when under pressure. Notice the differences in positively and negatively phrased goals in Figure 4.6.

FIGURE 4.6 Positive and negative goal statements

Negative Goal Statements	Positive Goal Statements
We can't afford to lose another client.	How can we strengthen our client relationships and loyalty?
The boss says to finish this, or else!	This is a top priority: so let's get on with it.
This had better be perfect.	Let's focus on making this really good.
If our competitors win that deal, we're in big trouble.	We've got back-up plans ready to activate.

An interesting exception ...

The exception to using positive goal statements is when doing something in which you are already very skilled. For example, if you are very familiar with adding up your weekly expense sheet but tend to make careless mistakes, you will make fewer errors by setting a goal to make no errors. However, if you are making an important presentation to the board, it is far better to focus on a positive goal, rather than telling yourself not to make an error.

SUMMARY

The global game challenges all Business Athletes to find a sense of direction in an environment where uncertainty and change are commonplace.

In this chapter, I have challenged you to consider the three factors that determine that sense of direction and to build these into your own personal practices. These three elements (passion, values and goals/strategies) will be revisited in Section Four when you begin to build and apply your Performance Model to your program.

5

Win Before You Begin

Whether you sit high in the stands at the Olympic Aquatic Centre to watch Ian Thorpe win another gold medal, or walk with Tiger Woods' group around the Augusta National Course during the U.S. Masters Golf Championship, it is easy to be seduced into believing that high performance is largely a matter of talent, combined with attitude on the day.

However, for a better reality-check, try watching Thorpe at the Australian Institute of Sport pool at six o'clock on a freezing Canberra morning, or go to the practice green after the day's competition, where Tiger Woods is endlessly honing his putting stroke.

High performers know that talent plus attitude on the day is critical, but even more important is the way they set up before the competition and what they do during the breaks between the action. This is what I call "Performance Set-up" and it is a key source of competitive and performance advantage for Business Athletes.

BUSINESS ATHLETE PERFORMANCE SET-UP

Four aspects of Performance Set-up are critical success factors across a wide variety of business environments. They are **physical**

environment, **information and communication systems**, **personal routines and rituals** and **support networks**. Getting these right, without being obsessive about everything, is a continuing challenge.

Changed game

The global game has significantly changed the principles of Performance Set-up. While most organizations have changed their set-up (new designs, systems, processes), there has not been the same focus on individual set-up. As a consequence, many workers still apply the same principles to the four areas described in Figure 5.1 as they did in the pre-global-game era. Figure 5.2 contrasts these practices with those of Business Athletes.

FIGURE 5.1   Critical success factors in Performance Set-up

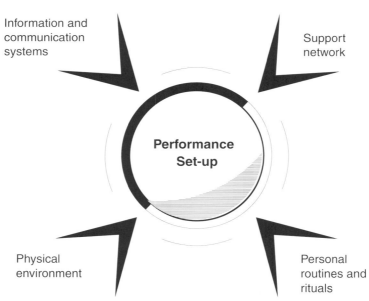

FIGURE 5.2 Shifts in Performance Set-up

	Pre-global game	Global game
General practice	Performance Set-up is done before the action begins, and then remains stable unless a major crisis or change occurs	Performance Set-up is fluid, and continuously refined as strategy is adjusted
Physical environment	Stable; work is defined by the physical environment	Mobile, adaptable, able to set up anywhere
Information and communication	Puts up blocks to avoid overload	Absorbs and filters large amounts of information; excellent coordination
Personal routines and rituals	Follows corporate rules, habit-driven, stereotyped	Performance-oriented, flexible, minimalist
Support networks	Family and little else	Has a close network, including coaches and in key support-performance areas

A CLASSIC HIGH-PERFORMANCE ENVIRONMENT

The environment in the lead-up to and during the Olympic Games is a fantastic place to observe how high performers manage their Performance Set-up in very challenging and dynamic conditions.

My objective in this chapter is to use that Olympic environment to illustrate practices that high performers employ to bring out their best performances. The similarities in performance environments between the Olympic Games and the typical global-game organization provide fertile ground in which to work. Figure 5.3 illustrates many of these similarities.

FIGURE 5.3 Similarities between the Olympic and business environments

Olympic Games	Global game of business
Member of a performance unit in a large team	In a networked organization
Busy Olympic Village	Complex, interlinked global game
Media and sponsor demands	Multiple stakeholder demands (increasing)
High performance expectations	World-class standards required
High rewards for winning	Performance consequences
Venue factors (crowd, distractions)	Venue factors (mobility, distractions)
Security	Controls
Rules and restrictions	Boundaries and gaps in knowledge

YOUR OWN OLYMPIC BRIEFING

The Olympic Games is a unique, powerful sporting and life experience for competitors and coaches. Special preparation and focus is needed to perform in the conditions of high expectation, media scrutiny, tough competition and multiple distractions. The strategies used by coaches and athletes to handle these demands offer great insights for Business Athletes who are experiencing similar challenges in the global game.

Come with me now on a journey into the cauldron of the ultimate global performance event: the Olympic Games. Assume that your business job/role has been installed as an Olympic event in the next Games. The Olympic Team is now a composite sport/business team comprising Olympic and Business Athletes and their coaches.

Your challenge is to ensure that you have strategies in place to deal with the unique features of the Olympic Games.

UNIQUE FEATURES OF YOUR OLYMPIC EXPERIENCE

Each element in this section is explained from three perspectives:

- Olympic Games
- Global-game equivalent
- Athlete performance strategies.

The headers describe the Olympic conditions, with the global-game equivalent given in brackets (except where they are the same, such as in "Performance Expectations").

Scale: Membership of a larger team (networked organization)

Your self-contained high-performance program (team) is a thing of the past. You've joined athletes, coaches and administrators from nearly 30 other sports and businesses to be part of a much larger team: your national Olympic team. As in the global game, this is a networked organization with lots of smaller high-performance units.

As a member of the national team, you are experiencing things in this Olympic (global) set-up that have not been a part of your normal competition processes. You are participating in pre-Games briefings, simulations and debriefing sessions, planning new strategies for travel and pre-competition, completing psychological, health and drug testing, getting fitted for your Olympic uniform, attending a team assembly just prior to the Games, marching in the Opening Ceremony, accessing the broader team-support services (for example, Athlete Services, Medical, Headquarters) and mingling with athletes from other sports (and businesses).

Can you enjoy it all but stay focused on what you are there to do? Can you sustain your training quality right up to the day of competition, despite everyone wanting to talk about finals and medals?

And, by the way, you're expected to participate in broader team activities such as team meetings and supporting your new team mates. More networking.

From my observations at four Olympics, there are four common features that separate the high performers from the average and below-average in how they deal with the scale of the Games.

The high performers know their "core business" (that is, what they are there to do and what they are not there to do).

They plan how to manage the extra demands and are assertive in managing expectations, creating their own micro-environment. This last point is very important because, through setting up their physical environment and following rituals or routines, they not only survive the demands of the Olympic build-up and competition, but often lift their performance to another level by staying in a much better emotional and physical state than the athletes who try to take it all in and become over-stimulated.

FIGURE 5.4 Practices of high performers in large-scale environments

	Performance Strategies			
	Core business	Scenario plan and execute	Assertion	Micro-environment
High performers	Athletes maintain fierce focus on pre-agreed priorities but coordinate well with others as required	Plan for distractions and simulate those plans	Refuse to be distracted by anyone who is irrelevant to the mission, irrespective of position	Create, manage and protect their personal environment and do the same for others
Average and below-average performers	Athletes engage in spur-of-the-moment, non-core activities and get frustrated by attempts to coordinate with others	Plan for routines with few contingencies	May waiver when pressured by officials	Fit into the environment as best they can: let others fend for themselves

Global-game lessons: Even the smallest Performance Units, from self-employed business people to teams inside companies, are part of large-scale performance environments. For example, you and your organization are part of a broader network of staff, customers, suppliers and stakeholders. Whereas it was once possible and, in fact, required for you to stay in your own area, deal just with a supervisor or single contact, and rarely venture much outside the core business, you are now expected to contribute in all manner of areas and ways. That increase in scale and reach has many implications for how you arrange your personal Performance Set-up.

Scale: Questions from the coach

Consider some of these questions and have your coach challenge you about how your set-up suits the scale of the global game.

- Are you now a member of a bigger team than in the past (think about your network, not just the boundaries of the organization)?
- What extra demands does this place on you?
- What impacts have these demands had on your Performance Set-up?
- What new capabilities have you developed to assist you to perform in this environment?

The medical retrieval system at the Royal Adelaide Hospital (RAH) is recognized and has been benchmarked as a world leader. Dr Bill Griggs, Director of Trauma Services at RAH, believes that the single most important factor in lifting the hospital's retrieval team from average to world-class level was the move to a better coordinated and integrated set-up of medical, fire service, ambulance and police services to respond to incidents that can be hundreds of kilometers away. Some of the skills needed include the capability to set up in harsh environments, such as desert or water, and in what Dr Griggs calls "shared space", that arise, say, when working to stabilize a patient while others work to cut that patient from a wrecked car. The details of this are further explained in Chapter 14 as we look at the importance of set-up to building the Performance Model for your program.

Enjoyment is a performance strategy

The scale of the Olympics is a unique performance factor, just as the scale of the business game has gone from neighborhood to global. Your fellow athletes will be familiar with World

Championships in their sport but the Olympics is like having nearly 30 World Championships in the one place at the one time. High performers thrive in these conditions, partly because they enjoy it and partly because they focus their attention more narrowly and do not let themselves get distracted.

As you stroll through the Olympic Village you will see how the swimming coaches manage these issues by working to disciplined daily plans, regularly briefing the athletes (twice-daily briefings) and maintaining their team as a team (through, for example, traveling and taking meals together).

You will see also how coaches work one-on-one with their athletes, imparting small pieces of information that help them to focus and to build confidence. Confidence comes from competency and a sense of control, so coaches constantly reinforce the core competencies of their performers.

THE OLYMPIC VILLAGE (COMPLEX GLOBAL GAME)

Two weeks before the Opening Ceremony, the athletes of the world begin to move into the Olympic Village. When full, the Village is, as the name suggests, a sizeable community of people of every size, shape, color and nationality. You will join more than 10,000 athletes and officials from over 150 countries, all packed into the space of a town block or two. There will be movie theaters, a free 24-hour dining hall seating 3,000 people, gyms, a discotheque, free soft-drinks, shops, some of the best-looking athletes you have ever seen and plenty of noise.

The Village is the greatest buzz of your career but also, potentially, your greatest enemy. You will need a fierce resolve not to get distracted and caught up in the high energy of Village life. Many of your predecessors have worn themselves out sampling all of the glitz and glamor of the Village.

In the Village, you will share your bedroom with another athlete and an apartment with maybe another six to eight athletes. There will be competition for bathrooms, sparsely furnished rooms, little personal space and the risk of chronic snorers and partying athletes to upset your sleep. The athletes' lounges may give some respite to watch television and relax but there will be competition for channels, seats and reading materials. Expect to get a little frazzled from time to time as you search for quiet time and space.

The leading athletes have similar core strategies for dealing with the complexity and chaos of the Olympic Village. On arrival, they settle quickly into a daily routine and they use structure and boundaries to avoid drifting from daily disciplines. They already know what to expect and accept it is a natural condition in a high-performance environment. They need only minimal order and system because they absorb, rather than react to, the environment. They also deal with conflict and resolve it quickly. Some of those practices are highlighted in Figure 5.5.

FIGURE 5.5 Practices of high performers in "high-noise" environments

Performance Strategies				
	Routines	**Chaos and complexity**	**Conflict**	**Quiet time**
High performers	Impose their minimalist routines from the outset	Expect and absorb the high-energy, high-chaos environment; work well in shared space	Deal with conflict and resolve it quickly, knowing that unresolved conflict affects everyone	Practice strategies to find own quietness: music, meditation, centering. Also negotiate with team for quiet space
Average and below-average performers	Get caught up in the excitement or try to apply fixed routines and become frustrated	Struggle against the environment; waste energy	Let conflict distract them, allow tension to build; liable to "explosions"	Try to get away from noise but find this difficult in team environment

The list in Figure 5.5 is for Olympic athletes but fits just as well as guidelines for astronauts, explorers and many Business Athletes. Where space is limited and "noise" in all forms arises, the high performers know they have an advantage because of their Performance Set-up.

Global-game lessons: The global game of business has many of the characteristics of the Olympic Village. You will be able to add to this list but some that are common include:

- open-space offices where people from all areas come together to work, talk, share, inspire and, at times, distract each other
- mergers and alliances that pull together people from different business cultures
- mobility, which means that we often work long distances from our home bases and live in hotel accommodation right next door to where we work (or inner-city living where people live in "business villages")
- constant on-line access to people, which means that your team and customers are always with you.

By following the practices of the high performers outlined in Figure 5.5, you will be in better shape to thrive in these situations. Further strategies are also discussed later in the chapter.

Rest and recover to perform

In the Olympic Village, coaches and psychologists will monitor your mood to make sure that you are getting enough rest and recovery. One of the first principles of sports training is the principle of recovery. You will notice a difference here between the Bosses and sports coaches.

Sports coaches will see recovery as a natural and essential part of the performance cycle. They know that there is a bandwidth in which athletes train and perform at their best. Too little workload and the athlete under-trains and under-performs: too much and they slowly wear down and lose the performance edge.

Bosses will be less aware of the importance of recovery, expecting that you will do this yourself. They equate performance with effort, whereas the sports coach knows that athletes who do not recover put in even more effort and yet get lower results.

Global-game lessons: The coach still keeps the athletes training but varies the type and load. The business manager who is trained in High-Performance Leadership does the same, scheduling project cycles and allocating roles so that you recover and refresh. This won't mean sending you to the beach but, more likely, getting you to do tasks that require different skills. Four options for refreshing Business Athletes in the workplace are:

- coaching and mentoring
- de-briefing other projects — working on evaluation and coaching instead of high-activity project work
- reading and renewing their knowledge at courses and forums, and in group discussions
- designing "franchise systems" that capture the knowledge from activities and build it into business systems (for example, packaging the project-management approach into a business module that can be used to train others).

Other activities of the Olympic athlete are also useful, including massage, swimming, aerobic exercise and meditation because, as we will see in the next chapter, these renew energy.

Access to food (many opportunities)

Twenty-four hour access to just about every type of food imaginable will test your resolve and commitment. Athletes get bored when they taper for big competition and it is easy to fall into the habit of sitting in the food areas and snacking on ice-creams and any other piece of food that catches your interest. Free burgers and cola 24 hours a day is quite a test; so, if your coaches are smart, they will use the power of peer pressure and make sure that you eat with your team mates and monitor each other.

Global-game lessons: Business Athletes have to avoid their bite-size temptations, including the constant "snack" of e-mails that comes through their laptops. The global game offers myriad opportunities to sample and yet, like the athlete's food, this draws energy away from what we really want to do.

Impacts of competitors and officials

At post-Olympic debriefing sessions athletes often express surprise at how they let themselves get psyched out/distracted by the presence of so many high-profile and physically well-tuned athletes (even though many of these athletes are in other sports).

In the Olympic Games and the global game of business, the best athletes and Performance Leaders/Coaches know and study the patterns of their competitors. They prepare for the competitor who appears unexpectedly or introduces a new strategy. Being prepared for an opposition tactic is important, but being able to adapt to previously unknown tactics in the heat of competition is where real advantage lies. To do this, it requires coaches and support staff who can formulate tactics, and leaders and athletes who are empowered to execute those tactics quickly. It also requires teams to organize themselves.

Global-game lessons: Business Athletes are in tune with this type of Performance Set-up (flexible, scenario-based, feedback) and the mix of practice, strong performance-feedback and empowerment needed to get fast execution of strategies. As Mike Heard, Codan CEO, says, "It is hard for 'driven managers' to let go but we must if we want genuine empowerment at all levels".[1] This is discussed further in Chapter 14.

Rules and restrictions (boundaries)

On arrival in the Olympic city you will go straight to the accreditation center. The process will be slow and tedious, as you have all your gear examined, pictures taken and all existing

FIGURE 5.6 Strategies that help athletes to adapt rapidly to new conditions

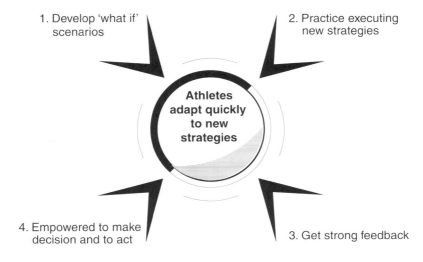

accreditation checked and re-checked. Expect anything up to eight hours until you are reunited with your luggage in the Village.

Whenever you want to leave the Village you will be checked. From time to time, your accreditation card might fail to pass the check, so expect more delays.

Olympic transport is like a supply chain of networked teams in full operation. A fleet of buses and cars running to tight time schedules deliver you to and from your training and competition venues using a prescribed corridor of roads. It all starts and finishes at the point of maximum demand: the transport mall located in a secure area (akin to a demilitarized zone) next to the Village. (You cannot travel by yourself to a venue — try it and you'll meet half an army in your path!) Security will be both highly visible and invisible.

For venues more than a few kilometers away, expect the bus drivers to get lost from time to time. This will disrupt your training. On competition day, you will plan to arrive at the venue very early to avoid any nasty surprises.

Travel into the city itself it will cost you nothing except time to make your way through the huge crowds. If you are a well-known athlete, this will not be an option, so you will have to find some other way of relaxing and enjoying the Olympic atmosphere.

Global-game lessons: Business people used to be able to work alone, but getting to a business deal these days needs teamwork and strategic alliances. Supply chains (networks) depend on other people getting their logistics organized so that products arrive at a competitive price and on time. As with the relay baton, everything must be passed at full speed and with precision to compete at world-class level. Accreditation can be as specific as an ISO quality requirement, or as general as being known well enough to be included on a selective tender. Similarly, cross-boundary opportunities mean new forms of alliances that can include working with your competitors to meet the needs of customers in ways that would have been seen as ridiculous just a few years ago.

Mitigating risk can seem to be unnecessarily bureaucratic but, having been in Atlanta when the bomb exploded in Olympic Park, to me the message seems very clear. September 11, made Olympic-like security a given for the business air traveler.

In the global game, risk management is now core business and starts with how you are set up to use risk as a business asset. This means knowing your personal rules. As Allan Moss, Macquarie Bank CEO, says, "External shocks occur and if you have appropriate risk-management arrangements, then you are in good shape".[2]

Media and sponsor demands (multiple-stakeholder demands)

If the Olympic Village seems fairly large with 10,000 people, it may surprise you to know that the Media Village will house 15,000. Media attention at the Games will be higher than at any other sporting event. This has many positive benefits for the careers of successful athletes but has also been shown in the past to have a negative impact on some athletes' performances.

Coaches in all sports will manage the potential distraction from cameras and journalists at training, but you will be scheduled to attend press conferences and sponsors' events and, of course, there will be lots of media attention at events.

The Performance Set-up strategy used successfully by the Australian Olympic team over recent Games has been to allocate an experienced journalist to act as a liaison officer between each sport and the media. This person understands the needs and tactics of journalists, and helps to coach the athletes in how to capitalize on the media attention without it becoming a distraction. Press conferences are planned, media releases prepared and individual athletes counseled on controversial issues, all to ensure that the media does not cause the athletes to lose before they begin.

Sponsors want maximum value from their association with the Games. The benefits of sponsoring a national team include getting access to the top athletes and coaches, and being able to use this to link products and services. Corporate functions attended by leading athletes provide great value for corporations and for the athletes concerned. Athletes must find the balance between their needs for pre-event preparation and the requirements of media and sponsors.

Global-game lessons: The business equivalents of media and sponsors are the multiple stakeholders that you meet in the global game. These can include shareholders, the board, community, customers, colleagues and staff, together with family and others.

Whether leading a change initiative or running a business unit, one of the challenges in the global game is to manage your sponsors and provide benefits, while also making sure, like the athlete, that results happen on the track. Without results, the sponsors will drop you instantly. Nothing is surer. The balancing act highlighted in Figure 5.7 is one of the challenges of the global game.

FIGURE 5.7 Performance balancing act

Do what is needed to produce the results	**AND**	Manage the demands and requirements of sponsors and other stakeholders

Managing multiple stakeholders is the other factor that many CEOs have identified as one of their biggest challenges, requiring time, effort and skill. In Chapter 8, we will explore some of the strategies that Business Athletes can use to foster relationships in a networked world.

Venue (Business Conditions)

The venue for your performance, like those for all the sporting athletes, will have its own special features for which you must be prepared. In conditions of complexity, the initial conditions can greatly influence performance (for example, getting to market first).

Television changed forever the timing and nature of many events. Archers and shooters now face off against each other in sudden-death finals; marathoners and cyclists share their routes with strange-looking vehicles with cameras pointed in their faces; and divers are followed from the top of the tower to the bottom of the pool by track cameras. Finals are held in prime time to meet the needs of networks; journalists shove microphones under the noses of athletes seconds after they have crossed the line; and even the least-known athletes find themselves squaring off against hundreds of reporters and cameras as their moment of fame is flashed across the world.

Global-game lessons: Business Athletes must know how to capture the attention of sponsors (see Chapter 7), how to keep focused on their core business when needed and, most importantly, how to get the private space that they need to prepare and perform. Increasingly that private space is inside them and portable, rather than a physical place where they can go to escape. We explore techniques to do this in the next chapter.

Creating a team and a set of disciplines that you can trust is also central to Performance Set-up in the global game. As HSBC Holdings Group Chairman Sir John Bond says, "Half our profit is made while I sleep. So I had better know that there are people on the other side of the world who are doing things the HSBC way."[3] Being able to operate in a team set-up is an essential capability for the global game.

PERFORMANCE EXPECTATIONS AND CONSEQUENCES

Amongst the most common characteristics of high-performance environments are high and public performance expectations and consequences.

The Olympic Games creates huge expectations. The biggest global festival of sport, held only once every four years, with the biggest television audience of any event and the participation of virtually every country, means big opportunities and, therefore, huge expectations.

The pressure of expectation

FIGURE 5.8 High-performance environments

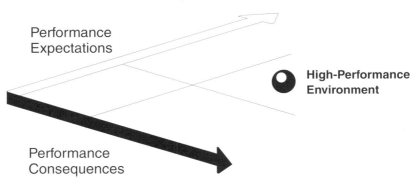

Performance
Expectations

High-Performance
Environment

Performance
Consequences

Pressure lifts performance but only to the point just before athletes and coaches begin to feel overwhelmed. At that point, performance begins to diminish. The best athletes and coaches handle these conditions.

As an athlete, you will work one-to-one with your Performance Leader/Coach and in teams to discuss and resolve these expectations before you compete (scenario planning and goal setting). You will be briefed well in advance by team psychologists and given "active calmness training" to create a mindset of control and confidence in a turbulent and changeable environment. And you will also hear from athletes who have succeeded at this level about their experiences (mentors).

Global-game lessons: Performers enjoy an environment of challenge and global competition but the rules are different from in the past. Whereas winning may have been easier at a local level, this is a bigger game where winning can be defined in different ways. What may be considered fast at home will now be well off the pace and yet shareholders and other stakeholders expect results.

Try the three strategies of the Olympian:

- Use Performance Coaches to facilitate your planning and preparation (or play this role for others)
- Learn the skills of active calmness (see Chapter 6)
- Seek out those with capabilities and experience from whom you can learn.

Performance consequences

Success at the Olympics is not a guarantee of future wealth and fame but it opens doors. Sports agents roam the sporting corridors looking for the Thorpes and Kournikovas who can become global brands in their own right. Top athletes are expert at marketing themselves. They appoint agents who brand and position them to get the best exposure and the best deals.

Global-game lessons: Personal marketing means knowing your market, the brand you (personally) want to project and how to position it and yourself. The global game depends so much on knowing people and being known. Your career progression, getting a project sponsor or taking a new technology or service to market each requires marketing and selling skills, together with a strong network of contacts. (These capabilities and strategies are covered in Chapters 7 and 8.)

The Olympics also delivers its share of failures. Each athlete and coach has succeeded in getting to the Games but failure can turn gold to dust. Such is the pressure.

Global-game lessons: High-performance programs/ organizations deal quickly and effectively with people who do not meet the performance standards. Typically, they will try to develop the person but you can expect less space in which to make the improvement than you had some years ago. Some give no second chances, such is the performance orientation of the global game.

Win Before You Begin: The High Performance Leadership Strategy

The Olympic Games provides an interesting analogy for the Business Athlete in the global game. Let's now address the success factors that were described earlier and explore some additional strategies for each.

Business Athletes ensure a lean, simple and functional set-up that is consistent with their overall vision and goals. In a changeable environment the challenge is to find a Performance Set-up that gives you stability but also flexibility to change as your aims and/ or conditions shift.

Physical environment

The physical environment in which you work has a direct impact on performance, so it is essential to consider if there is anything that you can do to create a better physical space for your work. Look around your own workspace. Is it an energy-enhancing environment in which you work creatively and effectively, or is it sterile and energy-draining?

Most offices and work areas are designed for efficiency and good looks (or expediency) and not for people. They are to people what corrals are for horses: places to restrict and control.

Join the retrieval team

Challenge the way that your environment is set up (and the assumptions that were used to create it). Work with what you've got and turn it to your advantage. Think as if you are part of a medical retrieval team: develop the tools and mindset to set up anywhere, anytime. As Dr Bill Griggs suggests of a retrieval situation, "You do what you can with what you've got".[4]

When implementing High Performance Leadership Programmes, we often visit clients at their worksites to observe their Performance Set-up. We find that too many people just take what they are provided with and give little thought to what might make their physical space more effective. There are countless examples:

- Bob's workspace faced a walkway and, therefore, constant interruptions by people who caught his gaze.
- Julie's new desk and computer set-up was too small to fit the sketch pads that she used to draw mind maps.
- The production team didn't have a cupboard to store meeting files.
- Chad still longed for his own office and had resisted designing a set of tools to suit the hot-desking at his company.

Some people never have enough resources. They use their lack of resources as an excuse for their own shortcomings. The world is full of people who have overcome a lack of resources to achieve great things. If Kenyan athletes can win Olympic gold medals, then you and I can find a way to do what we want to do. If it really is that necessary, then put a business case together and get the capital. If you fail, then maybe you and the business might be better off if you go somewhere else.

Fix it in five

Are you one of those people who work for years putting up with annoyances that could be fixed in five minutes? Have you created or inherited and maintained a dull, boring and toxic environment? Most importantly does the environment give you the energy and creativity that you need to succeed in this global game?

Business Athletes of the 21st century are far more likely to be into fresh air, interesting pictures, non-business magazines, fresh flowers, music and quiet spaces. Their homes and offices are designed for performers, not workers.

Take a good look at your office, your car and your home. Are they set up for you and those who are important to you and your vision or are they some sort of relic from the past? What can you do to freshen them up? Get your coach to challenge you about this.

The global game has put Business Athletes into open and mobile environments that are quite different from the boxed office. The upside is more freedom, more informal people-contact and less hierarchy; but the downside for many people is lack of quiet space in which to focus and recover. As you review your own physical space, make sure that you are setting it up to give you the opportunity to focus.

Think mobile

Business Athletes are super-mobile. If you can't give a presentation at a moment's notice, jump on a plane to capture a business opportunity a few thousand miles away, or work through a distant communication hub, you are simply not ready for the global game.

Performers train and equip themselves for this task. Stuart Ellis, a former SAS member and now a leadership consultant, says that when an SAS commando unit parachutes into harsh terrain their survival depends on their capability to adapt to the environment and to create the portable micro-environment that we have heard about from retrieval teams and athletes.[5]

This rapid-response, minimalist approach suits the demands of dynamic performance environments. When conditions are changeable and unpredictable, mobility and flexibility wins.

Minimize your set-up. Go with just key pieces of equipment; eliminate reliance on the physical workspace; form small teams and encourage simple command structures. In a world where opportunities fly past at warp speed, the old set-ups are too slow.

Personal routines and rituals

In team games, such as Olympic basketball, one of the best strategies to reduce the performance of your opponents is to flood as many defenders as possible into the defensive half of the field or court. With less space, the attacking team's forward movement is slowed down and players are forced to speed up their passing just to maintain clear possession. Each player becomes more isolated or blocked, working in less space, receiving poorer and unexpected passes, which all leads to more errors that result in turnovers.

Is business any different? Workers are flooded by meetings, calls, e-mails, conversations, memos, reports, plans and problem-solving exercises. There is less space to share with team mates, faster demands, and shifting and unexpected tasks that come because of pressures in other parts of the business.

Game strategists have developed tactics to minimize flooding that have direct relevance to business. The three most effective tactics are **the fast break**, **running interference** and taking **the three-point shot**. Each tactic is designed before the game and then practiced until it works under the pressure of full-speed competition.

These tactics will have direct benefits for you if your time is currently being swamped by day-to-day issues that leave little time to coach, develop and strategize. They are also effective business strategies to introduce to others in your program.

HOW TO USE THE FAST BREAK IN BUSINESS

Because flooding only works when teams are slow to enter their offensive area, the most effective strategy is to get ahead of the game. Long passes, fast teamwork and preparedness to work hard and fast up and down the field or court are the key. Some years ago, teams did not use the fast break. There were unwritten rules that suggested that the ball should be brought slowly down the court (the slow break!). Everyone then arranged themselves into pairs and the players ritually went through the process of trying to reach the basket or stop their opponents. Also, the level of aerobic fitness of players was not good enough for them to sprint up and down the field.

Pre-global-game businesses operate to a set of rules not dissimilar to those that existed in team sport a few years ago. Some of these include:

- Everyone must attend a meeting (i.e. we all move down the court together).
- Everyone is needed for the whole meeting (i.e. everyone should be involved in any scoring process).
- All e-mails must be answered (i.e. when a player leads, they must be given the ball).
- It is OK to interrupt people when they are doing tasks (i.e. stop players on a fast break).
- Let other people determine how your day operates (i.e. accept bad passes as part of the game...don't challenge the game plan or fitness levels).
- Only coach others when there is time (i.e. do not coach during the game; just let people do what they are doing).

Business fast break

The fast break is an essential business strategy to capture opportunities and get to the real value-adding activities that Performance Leaders should be doing. It requires you to do three things:

- Create space ahead of you
- Agree team rules that foster the maximum number of fast breaks
- Trust players to make decisions.

FIGURE 5.9 Business fast break

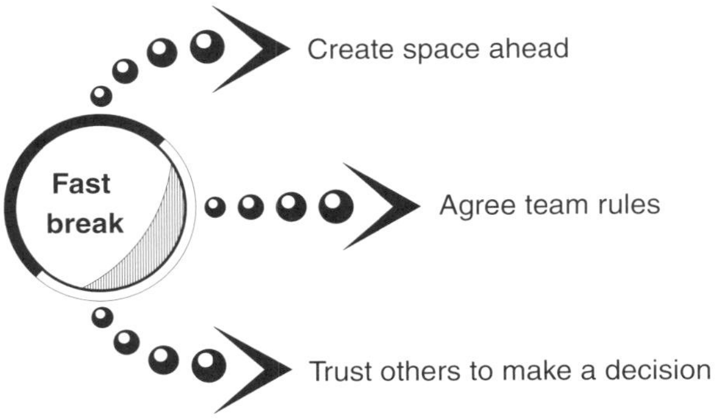

Create space ahead of you by getting to your schedule before other people start to fill it with their priorities, such as meetings and appointments. Two well-used strategies are as basic and essential here as the golf grip is to the professional golfer.

Space strategy one: Block your schedule/diary into chunks of time, including spaces for tasks that are one to three hours long, and spaces for three or four back-to-back appointments. As a starting strategy, put three task blocks and three appointment blocks into your schedule a few weeks ahead and then retain them. The principle is to create space in which you can focus on important tasks and get them done. *Focus time* is a key to achieving high performance.

FIGURE 5.10 Put focus times in the schedule

	Monday	**Tuesday**	**Wednesday**	**Thursday**	**Friday**
9am		APPOINT-MENT			
11am			APPOINT-MENT		TASK
1pm	APPOINT-MENT		TASK		
3pm		TASK			
5pm					

Space strategy two: Back-fill and front-fill your appointment spaces. Assume that you have an appointment block from 1pm to 5pm and you usually operate on one-hour meetings. The principle of creating space suggests that when the first person calls to seek an appointment you offer them the first or last appointment, that is 1pm or 4pm. Assuming that they accept 1pm, the next person will be offered 2pm and, if that does not suit, they will be offered the last appointment. The principles here are simple and effective. Firstly, create a block of appointments instead of scheduling them over the day (in ways that cause you to be constantly interrupted) and, secondly, put them together or as far apart as possible to create the focus time needed to deal with other tasks.

Agree team rules that foster fast breaks by addressing issues such as:

- who attends meetings and for how long
- e-mail rules/etiquette
- focus-time strategies for the team
- non-value-adding work activities.

Fast breaks will only occur when you trust others to make decisions. This comes from knowing each others' competencies, installing good monitoring processes and having a mindset that says "It's OK to let go". Building trust amongst others in your program is an essential aspect of Win Before You Begin.

How High-Performance Programs "Run Interference"

Many organizations think they have adopted the fast break but, instead of having one or two players take off while others cover for them, they actually compete with each other for activity. Around these people there is lots of activity, plenty of passing of e-mails and work but are they really creating value? Let's look at how interference adds to the potential of the fast break as a business strategy.

Sports coaches reduce flooding by devising a team plan that creates a pathway to goal by drawing the flooding players away from the offensive zone. Players either run interference (screening or blocking opponents) to create space for their team mates, or they draw their opponents away from the contest by making fake leads. Either tactic gives the "go to" player an opportunity for freedom that is similar to the fast break.

Business interference

Few Bosses and business people actually think strategically about running interference for each other. Usually they just all take off independently amidst the maelstrom of calls, meetings, projects and other demands. When people run interference for you they give you time to focus on a given task and get it done with quality and speed. The global game rarely gives you this chance. Instead, workers battle with shifting their focus from one interruption to another each. A task that might take an hour takes two and delivers less quality.

The High-Performance Leadership approach is to:

- Get people to run interference for you so that you can focus on a task and get it done
- Run interference for others
- Recruit people who you can delegate to — and then run interference for them so they can get on with it.

While running interference for the people who report to you, remember the words of Theodore Roosevelt: "The best executive is the one who has sense enough to pick good people to do what he wants done and the self-restraint to keep from meddling with them while they do it."

Interference strategy

Agree with your team that during your "focus times" someone else will run interference by taking your calls and attending meetings (that might be your personal assistant or a team member). When people call, the person who runs interference tells them that you are in a meeting but can be interrupted if it is urgent. Most people will not interrupt you and, in fact, will give your team mate the times that they will be available to take your call. This is a *double win* because you do not have to play telephone tag with them. Of course, this strategy needs support from your team and, at times, you will also need to play an interference role for others. Use these times to do tasks that can be done between interruptions.

TAKE THE THREE-POINT SHOT: APPLY THE 80/20 PRINCIPLE

The third strategy to defeat the crowded infield is to shoot from outside the flooded area. The U.S. Dream Team uses specialist three-point shooters to land the big bomb from outside the range of the opposition who are guarding closer to the basket. Is there an analogy here for business? What is the equivalent of the three-point shot in business? I believe it is the 80/20 principle.

Just as basketball rewards players with more points for longer shots, so the global game rewards those who can sort out the 20% of activities that are going to give the bigger (80%) return. These are the high-value strategies. When basketballers shoot from outside, they are rejecting their usual options and taking a risk.

Business three-point shooting

The danger of the global game for you and your business is that there are so many opportunities to shoot close to goal that you try to take them all but then find each route to goal is jammed. In such circumstances, Shane Garland, former Qantas general manager at Sydney Airport notes, "Changes are swamping you. You must decide which is the kite (of 15 or so) that has the best chances of success. That's where your experience counts. It gives you a feel for what is critical."[6]

The High-Performance Leadership three-point strategy is to:

- Use your experience to sort out what is high value and take a shot at these
- Say "No" to some closer options
- Put up some "big shots", knowing that they will not all land, although often they lead to rebound opportunities (for example, new network contacts).

Three-point strategy 1: Say "No" to many opportunities and choose the ones that are going to land the best results. Ignore some e-mails or faxes, choose your priorities carefully and don't take on things that can't be done. Challenge yourself: What have you said "No" to in the past month, and what have you exited?

Three-point strategy 2: Look critically at your business activities. If you could only tackle one-fifth of what you are currently doing, what tasks would you choose to give you the "biggest bang for the buck"? Apply the 80/20 rule and start to see things for their pay-off value.

Three-point strategy 3: Get up to a dozen balls in the air. No one shoots 100%, so common sense tells us that we have to put up some extra shots. John McGrath, one of Australia's youngest and most successful real-estate entrepreneurs, says that life has taught him many lessons in this regard. "One important one, which I utilize consistently," he says, "is that to be successful you need to have a dozen balls in the air at one time, because inevitably five or six of them are going to fall to ground."[7]

This is not contradictory to saying "No". Those extra shots are your future and they are the ones that often get forgotten in the business of today. Even if you miss, there is the chance of a rebound in the form of new contacts and learning.

Personal routines and rituals: Questions from the coach

Win Before You Begin is absolutely fundamental to creating the platform for high performance in the global game. Take a few moments to reflect on each of the questions about your personal routines and rituals before moving on.

- Is flooding reducing your personal performance?
- How can you use the fast-break strategy of creating space in your schedule?
- Is there value in back-filling and front-filling appointments to create more focus time?
- Who runs interference for you?
- Who do you run interference for in your program?
- Have you got enough balls in the air?
- Is saying "No" a strategy that you could employ better?

Information and communications systems

There are many excellent books and training programs that deal specifically with strategies for managing information including e-mails, data storage and retrieval and knowledge management. I direct you to these for detailed instruction on how to manage information. It is a major topic and not one that can be given sufficient coverage here. Two sources of expertise that clients I coach have found helpful are the training programs conducted by the Priority Management Group and Hugh Garai's book on the subject.[8]

As a brief summary, the leaders that I work with who are most effective in managing information have four things in common:

- clear goals and priorities
- a system that is set up to filter and sort information according to content and importance
- communication disciplines for what and how they pass on information
- an ability to act effectively.

These four practices help them to absorb large amounts of information and move it onwards. This is essential in networked organizations, where leaders can easily jam the system if they manage information poorly.

Support network

In interviews for this book, Louise Sauvage commented on how important her support team of two coaches and a manager is to helping her manage the pressures of travel, training, media, sponsors and competition.

"Support" is a word that does not always sit well with the image of the business leader, particularly among many male Bosses, who have been conditioned to believe that needing support is a sign of weakness. Business Athletes are sure about themselves and not threatened by support: they welcome it and gain energy from it.

If you do not have a support team (or, as some of our clients prefer, "pit crew"), your chances of success are diminished. The global game takes a massive flow of mental, physical and emotional energy away from you.

The High-Performance Leadership approach is to use a support team to:

- handle tasks so that you focus on high-value activities
- sustain and direct your energy
- provide perspective.

Who Handles Your Tasks?

Just as your business will struggle if it does not understand its core activities and allocate resources accordingly, so will you. This applies not just to business activities but to all facets of your life.

Business Athletes apply dual tests to their business activities:

- This adds value
- It is best done by me because of my capabilities or resources.

For example, Jane is a director of a small public-relations consultancy. She has one partner and three full-time staff, including a personal assistant whom she shares with her partner. Through working with a coach, Jane identified that over 30% of the time that she had been allocating to business did not meet these criteria. Through rearranging tasks and adding a part-time assistant to her staff, Jane expanded her profit contribution to the business and actually created extra time for herself that she now uses to take an on-line university course. Jane challenged her set-up, invested in support people to handle the basic tasks and trusted herself to make better value from her own time. Can this apply to you?

RESOURCES

Avoid using the "I don't have the resources" excuse.

At a High Performance Leadership workshop a participant asked the team: "If we were an orchestra, do you think people would come to listen to us if we offered the excuse that we did not sound good because our budget is too small?"

This organization, a government agency, has suffered huge increases in demand and cuts in budget allocation. Despite this, its service levels have increased as it sorted out what had to be done, worked the team interference strategies that we discussed earlier and refused to use prevailing conditions as an excuse for anything.

If you really believe that you do not have the resources, then change the goal or, if that is not within your power, leave and allow the organization to try someone else in your role. Keep in mind that one of the most fundamental principles of High-Performance Leadership is to "Pick Winners". This means picking niches in which you are competitive or can assemble the required capabilities.

WHO SUSTAINS YOUR ENERGY?

Many people fit into the broader definition of support team. Family, friends, associates, team mates, doctors, physical therapists, psychologists, accountants, lawyers, dentists, and so on, can all be part of our support network.

On the professional sports tours, you will see the most vivid example of the support networks that surround the Formula One teams, the tennis players, golfers and boxers.

Who do you need in your support team?

The answer is rarely static because there will be different needs from time to time. Nevertheless, part of Win Before You Begin is assembling a top support team that can help you to perform at your best.

Olympic support teams are assembled in accordance with the physical, psychological, technical and economic needs of the athletes. For example, all top athletes have agents or managers who handle business issues such as sponsorships, endorsements and sporting contracts. They also have physical trainers and psychologists to assist with their needs. Coaches are a given for all athletes. Around these are administrative support teams who arrange training, competition and general travel activities. Not to be forgotten are the family, partners and close friends. Each plays a part.

FIGURE 5.11   Support teams in sport and business

Support teams are an integral part of high-performance environments.

- Family
- Agent
- Assistant
- Coach
- Doctor
- Physical therapist
- Performance psychologist
- Team mate
- Technician

Who will help your business performance?

Use a coach

Leaders in high-performing organizations are increasingly following the lead of the sporting world by engaging personal coaches and mentors. I once again recommend having at least one coach with skills in relationships and personal management and a good knowledge of business. Use this person as a sounding board and then add specialist coaches in areas of technology, physical health and business specifics (for example, supply chain, marketing, finance etc) as required.

SUMMARY: CHANGE THE GOAL, CHANGE THE PERFORMANCE SET-UP

Like most people, you probably rate yourself as a good manager of change — ready, willing and able to adapt to the global game. If so, that's great. But, before we leave this chapter, have a good look at what you have done in the last six months to change your Performance Set-up.

The following questions will help that process:

- Can you genuinely say that the way you allocate priorities to your daily activities is as it needs to be for your goals and the conditions?
- What of your physical environment and mobility? Do they serve your needs or are there relics of past dreams?
- How are you set up to manage the flow of information that crosses your path? Are you filtering effectively or choosing between drowning or ignoring the information?
- Who runs interference for you?
- Is your support team in place and working well? Have you adjusted their roles to fit the demands of a new vision or do they still work to the beat of an old drum and make you less effective?

These are the questions that might best be asked by your coach, who can challenge your set-up in the manner that Olympic athletes expect of their coaches. They each address an issue that is central to making sure that you Win Before You Begin.

6

Performance Energy

What does "energy" mean to you?

Ask a NASA engineer how to create speed and, chances are, he will tell you that you need energy, and lots of it. Speed uses up energy and, unless it is a short flight, there must be a way to replenish what is used. In business we need speed *and* we need endurance. That means we need a source of fuel and replenishment.

And it is not just *physical* energy that is important.

Ask any chief executive what they need when juggling the often conflicting demands of the board, shareholders, staff and customers, and during the conversation you might hear the word "resilience". That's *emotional* energy and is every bit as important as physical energy to Business Athletes, who are faced with many drains on their energy.

Are there other types of energy? What about brain power: the energy of the mind to solve problems, create ideas, focus on issues and turn resources into assets? *Mental* energy is a currency in business. The power of knowledge and creativity is core business in a value-adding world.

Three forms of energy: *physical*, *mental* and *emotional* — each vital to performance, and yet too often neglected in business.

Let me add a fourth dimension to this discussion (which we will cover more fully in Chapter 8): the energy of the *relationship* — the network with its quantity and quality of relationships. *Relationship* energy might seem different from the other three, but I believe that Performance Leaders must be aware and skilled in observing the energy of their people and how it flows via relationships through the complex networks that are a feature of the global game. In particular, they must be able to form and foster relationships that add value to their program.

FIGURE 6.1   The four energies

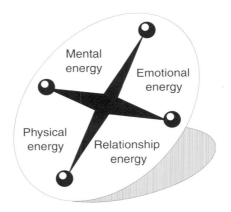

Mental energy:	the mix of your *knowledge, creativity and problem-solving capabilities*. Knowledge, ideas and intellect separate the Performance Leader from those who just manage the status quo.
Physical energy:	the *energy of your body* and its capacity to do the things that you want to do at speed and over time.
Emotional energy:	your *resilience* — your capacity to handle the emotional demands of the things that you experience.
Relationship energy:	the *extent and quality of your relationships* and network. In an Internet world, business happens through relationships, partnerships and alliances.

Energy for the Global Game

I have found through many hours of coaching leaders of organizations that self-awareness and the personal skills to manage and renew energy in all its forms are essential for High-Performance Leadership. However, it is a paradox of the global game that the reasons why leaders need energy are often the reasons why they can't find the sources to replenish it. This is highlighted in Figure 6.2.

FIGURE 6.2 Energy and the global game

	Impact of global game	Potential downside
Mental	Less time for creative thinking; information overload; knowledge becomes obsolete	Less creativity
Physical	Erratic time schedules; less time to exercise; meals on the run	Less endurance
Emotional	Isolated; change and career insecurity; high public accountability; pressures	Less resilience
Relationship	Demands of all stakeholders; less time for personal relationships; everyone is busy	Less support

Let's focus firstly on those two energies that are the "performance drivers" — mental and relationship energy — and then on the "performance enablers" — physical and emotional energy.

The Performance Drivers: Mental and Relationship Energy

Success in business requires two fundamentals: a product or service (something created with mental energy) and a network of either customers or alliances.

In the global game we have all effectively become freelance contractors with something to offer (product/service) and a network into which it is offered. If you are currently employed inside a large corporation, then you must have a skill or knowledge that the organization needs (a mental energy) and you had to create and now sustain a relationship with that organization in order to

FIGURE 6.3 Two business essentials

find and maintain your employment. If you are self-employed, then the same principles apply: you need mental energy (something to offer) and a network in which to sell your goods or services. Changes in career security suggest that we are all what Charles Handy calls "self-managers of our own assets".[1]

If you look at your career in this way it becomes very obvious that your career is at risk if your mental energy or network energy falls. Your mental energy (knowledge, creativity, intellect) and networks (relationships) are therefore key drivers of your performance. They cannot be ignored but, rather, must be developed. Fortunately the global game, despite its pressures, does tend to give us a lot more opportunities to do this than the old-style bureaucratic world, where information and networks were tightly controlled.

Mental energy: Questions from the coach

Challenge yourself with these questions or get your coach to probe the area:

- What has happened to your mental energy over the past year?
- Has your work given you a lot of intellectual stimulation?
- Have your problem-solving and creative skills been stretched and strengthened, or has your mental edge diminished?

If you believe that your creativity and knowledge has decreased (other than through tiredness — we'll get to that in a minute), then change jobs as soon as possible. Anyone who is not having their brains stretched to the limits at the moment is in deep trouble.

Relationship energy: Questions from the coach

Try these questions to check your relationship energy:

- Has the size and quality of your network increased or decreased over the past year?
- Have you developed deeper relationships with key people?
- What has happened to your personal relationships?

If your network isn't stronger now than a year ago, then consider whether it is you or your role that is shrinking the power of your relationships. Without a growing and valuable network a freelancer will starve (we cover this in detail in Chapter 8).

THE PERFORMANCE ENABLERS: PHYSICAL AND EMOTIONAL ENERGY

As much as mental energy and relationship energy are drivers of performance in the global game, so physical and emotional energy are the performance enablers (or potentially the blockers).

Performance Leaders cannot build and capitalize on knowledge, creativity and relationships unless their physical energy (endurance) and their emotional energy (resilience) permit. In fact, many leaders invest vast amounts of time and effort increasing their knowledge and relationships and then fail to use these resources because of physical and emotional fatigue.

Physical energy: Questions from the coach

Use these questions to consider your current physical energy:

- Do you have the physical energy to keep up with the game?
- Are you fast and agile from start to finish of a business day?
- Do you joke about your physical condition?
- Do you rationalize that business is a mind game, not a physical game?
- Are you fitter then 75% of your peers?

The traditional Boss, like the average tennis player, says that physical condition doesn't matter because performance is mostly about skill. Well, perhaps it didn't matter last century but welcome to the global game. Professional golfers used the same argument until Tiger Woods arrived. Simple message: get fit or prepare to under-perform. It is not a luxury: it should be an edge.

Irrespective of their personal emotional style, high performers also recognize the importance of managing the emotional drains of a fast, uncertain and risky game. Acclaimed artistic director Peter Sellars illustrated this when he said, "Because everyone is so harried, so rushed, so pushed in the theatre, I try and allow some repose, some space".[2]

Dealing with the emotional area in business is still a difficult issue, particularly for many male business leaders who have been conditioned to conceal and control their emotions. However, as psychologist Steven Biddulph has pointed out, "If you think about it, the great men in history — Gandhi, Martin Luther King, Buddha and Jesus — had a courage and determination, along with sensitivity and a love for others".[3]

Concealing emotions and being totally independent might give you the impression of great strength but it is a wooden approach that doesn't help you to move on and grow from experiences, and makes it less easy to relate to others at a human level. In sport, this is a particular issue with both genders, and only in recent years have sporting clubs started to recognize and deal with the links between emotional well-being and high performance.

For those reasons again, the use of a coach who can help, particularly with debriefing tough events and situations, is an important part of High-Performance Leadership. Dr Bill Griggs acknowledges this as an important aspect in helping people in his program deal with the tragedies that they encounter at accident scenes. Similarly, the Australian sport system has a network that provides emotional debriefing and support services to athletes.

Mental energy: Questions from the coach

Challenge yourself with these questions or get your coach to probe the area.

- How do you rate your emotional resilience?
- Are you clear in mind during the tough situations?
- Do emotions cloud your actions and judgment?
- Do you struggle to find a quiet space in your mind?
- Do you do something regularly that renews your inner strength?

Lifting the energy

There are principles and practices of High-Performance Leadership covered throughout the book that will help you to lift your mental and relationship energy. In fact, Chapter 8 is devoted entirely to the topic of network relationships, and Sections Three and Four contain many ideas that will stimulate your thinking about how to create a high-performance program. Therefore, in the remainder of this chapter the focus will be on strategies for lifting your mental energy, with a few reminders on physical energy.

Lifting emotional energy

A surfer peels away from line-up and paddles into the pit forming in front of the largest Waimea wave yet seen on a sunny Hawaiian afternoon. Oblivious to the crowd on the cliffs and the rescue helicopter hovering overhead, he gathers speed. In one movement, he slips to his feet and drops almost vertically down the face of the 30-foot monster before turning to tune the board under the line of the massive curl that threatens to swallow him without trace. He is totally focused, calm and yet alert, ready to change direction in an instant.

Replace hype with Active Calmness

If the surfer followed the rules of many "new economy" experts, he would have hyped himself to the max; but it doesn't make sense, does it? Performance at top level, under really demanding conditions, requires a mix of courage, physical and mental balance, inner calmness and focus.

Hype is for the next level down: it is not High-Performance Leadership. Don't let anyone convince you that the way to succeed in this fast-moving world is to be on the edge and to keep people on the edge all of the time. Performance Leaders exude an energy but it's not frenetic energy: it is a calmness and poise, despite all that they are doing and all that is happening around them. It is the dynamic performance zone: flow.

I use the term "Active Calmness" to refer to this mental state in which you are alert and in control. Active Calmness is a feature of the mindset of Formula One racing drivers, pilots and others who perform consistently under fast, dynamic conditions. It provides the alertness and vigilance needed in volatile environments and the control to make clear judgments. That the absence of Active Calmness in leaders places the program at risk is reflected in the comments of Air Transport Safety Investigator Steve Wilson: "What is the cause of most aviation accidents? Usually it is because someone does too much too soon, followed very quickly by too little too late."[4]

As we saw in Chapter 3, one of the most important triggers to the zone is balancing the perception of the extent of the challenge with your perception of your capabilities. Active Calmness lowers the anxiety about the demands (reducing the perception of challenge) and increases the perception of capability, enabling you to deal with higher levels of challenge.

Three Active Calmness strategies

Active Calmness comes from attitude or mindset and through your physical actions. Three techniques that we have found helpful in developing a skill that works under typical global-game business pressures are buffers, quietening and centering.

Buffers

The roles that we fill every day take a large amount of energy and it is easy to "become" the roles and to lose ourselves in them.

FIGURE 6.4 Active Calmness increases performance

However, one of the beliefs of many top performers is that they are separate from the roles they fill in their lives. For example, Michael Johnson, the great U.S. 400-meter runner, describes running as something that he *does*, not that he *is*. He doesn't want to lose himself to a role. If I were to take this perspective and apply it to myself, then Figure 6.5 illustrates the differences.

You are not the roles that you fill, even though some are central to your identity and your life. This is a very important point, because what you give to each of the roles in your life is energy. That energy has to be replenished, and it will come from two sources: other roles (for example, exercise, socializing) that create a different state of mind from the usual draining roles, and time when you can step out of all of your roles and just be yourself (for example, when you are by yourself or meditating).

Nurture your inner mental energy when you are facing the demands of a high-performance world. For me, for example,

FIGURE 6.5 Separation between self and roles

surfing, a quiet weekend at our country retreat, aerobic exercise and kicking a football with my sons are activities that take me out of my "business mind" and freshen up my thinking. Meditation also helps me to create my own quiet space, particularly when I am traveling on business. Shane Gould describes this as having a "release activity" which helps to balance the performance pressures.

Active Calmness: Questions from the coach

Take a few moments to consider each of the following questions and jot down your thoughts:

- Which of your roles takes the most emotional energy?
- Can you see the distinction between you and the roles you play?

- How do you replenish your energy?
- What activities naturally freshen up your mind?
- When do you allocate time for your emotional needs?

Quietening

Herb Elliott has written of his ability as an athlete to "develop a sense of power within me that was peaceful and quiet".[5]

Most Olympic athletes learn a quietening technique designed to shift them from their active mind and body state, into this state of quietness that speeds up mental and physical recovery and builds personal power.

This notion of creating the experience of inner calm is a core concept in just about every human-development process, including religions and martial arts.

One of the projects for participants in the High Performance Leadership Programme is to learn a quietening technique that suits their personal preferences. For example, some find the combination of physical movement and mental concentration in yoga or Tai Chi to be useful, while others like the quietness of meditation or massage. Some find that learning the fundamentals of a martial art, particularly *aikido*, to be powerful in both developing quietness and in understanding a philosophy that integrates with the Business Athlete principles.

We also include training in a simple and effective quietening technique as part of the workshop program. The fundamentals of this technique, which reduces muscle tension and clears and quietens the mind, are outlined in the following section.

Background to the Active Calmness technique

The Active Calmness technique requires a quiet, distraction-free environment and between 14 and 21 days to develop a baseline of calmness. To achieve full ongoing benefits, the training needs to be continued on a regular basis as a part of daily routines and combined with the centering approach described later in this chapter.

Instructions

The instructions that follow describe a simple training process that will introduce you to the process of quietening. If you want to go further with this, or have any concerns about practicing a quietening technique, then speak with a psychologist, who will be able to guide you through the process or suggest alternatives.

- Find a place that is quiet, distraction-free, comfortable and warm. Allocate between 20–30 minutes, avoiding times straight after meals (digestion affects the calming) or when you are very tired. Wear loose-fitting clothes and no shoes (loose slippers are OK).
- Sit in a comfortable chair and adopt a symmetrical posture. This means a comfortable position with straight back, hands loosely clasped in the lap and feet flat on the floor about shoulder-width apart. Avoid slouching or leaning forward.
- Begin with three to five minutes of very light stretching and loosening your muscles, including your arms, shoulders, back, chest and legs. Lightly stretch each muscle group and then exhale as you relax the muscles and then let them be as limp as possible. Focus on a point directly in front of you. While you may wish to close your eyes, it is important not to. (The transfer of quietening skills from this non-stressful situation into a performance situation will be most effective when you have learned the skill with your eyes open.)
- While focusing your gaze on the chosen point, breathe in slowly, smoothly and quietly, giving as little interruption to your mind and body as possible. Let the air push out your lower stomach and abdomen. Breathe out even more slowly. Imagine that tension is leaving your body with each breath. When you have exhaled, focus on the stillness that can occur between one breath and another.

It may take quite a few sessions for you to become aware of the stillness; however, this is the feeling to capture, so perseverance will be rewarded. Do not force it, simply repeat the same slow, effortless, natural abdominal breathing pattern over and over. (Make sure that you do not wait too long between breaths or breathe in too slowly, because this will just restrict oxygen and reduce the value of the whole activity.)

Figure 6.6 highlights the simplicity of the process, using the shape of the triangle as a guide for your breathing. That is, breathe in as your attention moves up the left side, then relax as you breathe out and enjoy the moments of stillness before the next breath.

During the whole activity, focus your attention on a specific point and develop the feeling that there is nothing but the feeling of stillness and the point on which you are focusing.

Your mind will probably not want to clear itself of all other thoughts, but this is quite natural and is experienced by virtually all Olympic and Business Athletes when they begin the training. Let your response to intrusive thoughts be no more than to simply

FIGURE 6.6   Active Calmness training

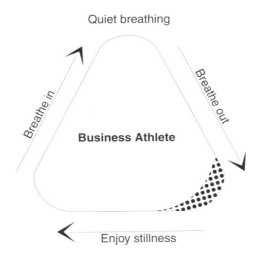

acknowledge what your mind drifted towards and to re-focus on your breathing, on stillness and the focal point.

The active mind fights back

The biggest challenge for most high performers in learning the quietening technique is to accept that it takes time and that their minds will seem at times to be actively opposed to the process. This is fine: remember that your mind is accustomed to being active and it is certainly not used to the calmness that can occur during this process. Be satisfied if at any time during the practice, even if only for a moment, you experience the feeling of stillness.

Centering

In the midst of a business day when you are juggling phone calls, e-mails, meetings, negotiations and the like, centering is a useful tool to have in your personal armory. This simple and well-known technique is widely practiced in the martial arts and in sports such as archery, golf, shooting and basketball (when attempting free throws).

Centering in its most basic form is no more than the breathing technique used in the quietening training, except that it is used at the start of or, in some cases, during activity to create that sense of inner calmness.

Watch the leading tennis players before they serve, or divers before they take up their position on the board. They build centering into their pre-performance routine.

Experiment with using centering during negotiations, prior to a phone call or between activities. With practice, you will find that you can achieve lots of centering moments without anyone else being aware. In a rapidly changing environment, where lots of things are competing for your attention, the use of centering can increase your energy and improve your creativity and decision-making.

Emotional energy is OK

Leaders who are sensitive to the impact of emotional energy on their own performance are more likely to understand and manage the emotional pressures faced by the people in their programs. High-performance environments are emotionally demanding and, as Margaret Hansford, CEO of FPA Health, says, "If we don't deal with feelings, people are distracted from their work and can't hear each other and ultimately can't perform."[6]

When you set the example by building performance buffers and modeling Active Calmness in pressure situations, you increase the likelihood that you and others in your program will perform to full potential.

Physical Energy

The typical business professional can usually complete their work tasks on a given day with a relatively poor level of fitness compared with that needed for even moderately demanding activities, such as playing tennis, walking briskly up a hill or shoveling a few loads of sand. However, as business has become both a speed and endurance event, there are numerous potential benefits in maintaining an adequate level of physical fitness. These include:

- more energy to devote to each work task
- more energy for family activities
- clearer thinking because of reduced tension
- better overall quality of life
- more endurance to cope with demanding work periods
- fewer aches and pains (headaches, back pain).

Many global-game organizations offer physical training programs to staff and some are now making it a part of the work routine. It makes great sense to have your people work out together because they get to communicate informally and good ideas often flow as the endorphins from exercise are released into their bodies.

Go for activity not intensity

Alex is a partner in a medium-sized national legal practice. She attended a conference on the theme of "Better Fitness, Better Performance" and, following the conference, decided to put the concept into practice and join a local health club. She did two sessions of aerobics and two sessions of a super-circuit (a timed circuit of weights) each week.

During the first month, she improved quickly and had more energy at work and felt much better about herself.

In the second month, she started to set progressively more difficult goals for herself. This meant doing an extra hour of the most advanced aerobics class and increasing weights and repetitions during the super-circuit. Soon, she was feeling tired at work and was struggling to meet her training goals.

By the third month, Alex was skipping training sessions and by mid-way through the next month had sustained an injury to her back. A week later, she decided to give up exercising.

Have you ever been through an experience like Alex's? She lost sight of her original goal and let her natural achievement motivation take over. Her training moved rapidly from active and rejuvenating to over-intense and exhausting.

Athletes and coaches sometimes fall into the trap of believing that if a bit of activity is good for you, then twice as much must be twice as good. For Business Athletes, the key to fitness training is viewing activity as the goal, rather than wanting to reach Olympic levels of fitness. This means asking three key questions:

- What is my current level of health and fitness?
- What is a realistic health and fitness goal?
- How is my current activity helping me to achieve my goal?

Give some thought to your current level of health and fitness, and always discuss your program with a trained professional who can design something that suits you and the demands of your role.

SUMMARY

This chapter is intended to prompt you to review and refine the way you manage your energy and, in particular, your emotional and physical energy. Performance Leadership places great demands on your mind and body. It is essential that you are aware of this and take steps to nurture and renew your energy. This is not a selfish indulgence but, rather, a core skill of Business Athletes in the global game.

7

Becoming A High-Performance Brand

The high performers of business, sport, science and politics have more than just the core skills of their trade. Individuals such as former U.S. President Bill Clinton, former GE chief Jack Welch and golfer Tiger Woods are also clever and effective marketers of their own *high-performance brand*, and this is how they attract money, media, opportunities and more power.

You also have a brand: in your company, your industry, profession and community. By effectively creating a brand identity of "high performance" you will also attract many opportunities.

A Different Ticket to the Top

From the industrial revolution to the last decades of the 20th century, "the establishment" or "old money" controlled the world of business. Deals were done behind the closed doors of clubs to which only those from the right schools and the right families were permitted entry.

Membership was male and usually of some professional background such as law, accountancy or stock-broking. Conservatism and hierarchy dictated the terms.

Being in the establishment network guaranteed a ticket to personal wealth and access to all manner of opportunities in business and politics. From Britain to the U.S. and China, the same basic principles of power prevailed.

Over the past two decades, the growth in communications and information technology and travel, and the reductions in trade barriers, have acted to shift power away from the old networks. Obviously banks, corporations and governments still hold considerable power, but there is an increasing shift of power towards the individual and small business.

For example, publishing houses traditionally held most of the power over authors but now it is the brand-name authors who hold a lot of the power. This rise of *personal* power has come about because people with a special skill, knowledge or product can assemble whatever they need to commercialize it in the global game. The stronger the brand identity of the person involved, the greater their power.

Personal power is also a key factor in career progression. The days of promoting people slowly and steadily through an organization have been replaced by fast-tracking those who are perceived to have high potential. Once again, personal power lies with those who demonstrate capability and who create and market themselves as a high-performance brand. Figure 7.1 illustrates some of the shifts in power that have accompanied the global game.

FIGURE 7.1 Power shifts in the global game

	Pre-global game	Global game
Capital	The "top end of town" controls the money	Many sources of capital attracted to ideas
Production and distribution	Establishment network and big business decide what gets made and where	Ideas are commercialized through organizations assembled from anywhere
Boundaries	Tight network boundaries — little social contact across networks	Strong networks, greater variety and movement across networks
Career progression	Promotion based on seniority	Promotion based on performance

HIGH-PERFORMANCE BRAND OR COMMODITY?

High-performance brands influence the purchasing decisions of people all over the world. Nike, Starbucks, Xerox and Virgin each occupies a piece of the consumer's mind and represents quality, image and value.

Brand is another word for magnet. Top brands are like magnets and attract the best employees, investors, partners and customers.

Do you want to be a distinctive high-performance brand? It makes good sense to answer "Yes" because the best "people brands" get the best promotions, are invited to join the most interesting projects and attract people and power. If they work for themselves, they get the best clients, the best assignments and charge the highest fees.

The risk of not focusing on building a distinctive brand is that you become like everyone else: a commodity. Commodities don't attract the same opportunities, even though they might have the same skills and knowledge.

Personal brand: Questions from the coach

Try these thought starters or get your coach to probe your thinking about branding:

- Which well-known brand is most like you (BMW, Dell, Microsoft etc)?
- Where is your brand as a Performance Leader positioned between commodity and high value?
- What value do you currently gain from your brand?
- What are the risks of your current brand positioning?

In the global game, it is not just corporations and celebrities that are actively building their brand value. Individuals and teams create and communicate a brand that acts as an attractor to others in the game. The following sections explain how to do this.

BUILDING A HIGH-PERFORMANCE BRAND

The way to build your personal brand is to follow the principles that are commonly adopted by sports and celebrity manager/agents when they build their clients into global brands. Top managers such as Australia's Elite Sport Properties (ESP) have a feel for the chemistry between an individual athlete and a potential sponsor. As ESP director Craig Kelly says, "Matching an athlete with a sponsor is not a simple process. A manager must take into account a number of considerations — Does the athlete appeal to the target audience? Does the sponsor fit with the athlete's brand strategy? Is there scope to grow the athlete's brand with the sponsor?"[1]

Ian Thorpe, Olympic and World swimming champion and 2002 International Athlete of the Year, is a highly visible emerging story of high-performance branding that illustrates the key principles.

In Japan in 2001, Thorpe became a marketing sensation. His management (Grand Slam International) aligned his performance qualities (world-champion swimmer) with his personal qualities (young, fresh-faced, articulate, friendly, humble) and matched them to the needs and interests of Japanese teenagers.

The chemistry between "Brand Thorpe" and the market was near to perfect. Japanese teenagers like swimming, and couldn't get enough of the tall, rich, good-looking (and yet humble) Thorpe. To emulate him, they bought the products and services that he endorsed.

Supporting Ian Thorpe has become a cult-fashion in Japan and if his management continue to be as successful in promoting Brand Thorpe internationally as Thorpe is in the pool, the same phenomenon will spread world-wide.

Four elements of Brand Thorpe have direct relevance to Business Athletes and to positioning yourself as a high-performance brand:

- Know what your brand communicates (and to whom)
- Deliver results (Success in the pool underpins everything)
- Package and promote the brand
- Mold the person (Thorpe) into the brand.

KNOW WHAT YOUR BRAND COMMUNICATES (AND TO WHOM)

Ian Thorpe seems to know very clearly what his brand communicates and to whom. Do you know what your brand is communicating?

FIGURE 7.2 Building your high-performance brand

Know what the brand communicates

Deliver results

Building your brand

Package and promote

Mold yourself to the brand

When the 17-year-old Thorpe's website registered 3.5 million hits in the week after he won two gold medals on the opening day of Olympic swimming competition in Sydney, his management knew they were on a winner and a potential global product.

Traditionally, the only way that an Australian athlete or celebrity could become an international brand was to move to the United States. Greg Norman, Karrie Webb, Nicole Kidman, Mel Gibson and even Rupert Murdoch only became global brands after they positioned themselves physically in the U.S.

Thorpe's management capitalized on the unique opportunity presented by Thorpe's success in the lead-up to the Sydney Olympics to make him an international brand. Media coverage was organized that led to a big break when Thorpe was offered the opportunity to be one of the faces of the Olympics for Coca-Cola in Japan.

Thorpe was the face of the 2001 World Swimming Championships in Fukuoka while, behind the scenes, his management capitalized on the commercial opportunities that came from the chemistry between Thorpe and his audience. Thorpe left with five gold medals, equaling the all-time record, and took a huge step towards Brand Thorpe becoming an international phenomenon.

Thorpe's management were very astute in spotting the Japanese opportunity and building the chemistry between their high-performance brand and the teenage market. They shaped the four elements that create and sustain that chemistry: value-promise, attractive values, position and portfolio.

Each of these elements is as relevant to your branding strategy as to any high-performance athlete.

Define your value-promise

Your employer, customers, investors, partners and employees are all interested in the value-promise that you offer. For example, Richard Branson promises adventure, the unconventional, value for money

FIGURE 7.3 Chemistry between brand and audience

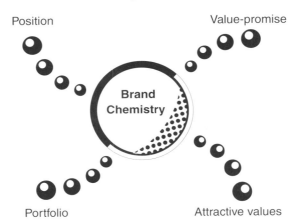

and fun. Ian Thorpe promises Japanese teenagers a self-image: a feeling of being successful, good-looking, international and nice. The promise is relevant and valuable.

What does your brand promise that is relevant and valuable to the people who are central to your vision and plans? Think about each segment, including employers, customers, alliance partners and employees, and identify their current and emerging values and needs. For example, organizations in the global game are looking for Performance Leaders who can create and lead vibrant, agile, high-performing teams that collaborate with others in the total program. Is this what you offer? Getting the chemistry right between your high-performance brand and your "audience" is very much about getting the right value-promise.

Make your values attractive to your audience

When celebrities invest in community programs, they do so with a very close eye on the values that they want to project to the market. Thorpe chose to involve himself in an anti-drugs campaign in Japan, while Pat Rafter and Tiger Woods are well known for their work with disadvantaged children. These activities are all part of projecting values that are attractive to their target audience and making a genuine contribution to society. Louise Sauvage has created a program called "Aspire to be a Champion" (www.aspire.au.com), which raises funding for grants to aspiring young athletes with a disability. It is both remarkable and refreshing that so many top athletes make a contribution outside of their sport.

People will have a view about your values because of your profession, industry, culture and a hundred other factors. Think long and hard about the values that are important to you and your target audience and how you want to project them in tangible and intangible ways.

Values show in your behavior. In particular, when times are tough people will see your values in the decisions you make, the way you treat people and how you carry yourself. High performers are disciplined and consistent in their actions around their core values. This does not always mean being clean-cut and polite or having apple-pie looks. People respond to something different, as Nike has shown over the years by associating itself with athletes who have "attitude". Sometimes you may not agree with those values, but from punk-rock stars to athletes and business gurus the chemistry is built by projecting values that are attractive to the audience.

Celebrity agent Max Markson claims that he can make anyone famous, even the unknown.[2] Max's view is that positioning for publicity comes down to either getting extraordinary people to do ordinary things (for example, getting Bill Clinton to walk down the street) or getting ordinary people to do extraordinary things (as, for example, when the father of Derek Raymond, the British runner who injured his leg at the Barcelona Olympics, jumped the fence to help his son and together they shuffled across the line).

It is the combination of values and the point of difference that sits in the customer's mind to really create the chemistry.

FIGURE 7.4   Values projected by celebrities

Celebrity	Values
Billy Connolly (Actor/Comedian)	Irreverence, fun
Mother Teresa (Nun)	Compassion, selflessness
Bill Clinton (President)	Power
Eminem (Rap singer)	Anti-establishment
Lance Armstrong (Cyclist)	Courage, achievement
Nelson Mandela (Political leader)	Belief, justice

Position yourself

Many young athletes expect that winning an Olympic gold medal will open the door to endorsements, sponsorships, wealth and fame. Unfortunately, many fail to secure even a single endorsement from their victory, proving very clearly that all Olympic medals are not of equal worth.

Winning a gold medal is not much different from getting a university degree. It's a good start, but you need something distinctive, even unique, to offer the world. So, just as Bill Gates didn't hang around at Harvard to finish his degree, some athletes are so unique that they don't even have to win gold medals. For example, at the Sydney 2000 Olympics, Australian pole-vaulter Tatiana Grigorieva became arguably the most commercially successful silver medallist in Olympic history. A number of factors helped, including a home Olympics and prime-time television coverage. But the real clincher was that Tatiana is a "drop-dead" gorgeous model, with blonde hair and long tanned legs. Companies went crazy with offers to have this lady associated with their products and services.

Marketing experts always suggest narrowing your brand to distinguish it from competitors and general "noise". For example, one of my clients, who works in a biotechnology company, positioned herself as a commercial facilitator. It was a new concept for that business and has since been instrumental in her gaining access to some of the most exciting projects. As marketing gurus Al and Laura Ries suggest, "the best way to make news is to announce a new category".[3]

As you reflect on how to define your brand and to distinguish it from others who are in the market for promotions, assignments and other opportunities, keep in mind the sage advice of R.L. Wing in his translation of *The Art of War*: "Brilliant leaders align themselves and their organizations with the larger trends and evolving sentiments of society."[4]

Refine your portfolio

Most multinationals operate a number of brands and sub-brands; however, unless each fits into a meaningful pattern, there will be brand confusion.

Most of us start our careers with a predominant brand, such as "engineer", but over time we move away from that role and gather many other brands — manager, facilitator, designer and consultant. What was your starting brand and how has it changed?

Brand Thorpe started as a swimmer and retains that, at least for some time. But, if successful, he will become like Michael Jordan, who is still linked to basketball but is now branded as a celebrity.

When managing your career be mindful of pulling together a congruent portfolio of activities that reflect your high-performance brand. One of my challenges has been to manage the branding between sports psychology and corporate activities. Despite having done my training and professional supervision in organizational psychology and spending well over 75% of my total career time in the corporate consulting world, I am still seen by some people as a sports psychologist. Sport and, particularly, the connection to the Olympics is a great point of differentiation but sometimes when I get calls asking me to give a pep talk it reminds me that the sports psychology brand has its disadvantages and needs to be managed.

Consider how your current portfolio looks now, and how you might shape it over the next few years. For Business Athletes, the advice of Tom Peters to update your resume every three months is a sound practice for maintaining a relevant portfolio in the global game.[5]

DELIVERING RESULTS

Three gold and two silver medals at the Sydney Olympics made Ian Thorpe Australia's most successful athlete of the previous seven Olympiads.

It would have been easy for him to use the post-Olympics period to reap the benefits of that success through focusing totally on media and corporate activity. But Thorpe's management, and Ian himself, decided that success would be short-lived if he did not continue to deliver in the pool. And so he set his sights on beating his Olympic performance at the World Championships in Fukuoka.

Thorpe and his support team knew that to "win before you begin" at the World Championships, he had to:

- strengthen his swimming capabilities
- get better at repeating high-level performance throughout a gruelling meet
- rest enough to recover from the physical and mental stress of competition and training.

And he still had to maintain a high media profile for his long-term brand strategy.

That he turned in a remarkable World Championship performance of individual gold medals (in the 200m, 400m and 800m — all in world-record time) and two relay gold medals while becoming a media sensation in Japan illustrates the power of combining high performance with an effective branding strategy.

Delivering the results for Brand Thorpe means not losing sight of his unique selling points, which are a combination of swimming ability and personality.

The test of "Brand You" is delivery on "the promise". In business, that means delivering results for people in a manner that meets or exceeds their needs or perceptions. Be mindful also that short-term decisions such as taking a new job or project, partnering or choosing a mentor don't harm your brand in the longer term. As ESP's Craig Kelly says, it is important for the manager to be sure that there are no "conflicts or missed opportunities if an athlete signs with a particular sponsor, or that the sponsor affects the athlete's ability to do his or her main job, and that is to perform well".[6]

Delivering results: Questions from the coach

Consider these questions to review your current branding strategy:

- What are your unique selling points?
- Do you have a reputation for delivering results?
- What long-term value do you expect from enhancing your brand?

PACKAGE AND PROMOTE YOUR BRAND

Brand Thorpe is a well-packaged, high-quality product that is actively promoted but not overexposed. Like all products, it has a lifespan and will need to evolve in order to fit with the marketplace of the future. However, the Athens and Beijing Olympics are major opportunities that lie ahead.

The promotion of brands like Thorpe, Tiger Woods and others requires careful packaging and a combination of strategic and opportunistic promotion and marketing. The same applies to Business Athletes in the global game.

Packaging

Your packaging is everything that people see and sense about you as a person. It is your clothing, accessories (pens, technology), color choices, stationery, motor vehicle, office location and layout, travel preferences (airline, seating, hotel) and a host of other such factors. It is also verbal style and personal style, the standards that you apply to things like punctuality and returning messages, and every piece of work that you produce.

Next time you prepare a report, give thought to how you package it, and what you want it to communicate about you and your brand. Packaging is easily forgotten when you are familiar with the product, but it is so obvious and important to the person who is forming an opinion about you.

A word of warning. There are many people who completely lose their identity in an attempt to fit the stereotype of what they think will appeal to other people. Be realistic about the notion of packaging and make some judgments about what you are prepared to do and what you are not prepared to do. For example, do you want to add another $200,000 to your mortgage to buy that waterfront weekend-retreat that seems to be fashionable at the moment?

Packaging: Questions from the coach

Challenge yourself with these questions about the way you are packaging yourself:

- What messages are you, as a Performance Leader, projecting through your packaging?
- Are they consistent with your vision and values?
- Are they consistent with the values of your target audience(s)?
- What needs to change?
- What are you not prepared to change?

Promotion

Brands need promotion, but be careful how you do it.

The options range from traditional "push" activities, such as direct selling and advertising, to "pull" activities such as public relations (articles, stories and attendance at events) intended to encourage people to come to you.

As a general rule, the higher the value of the brand, the less the need for push and, in fact, the greater the risk that it will actually damage the brand. The very nature of product endorsement by top athletes and other celebrities is a prime example of companies trying to sell their products through association rather than hard selling.

Work closely with your coach or, if appropriate, a public relations expert to decide how to promote your high-performance brand.

In our consulting business, some of the options for "pull" strategies include speaking at conferences, attending networking functions, writing articles and books, and facilitating meetings. These are opportunities to project a brand image and value-promise without selling directly. There are times, however, when a direct approach is best, particularly when we believe that we have an offering that solves a problem for a client or potential client.

SUMMARY

The global game has increased the power of individuals and made the high-performance brand more valuable and essential. The example of Brand Thorpe illustrates the brand-development and promotion process that you can use to create and sustain your personal high-performance brand.

High-performance brands: Questions from the coach

Take a few moments to reflect on the key issues covered during this chapter by considering the coaching questions below.

- What is your overall career strategy?
- What relevance does branding have to that strategy?
- What is your current brand awareness amongst key segments?
- What results do you expect from branding?
- What threatens your brand and how can you protect it?
- How do you plan to enhance your brand?

Keep your personal brand in mind as you go about developing and implementing the High Performance Leadership strategies outlined in Sections Three and Four.

High-Performance Networking

The driving forces of the global game have fostered the growth of a complex network of organizations, markets, economies, societies and information.

Stock-market crashes, terrorist attacks and computer viruses remind us that we are all connected in this complex web, and we need new skills and approaches to perform amongst the challenges that this presents.

For organizations and their leaders, one of the biggest paradigm shifts is to move from looking at teams, organizations and nations as individual units or entities, to understanding and engaging with the networks of which they are a part.

For example, leaders have always valued organizational structure but few have put much value on the network relationships of employees, customers, partners or suppliers. In fact, traditional management practice was to restrict the influence of informal networks (for example, the "grapevine") and to tightly control any cross-boundary activity (such as gaining customer feedback or dealing with someone higher up the hierarchy). Stifling informal networks is now more likely to destroy value.

One of the most remarkable examples of networking that I came across when researching this book was Duncan Chessell's account of its value during the Everest expedition. Duncan explained how the network relationships gained from "immersing myself in climbing for six years" meant that he knew people "all over the mountain who shared little bits of information over the radio". That information was invaluable in guiding him to the summit. He also spoke of the networking high up on the mountain, where competitiveness was replaced by cooperation and the sharing of information and of resources such as ropes, oxygen and support climbers.[1]

In the previous chapter, we highlighted the closed "establishment" networks of pre-global-game days. Figure 8.1 further explains some of the shifts in the nature of network relationships.

FIGURE 8.1 Changes in network relationships

	Pre-global game	Global game
Formality	Club-like membership — long-term, little change	Informal networks — forming and evolving
Value	Little value in informal networks	Encourage and foster to capitalize on networks
Control	Eliminate or ignore most networks — they lack control	Formalize some networks but give them freedom
Types of networks	Top end of organization — professional and for sales: not with competitors and suppliers	Very broad — including with competitors, partners and suppliers
Hierarchy	Viewed networks as a threat to hierarchy	Seeks to find balance between hierarchy and networks
Networking skills	Not an important capability	Essential capability at all levels

Networking: Questions from the coach

Before we look further at the principles and practices of networking, consider these questions:

- What value do you place on the network relationships of your employees or colleagues?
- How do you help others to foster their networks?
- What restrictions make it difficult for you to build and maintain networks?
- What are the strengths of your personal network(s)?
- What are the weaknesses or gaps in your current network?

THE CHALLENGES

In a networked world, it is difficult to argue against the notion that forming and fostering network relationships between people, organizations and communities will enhance performance. Nevertheless we find, when introducing High Performance Leadership Programmes into medium-to-large organizations, that there are vast untapped opportunities to network within the organization and to share contacts and linkages.

Performance Leaders and Business Athletes take a different view of network relationships from that of the traditional Boss. For example they:

- put a value on network relationships and give priority to building and enhancing these relationships
- define their program as a network, not a closed organization structure, so their planning takes into account the broader system
- view informal networks such as the "grapevine" as an untapped resource (not as an enemy of management and a leakage of power)
- know when and how to formalize network relationships without stifling flexibility
- develop the interpersonal skills needed to work across diverse and changing networks.

For Greg Bourne, President of BP's Australasia region, "Networking is key to being able to adapt quickly. Networks provide information, support and influence" and enable you to "call on your strengths wherever they are".[2]

In this chapter, we address these high-performance networking practices by providing a practical set of principles and techniques for forming and maintaining network relationships. The organizational-design issues that networks present will be dealt with in Chapter 14.

NETWORKING ADDS VALUE TO YOUR BUSINESS

Networking is the formal and informal process of building and maintaining mutually beneficial (network) relationships. These relationships can be with peers, staff, mentors, advisors, partners, customers, prospects, suppliers, colleagues — in fact, anyone.

The process of networking includes activities such as socializing before and after meetings and forums, conducting tours and entertaining influential people, sharing information and providing assistance across an organization, mentoring, forming alliances, attending and arranging social functions and contacting and meeting with people in all manner of situations. Anytime you are mixing with people, you are potentially building network relationships.

Some of the personal benefits and value that come from network relationships are explained in the following table.

FIGURE 8.2 Benefits of network relationships

New business leads	Prospects, direct invitations to participate in an activity, or information on opportunities
Information	Things that you need to do your job more effectively, such as how to weave your way through a large organization to get to the decision-makers, how to move your business through a turnaround
Accessing resources	Resources to build the business such as finance, consultants, employees and alliance partners
Advice	Mentoring and advice that help you to make better personal and business decisions
Research	Informal research into markets and fields of information, such as the potential impact of a new technology or a change in government legislation
Opportunities	Access to opportunities such as presenting at a conference or pitching for a project
Coaching	How to best use a new piece of software, resolve a tricky interpersonal conflict or win a tender
Ideas	Fresh perspectives that inspire your creativity and lift your energy
Referrals	Referrals to people who can assist you to achieve your aims

While there are plenty of courses that encourage you to get out and expand your network, it is important to be strategic in choosing where you want to invest time to create and build relationships.

At any given time the value of your network relationships will depend upon the skills and knowledge of the people in your network, the quality of those relationships, and your aims. Be wary of building a big, widespread network and losing the value that can come from a closer, more selective network.

Centers of influence

In most organizations and communities there are people who are centers of influence. These people are "nodes" in networks because of their particular knowledge, relationships, experience or personal style. For example, accountants are important centers of influence for real-estate agents because they know who is in the market for investment properties.

Centers of influence often shape and influence decisions within and across networks. If you can build positive relationships with these people, you are well positioned to benefit from their influence and greatly expand your power.

Politicians use centers of influence to help with the introduction of new policies; sports coaches use them to influence the actions of the team on the field; and business leaders use them as agents of change. The two key characteristics of centers of influence are that they are well connected and influential. In a networked global game, connectedness and influence can become more powerful than traditional hierarchies.

A note of warning: the most influential people are often not the noisiest and most obvious. Look for the people who *really* influence decisions on strategy and priorities.

Mutually beneficial

People who network badly just build up a list of contacts and use them for their own ends. They pressure people for leads or to buy their services, ask favors, waste people's time, and never thank them or do something for them. Rather than creating value, they destroy it.

My view is that high-performance networking is about building long-term, mutually beneficial relationships. You cannot do that unless you take the time and effort to get to know the values, style and needs of the people in your network.

What follows is a process that acknowledges that networking is a business activity that must generate value, but one that is, once again, about sustainability.

READY, SET, NETWORK

As part of introducing the High Performance Leadership Programme into organizations, we coach leaders and teams in a process that we call "Ready, Set, Network". It is undertaken as an intensive project by each person and designed to expand the power of their networks. For most participants this means forming new relationships and strengthening current relationships.

The Ready, Set, Network process covers five stages for forming and strengthening network relationships:

- Define the game plan
- Profile and blend for rapport
- Create a positive impression
- Gain commitment and exit
- Deepen the relationship.

The relationship between these five stages is illustrated in Figure 8.3.

Let's look at each of these five stages in some detail.

DEFINE THE GAME PLAN

Your networking game plan begins by identifying your main network categories and goals for business-related networking. For example, Judith is a team leader in a technology services business. Her categories and goals for the Ready, Set, Network project are described in Figure 8.4.

FIGURE 8.4 Networking categories and goals

| Main Categories | • In-company |

FIGURE 8.3 Forming and strengthening network relationships

Define the game plan

Ready, Set, Network

Reconnect: deepen the relationship

Profile and blend for rapport

Gain commitment and exit

Create a positive impression

• Industry
• Professional

Goals

• Build a mentor relationship with a senior leader within the company
• Form five new "B-level" relationships across the industry
• Maintain relationships with colleagues

Reflect on your network categories and consider if you also want to include personal networks (social, family) or stay with core business networks.

As you identify the main categories, take time to consider the main sub-categories. For example, in the example above, Judith noted that her in-company network could be sub-divided into peers, her team, management, sales, professional/technical, administration and social club just to name a few. This is a good discipline to illustrate just how many interlinked networks exist in an organization.

Map your existing network

As with any performance activity, the key is to establish challenging and specific targets. A simple and effective strategy is to list your existing relationships and then place them into five categories, A, B, C, D and Z. The criteria for each category are explained in Figure 8.5.

FIGURE 8.5 Network relationship categories

Relationship level	Characteristics
A	Close, mutually beneficial relationship, high level of trust, important to your current and future plans
B	Respectful relationship usually based on views of competence and character, relevant to your business direction
C	Acquaintance, will acknowledge each other in the street, may be relevant to your business plans
D	Know of each other but a distant relationship, little one-to-one contact
Z	Distrustful, negative relationship — can have an impact on your future success

With your network relationships sorted into categories, it is relatively straightforward to identify targets for expanding the power of your network by:

- adding to the quality of relationships (for example, move them from B to A).
- increasing the size of your network (for example, meet some new Cs and Bs).
- maintaining your existing network.

The last point is very important because, in the hectic flow of the global game, it is easy to let existing network relationships slip and to lose contact with people. It is just as important to keep in touch with people in your current network as to develop an even bigger network.

Our experience from running Ready, Set, Network programs is that most people need a wake-up call to devote more productive time to maintaining their A-level relationships. Does this apply to you?

Profile and Blend to Build Rapport

Have you ever met someone in a business context and felt uncomfortable and distrustful of them? They sent out signals that you picked up at a subconscious level. They oozed a negative energy. You might have seen it in their dress, their hairstyle and body language, or heard it in their tone of voice or the content of their conversation. Because they didn't build rapport with you and the foundation for trust that is so essential to forming effective relationships, chances are that you didn't share important information or opinions with them.

Foundations for rapport

Skilled professionals build rapport by understanding the other person's needs and values, and projecting a personal style that blends with those characteristics.

For example when people blend their language and personal style to match yours and show understanding of your situation, they make you feel comfortable and a rapport begins to build. From that initial rapport, trust develops as you get to know each other's character and capabilities.

This process of analyzing another person's values, needs and personal style is what I call "profiling". An allied and equally important skill is that used by skilled counselors to match their behavior (tone of voice, level of assertion) to that of the other person. This is what I call "blending". The more accurate the profiling, the more likely it is that blending will be successful in making that all-important positive first impression.

These two skills will undoubtedly prove to be of great value to you as you expand your network relationships.

Blending

Blending is about reducing the perceived differences between you and the other person. This requires that you move to establish common ground.

There are three key elements of blending: *vocal* — in which you adapt your own style to suit that of the other person; *physical* — in which your dress, facial expressions, body posture and movements are adjusted to align with those of the other person; and *verbal* — in which you ask questions and discuss topics that you expect to be of interest to the other person.

All of this is, of course, common sense and is an approach you see every day in television advertisements in which the advertisers match their style to the needs and expectations of the audience, about whom they have gathered a great deal of information. Here, profiling and blending are used to good effect. Blending does not mean being a complete mirror of the other person but it does mean recognizing that people are generally more comfortable with other people who are in sympathy with their verbal, vocal and physical style range. Blending builds rapport.

As you get to know a person and as they get to know you, styles often start to change, with more openness and greater give and take on either side. The assumption that sits behind effective blending is that you know the other person's needs, interests, values and personal style. This is where the process of profiling is important.

A word of warning: Blending can leave itself (and you) open to accusations of being manipulative and unethical. This, of course, all depends on your motives and values. We work on the assumption that Performance Leaders act with integrity at all times.

Profiling

Top coaches are amongst the most skilful people at "reading" their athletes to understand their values, needs and personal style. Using skilled observation developed over years of experience, they pick up on signals that help them to build rapport and bring out the best in their athletes.

In the global game, where you are constantly meeting new people, the skill of "reading" other people gives you an advantage because you can form relationships quickly and match your products and services to their needs. This applies equally to the sales person selling a product and to a team leader motivating a new member of the team.

To develop your skills in reading people, begin by using a pro forma profiling sheet similar to the type used in High Performance Leadership Programmes. An example of a draft profiling sheet is displayed in Figure 8.6. You will notice that it is divided into two sections: Personal needs and Character.

How to read character

Psychologists use what are called "bipolar traits" to assess the dimensions of personality characteristics. The most common of those dimensions is extroversion/introversion which, in its simplest form, describes a person's level of sociability. For example, extroverted people are outgoing and gregarious, enjoy the company of others and are open and friendly. Introverted people, on the other hand, tend to keep to themselves and to be more serious and introspective.

Extroverts are often easier to identify by their behavior and also by their career choices (they gravitate towards careers that involve

FIGURE 8.6 Profiling pro forma.

Character

Introverted	⟵ ● ● ● ● ● ⟶	Extroverted
Passive	⟵ ● ● ● ● ● ⟶	Dominant
Data-oriented	⟵ ● ● ● ● ● ⟶	Intuitive
Emotional	⟵ ● ● ● ● ● ⟶	Controlled

Personal needs

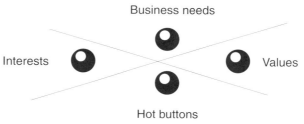

high levels of contact with people). Generally, it is not too difficult to get a fix on where a person might fit in regard to the dimensions of extroversion and introversion.

Introverted				Extroverted
✿	✿	✿	✿	✿
Always act in this way				Always act in this way

The majority of people in your program and broader network will fit between these extremes, being neither strongly introverted nor extroverted. Most, however, will lean towards one side or the other and this gives a guide as to how to blend.

For example, how would you best blend with a new staff member who is highly introverted? Would this person feel most comfortable in the company of really outgoing, loud, gregarious people, or people who are quieter and more reserved? Chances are that the best way to create rapport with this person will be to blend to their quiet and reserved style.

Three other dimensions are useful when using profiling in business situations to assist in blending. These are: passive/dominant; data-oriented/intuitive; and emotional/controlled.

Passive/dominant

Passive people accommodate the views of others and show little assertion or need to control people or things. Dominance is often seen in business as assertion, exercising control and shaping and influencing. In Olympic team sports you tend to find a large percentage of dominant characters. What is it like in your program?

Passive				Dominant
✿	✿	✿	✿	✿
Always act in this way				Always act in this way

To blend with dominant people, try matching but not exceeding their dominance. With those who are more passive, temper your own dominance but still remain at or just above their level.

Data-oriented/intuitive

This dimension is one that is useful in business because it often reveals itself in the decision-making style of leaders. Data- or detail-driven leaders favor numbers and objectivity, while intuitive leaders work happily in the abstract and with the big picture. If you try to blend with a data-driven person by offering pie-in-the-sky ideas, you'll quickly lose any rapport. They will respond much better to details and facts.

Data ✿   ✿   ✿   ✿   ✿ Intuitive

Always act in this way   Always act in this way

Emotional/controlled

Highly emotional people react to issues with their emotions and, until you get to know them, this can make them quite unpredictable. Once you do get to know them, however, they are usually very easy to read because their moods are transparent. Those at the other end of the dimension play their cards close to their chest and show little emotion. They are poker players and arguably the hardest people to blend with because they offer little feedback. They will test your Performance Leadership skills and particularly the questioning techniques covered in Chapter 11.

Emotional ✿   ✿   ✿   ✿   ✿ Controlled

Always act in this way   Always act in this way

Be careful not to show too much emotion when dealing with the poker players. On the other hand, highly emotional people respond to people who listen and empathize with whatever is sparking their emotions.

Profiling: Questions from the coach

Consider a person with whom you want to improve your network relationship. Can you identify any characteristics that might help you to blend to their style?

How to read personal needs

The profiling pro forma (Figure 8.6) asks questions about a person's needs, values, interests and passions.

As with character profiling, it is amazing how much we actually know about someone or can deduce before even meeting them. For example, if I want to build a relationship with a senior finance executive in a government agency, I will try to find a colleague who has met them or knows a little about them. Even before doing this, I can already assume from their role and professional background that minimizing risk, discipline, involvement in executive decision-making and getting the best value from assets are likely to be important to them.

If my colleague adds some extra personal background, such as the executive's career path, their personal needs (such as need for status), as well as things that are important to them (for example, family, sport, art or community interests), then a clear picture is emerging. Add to this a little basic research from the Net and business publications about their organization and I can prepare to meet them and discuss their likely interests. With this profile, I am also in a much better position to blend my style and conversation to suit their preferences.

When considering a person's needs, search for "hot buttons" to build a profile that gives you the best chance of building rapport. Hot buttons are the things that the person is passionate about. For example, if you know that a leader is passionate about integrating community services to produce the best value for the community, then you can ask questions and offer points of view to cover this area.

The profiling pro forma addresses both personal needs and character. The time spent in researching such matters will pay off in building better relationships and, in a networked world, that means business opportunities, inside and outside your program.

CREATE A POSITIVE IMPRESSION

It is perhaps something of a truism to say that first impressions are very important, but it bears repeating nevertheless. Whether meeting a person on a plane, at a cocktail party or at an interview you need an introduction.

The best self-introductions are brief and contain a tag line that the other person remembers and comments on. For example, a participant in a recent Ready, Set, Network program has the surname "Young" and she uses a play on this name when handing over her business card by grinning and saying, "You'll remember the name because we're never old and stodgy". It works really well for her and in this simple way she brands herself and her business as young, fresh and creative.

In their account of networking at the 2000 Olympic Games, John Rich and Lucille Orr wrote that an effective introduction "needs to be short, to the point and interesting enough to make them want to ask questions about your service or product".[3]

We recently worked with a client organization that had a number of staff who were about to attend the World Congress in Information Technology. With over 1,500 delegates at the Congress, the need for a distinctive introduction was obvious. Therefore, as part of this program, we worked with them on identifying the points of competitive advantage for their organization and their own unique capabilities and experiences. These were then included in introductions that were practiced prior to the Congress and later used successfully to create positive initial impressions.

A point of difference in your introduction might include a brief story of what you do, an interesting angle or maybe even a comment on your name. Much like the sustainable point of differentiation for your business, make sure that you have a point of difference in your introduction so that you make a positive and lasting impression.

Connect to the other person's interests

After your brief introduction, the next step is to say something that will connect with the needs and interests of the person with whom you are speaking.

Small talk can lead to profitable business. When you can get people to talk about themselves and their interests, it can open the door to all manner of opportunities.

Prepare your openers

If you know in advance who is to be in attendance at a conference or function, it is good to be prepared with a few questions or conversation "openers". Open questions are usually best, provided they do not put the person into an uncomfortable position. For example, extroverts will revel in being asked for their opinion so they can be the center of attention. An introvert, however, will appreciate it if you frame the opener so they can answer more briefly and in a way that doesn't embarrass them.

Cooperative networking: Disclose your goals

In the global game, it is often important to form relationships with people who may perceive themselves to be in competition with you. In business as in everyday life, finding common ground is always a good way to start. Try asking questions that lead towards finding shared, rather than competitive, goals. This is particularly important in professional networking, where people tend to be protective of their relationships with clients.

One of the most powerful shared goals is the desire to do the best possible job for a client so that a long-term relationship can be built. Achieving this, means understanding your core capabilities and being willing to introduce colleagues with complementary skills to your client. Where this happens in an environment of trust, everybody wins.

The traditional corporate hierarchy fosters an environment of competition, but this can be reduced when Performance Leaders actively build relationships across the barriers.

GAIN COMMITMENT AND EXIT

Networking happens in many situations and sometimes, particularly at functions such as conferences and networking dinners, you need to leave the person and move on.

When you have established rapport and want to move on, the two key points to remember are:

- **Secure commitment:** Arrange to contact the person again, ideally by allowing them some flexibility about where and when, but locking in a future contact.

- **Exit gracefully:** We have found this to be consistently the most challenging issue, because people do not have simple techniques that help them to move from one group to another at larger functions.

Securing the commitment is relatively straightforward and can include agreeing to send a note or some information, or arranging a meeting if you have really hit on a point of common interest.

Making an exit can be a little trickier but a couple of useful standbys are what we call **"Other Person"** ("It was nice meeting you...but Kerry has just caught my eye and I must pass on a message to her before the meeting recommences") and **"Organizer/Freshener"** ("Can you excuse me ... I need to freshen up/check with the conference manager before the next session"). These suggestions are, of course, fairly commonplace but it is always good to be armed in advance with a strategy, the lack of which may cause embarrassment to all concerned. And going to the bathroom or checking with event organizers are not just appropriate exits, they are also essential activities at many events! Needless to say, though, always show respect for the other person, and avoid leaving them by themselves.

RECONNECT: DEEPEN THE RELATIONSHIP

The final stage in the Ready, Set, Network process is reconnecting with the person after your initial meeting and building the relationship.

Network relationships will inevitably range in quality according to the rapport that you form and the common needs that emerge. The relationships that endure usually develop common understanding and trust, which comes from knowing each other's competencies, discovering the person beneath the role/title/job description and maintaining frequent contact.

Your game plan for maintaining and deepening relationships therefore needs to consider how to:

- define your goals/expectations for the relationship
- demonstrate competency
- build ongoing rapport
- maintain contact
- offer benefits (e.g. information, assistance).

Consider these issues for each key network relationship and use the tools and tactics outlined below to assist this process.

Tools of the Networking Trade

The three key tools that should be a part of the basic set-up of all Business Athletes are a diary, a contact system and business cards. There are numerous off-the-shelf contact-management systems to help you to keep track of contacts and to synchronize this with your diary. From the most basic card systems to the latest networked contact database, they all contain information outlining the name and contact details of the person concerned, their occupation and business interests and how you met. There will be room to record the date you were last in contact, a summary of your conversation and the names of any referrals from this person.

Having this data is useful, but you'll also need a diary or organizer to assist you to make the creation and maintenance of relationships a valuable and regular activity.

The final tool of networking is the business card. Cards are part of your branding and are absolutely essential in Asia as part of the ritual of forming new relationships.

Summary

This chapter has offered an introduction to the personal skills needed to form and maintain network relationships. These relationships are essential to doing business in the global game. While we are not yet at the point where organizations recognize and measure the full value of networks, the creation and maintenance of network relationships is a critical role for the Business Athlete and Performance Leader.

As organizations form more and more strategic alliances with partners, employees, suppliers, contractors and the like, the core capability of high-performance networking will continue to rise in importance and value.

In the next section, we move on from the practices of the Business Athlete to explore the role and skills of Performance Leadership. As we do this, you might keep in mind that one of the most powerful resources available to organizations is the network relationship. It is essential, therefore, that Performance Leaders are skilled in fostering those relationships and in developing the capabilities of others to create and develop all manner of relationships.

Section Three

The Performance Leader

9

In Search of a Performance Model

In this chapter you will learn a simple yet powerful Performance Model that has been developed, tested and refined in many high-performance settings and that has been shown to guide Performance Leaders and teams to create their own high-performance programs. In organizations from small technology operations, to multinationals and large government agencies, Performance Leaders have reported that the model gives them a practical and highly effective framework.

Many have commented on the value of having a Performance Model that can be understood and communicated to all employees, and applied by each Performance Unit in consistent but flexible fashion. This is the model that you will refine and customize in Section Four to become the basic framework for your high-performance program.

WHERE THE MODEL WAS BORN

As the global game began to affect my business clients during the second half of the last decade, I found myself in a unique position: I was head of psychology services for the Australian Olympic team, managing a consulting business and working in alliance with PricewaterhouseCoopers (PwC) Consulting.

The Olympic role allowed me to see how the full array of high-performance sports programs were created, and to participate at a strategic level in setting up the operations of one of the world's leading Olympic teams. From there, I had access to the best thinking in performance psychology and coaching, and could see it applied and tested in one of the world's most dynamic and competitive environments. Working in alliance with PwC, the world's largest professional-services firm, I witnessed the global game firsthand. Through observing and working with the firm's consultants and clients, I was able to adapt and evolve what I had learned into the High Performance Leadership Programme.

During that process, it became very clear that the global game was causing organizations to change their structures, customer relationships, information systems and value chains, to adapt to the demands and opportunities of globalization, new technologies and shifting customer requirements.

This led my focus increasingly towards the issues of agility and adaptability that were evident in high-performance programs that I had studied. Each of these programs had a capability to constantly scan the world, to develop strategies and to implement them quickly and effectively. This agility and adaptability seemed essential for organizations right across the corporate world. We adopted three words as a catchphrase for the process: **analyze** (scan the world), **strategize** (decide on positioning and action) and **energize** (mobilize people and resources to capitalize on the opportunity).

FIGURE 9.1   Three elements of agility and adaptability

The Performance Model was born out of my experiences of high-performance programs and the emerging needs of Performance Leaders for a practical model to guide the development of their programs. That model had to focus on how to create individuals, teams and total organizations with the agility and adaptability required in a global game.

Making Sense of Complexity

You will recall from Chapter 2 that in each sports program in the Australian Olympic sports system, a Performance Model was designed and brought to life through the actions of the Strategic Leaders, coaches, support staff and athletes.

My hypothesis was that if a similar model could be created for business leaders/coaches this would help them to make sense of the complexity of the global game, to organize their thoughts and resources and create a shared commitment amongst people in their program.

In search of such a model, I observed the Olympic head coaches and spoke at length with those who worked with them, particularly their assistant coaches and psychologists who were involved in creating and sustaining the performance culture. A common feature was the clarity of each coach's philosophy or ideology on how to create and sustain a culture in which athletes could perform at world-class level. While their individual philosophies may have varied, they were all very much focused on performance culture.

Ultimately, it seemed that what I was looking for was not a "packaged philosophy" but, rather, a mental model or template through which a Performance Leader could design, consolidate, communicate and implement their philosophy or performance culture. This template should contain common performance principles but also allow space for leaders to add their own flair and, most importantly, to adapt to and evolve with changes in the world around them. The template should also be understandable to everyone in the program so that leadership was on everyone's agenda and not just the Strategic Leader's.

An Example of a Mental Model

Let me give you an example of the type of model or template that I was seeking.

Suppose that a professional coach asks you to take over a soccer team and offers to train you for this task. One of the skills that you will learn is "bench coaching". This is the skill of watching a game, understanding and analyzing what is happening and then making decisions about game tactics. If you haven't seen this soccer team play before, you will need some frame of reference so that you can understand what is happening. To get this, you will need to become a skilled observer, which means learning and using an "expert model". It is this model or way of looking at the game that the coach will want to impart. For example, they will explain principles, rules and practices of their offensive strategy, thereby giving you a way of looking at the offensive set-up that brings order to what looks like chaos or chance. With experience, you will start to populate that model with your own ideas (philosophies) and start to see even more patterns.

Reflect on an area of your own life in which you have been trained. That training contains core assumptions/philosophies and a number of expert models. In my own field of psychology, the "personality assessment" is an example of a mental model that helps to bring order to complexity by sorting a person's individual characteristics into categories (traits) that allow me to make clearer judgments and predictions about behavior than would not be possible without such a model.

As an undergraduate student, I can remember scoffing at a professor who told us that there was nothing more practical than a simple and effective model. From experience, I can now see that what he was asking us to do was to see merit in templates that guide us to see patterns in the world, rather than looking at complexity with no way of making sense of it. Michael McMasters has said that complexity "is about making things simpler through patterns".[1] Examples of mental models that have been popularly used in business include the SWOT analysis, TQM and Six Sigma.

The value of mental models, such as that used in bench coaching, is that they direct our attention onto the things that are important. For Performance Leaders, this means understanding the elements that influence performance and then developing a point of view and techniques to do just that. Successful top-level Performance Leaders and coaches all seem to do this, either consciously or intuitively. Either way, they bring to their global game a Performance Model that they embed into their program and, ultimately, it is this model that underpins real and sustainable performance.

BUILDING THE MODEL

The Performance Model contains seven elements. These seven elements were common to all of the successful high-performance programs that I have studied and they are also the same elements that trigger in-the-zone performance in individuals. Accordingly, the framework contains exactly what we need in a global game: a model that helps us to make sense of performance for individuals and various types of organizations.

Let me use the example of a single shot from an archer to illustrate the seven elements.

Imagine the Olympic archer, her aim narrowing from the lifelong dream of winning the gold medal to intense focus through the sights towards the gold ring 70 meters away. Competitors span 50 meters each side of her, poised and waiting for a break in the tricky breeze to shoot. All day she has followed her pre-competition strategy: equipment checked, warm-up completed, she is set up to perform. She is "in the zone": relaxed yet alert, confident and focused as she almost automatically releases the arrow, straight at gold. It deviates slightly in the cross-breeze as she continues her follow-through before slipping almost silently into the target just above dead center. She pauses, reviews the total performance, seeking any opportunity to improve the next shot, while accepting the result as evidence of a strong process producing a strong result.

In this single shot the archer has brought seven elements into play that describe or define a template of performance:

- taking aim
- awareness of conditions
- preparation/set-up
- mindset
- executing the task

- learning and adapting
- achieving a result.

All performance programs, from that of the individual archer to those of the major corporations, must address these seven elements. You can use the seven elements (expanding the notion of mindset to include group mindset/culture) to design performance programs for all manner of activities, ranging from shooting a single arrow to engaging an entire corporation in a global mission. The content will change from one situation to another but the framework remains consistent.

High-Performance Leadership expands on these seven elements, guides you in how to apply them to yourself and then, as a Performance Leader, to your program in a way that suits the global game. You will find as you review the elements that they also offer a language that can be understood right across even the largest of organizations.

Exploring the Seven Elements

The basics of each of the seven elements in the Performance Model are outlined below and then expanded into separate chapters in Section Four.

Take Aim

Take Aim reminds us of the first and most obvious element in performance. That is that, even in the most uncertain of environments, the best performance starts with an aim.

Take Aim is the motivation, direction and focus required to create and sustain high performance. It is visualizing your ideal future, whether that be a business venture, relationship or personal health. It is also knowing your values; defining what is important and what you will do next.

Reflect on your analysis of your own performance zone and on the relationship between aim and zone. For example, how does clarity of purpose affect your performance? And what about the goals of the organization in which you are working? What impact do they have on your motivation and enjoyment? These factors are central to determining your level of personal or organizational performance.

Any model of performance needs to include this element and to describe how factors such as purpose, vision, values and goals influence performance. In Chapter 12 you will build your own performance philosophy for Take Aim.

High-performance environments challenge us to not only clarify our aim, but also to re-check and refine as the conditions shift. In such a changeable environment, we need stable guideposts. That is why I include values and principles as part of Take Aim, because they are likely to remain unchanged for a lot longer than your goals.

Scan: Know the Conditions

Complex performance environments are unpredictable. They can change in an instant, often as a result of a single event, which then completely alters the game and the requirements for success. Like the movement of a single grain of sand that brings down the whole sandcastle, the world is full of possible scenarios that can be triggered from small or large events. Of course, we can predict that a sandcastle will fall at some point if we keep adding sand. Social, political and economic systems, however, are not as easy to predict but they all have their patterns and trends and it is these that high performers notice.

Scan: Know the Conditions requires having a constant process for scanning the environment because in high-performance environments scanning is as important as planning. Where in years past senior managers set a plan and gave staff a sense of security from that plan, the new high performers "scan-plan-act" all at the same time. It is a different mental model for a different time and one that links Take Aim and Scan: Know the Conditions.

Scan: Know the Conditions poses two broad questions:

• How will the conditions influence our performance?
• How can we best scan the conditions?

It is important to point out that no scanning process is going to help you to predict everything. There will always be unforeseen events, but the best performers know and anticipate how various scenarios will test their resilience. For example, the petroleum industry experienced the Bhopal/Union Carbide and Exxon Valdez disasters but, as Greg Bourne of BP Australia suggests, "As an industry we learned from survival events. Some things are not predictable. You need to be ready for that and have the flexibility to respond."[2]

Scanning is always part of the preparation for an Olympics. As a global event, staged in different locations and under the glare of media attention, it is essential to understand the likely range of conditions and to throw in a few "What ifs?". Coaches prepare athletes for the conditions, including both macro issues (media and culture, for example) and micro issues (such as competitor behavior and venue conditions).

In business, the principle of Scan: Know the Conditions directs our attention towards customers, suppliers and alliance partners, and also to competitors and market conditions. It points to threats and constraints and also to opportunities and linkages. Like the yachtsman, the Performance Leader must maintain alertness to the conditions, anticipate the emerging patterns and changes and respond accordingly. As Catherine Livingstone, chair of CSIRO and former managing director of Cochlear, advises, "More than developing visions, the critical characteristic for the future will be the ability to see patterns — particularly evolving patterns."[3]

Performance Set-up

To the professional golfer, "Performance Set-up" means having the right support personnel (coaches, sports psychologist, manager, caddy), equipment, practice routine, course strategy and pre-shot routine. The professional knows that this basic set-up will go a long way to determining their performance. "Win before you begin" is the motto of many top sports coaches who know that time spent on Performance Set-up gives them a competitive advantage. The Williams and Ferrari Formula One teams are great examples of this principle at work.

The people in your program are professionals. What are their support networks, their daily planning systems, equipment and routines? Amateurs are lax in their set-up, leaving too many things to chance. Professionals set up to succeed.

Performance Set-up poses two core questions:

- What resources, structures, systems, processes and routines best suit our aim and the performance conditions?
- How can we create that Performance Set-up?

The demands and opportunities of the global game have seen massive change in the set-up of organizations (for example, in structure, information systems, supply chains and capabilities). Interestingly, many organizations have failed to capture the advantage of these changes, particularly the implementation of new technology. We will explore how to implement changes in, and capture the benefits of, Performance Set-up later. Not surprisingly the Performance Leader plays a key role in this activity.

The pre-global game was an era of rigid corporate set-up to suit a reasonably stable environment. Structures, processes, employment arrangements and organization boundaries were constant or slow to evolve. However, the speed and complexity of the global game is spawning new forms of set-up designed to suit a more dynamic, networked world. Organic structures, flexible employment contracts and knowledge systems are just some of the examples of the changes in Performance Set-up that we will be considering in Section Four as you create and refine your Performance Model.

Performance Culture

This element of the Performance Model deals with two components: individual mindset and collective mindset (culture). This is referred to in the model as "Performance Culture".

Your individual mindset is the thoughts, emotions and underlying values that you bring to the task, to yourself and to others. It is reflected in the choices you make, how you react to setbacks, the nature of your relationships, and your balance and poise under real pressure.

Mindset, particularly in challenging situations, often determines your success. As discussed throughout Section Two, it is a key ingredient in the make-up of the Business Athlete.

While individual mindset is important, our Performance Model must also extend to the collective mindset or culture of the organization and the all-important interpersonal relationships.

Culture is what has become popularly known as the "DNA" of an organization. It is a collective mindset that evolves over the history of an organization from all manner of influences including leadership, industry/specialization, shared values, relationships and experiences. It is a strong component of the Olympic campaign because creating a consistent high-performance culture is a key task for the architects of the total system.

Culture is seen by some businesspeople as "soft" and not as important as financial and related matters. The PwC 2001/2002 survey of leading Australian chief executives revealed that investing in shaping the culture is definitely on the "front page" of the best leaders. From other reports, it seems that it is yet to be accorded the same importance by many boards and market analysts, who prefer a simpler, short-term attention to the bottom line.

It is interesting that much of the corporate world is still working to a model that ignores culture as a key driver of performance. This is absurd because any Performance Model that ignores the importance of creating a high-performance mindset/culture does not address what is needed to create and sustain high performance.

Within Performance Culture, the Performance Model deals with issues of attitudes, leadership (including relationships), teamwork and performance themes. Each shapes the performance of your organization and must be addressed in your Performance Model.

Perform

We cannot have a Performance Model that misses the central element: action.

Performers get things done. They recognize that the best planning systems, the most original ideas and the latest technology only give them a performance advantage when they turn these into actions (and then into results). Equally, it is only through action that you will bring your values and overall Performance Model to life.

For many people it is the task itself that triggers the zone. What activities in your work put you and your colleagues into the zone? Which push you out of the zone?

High performers act in line with their aim and in concert with other people. They are effective and, in business, they regularly question and challenge the value of activities. They are not frightened to stop doing something that is no longer relevant even if they've invested a lot of time and effort in it.

Resilience, agility and adaptability are all evidenced in behavior. Our Performance Model must identify what people and organizations "do" that defines them as high-performing. This will vary from one situation to another but the bottom line is that they perform.

Learn and Adapt

High-Performance Leadership capitalizes on opportunities, and it will not be surprising therefore that one of the core elements of the Performance Model is Learn and Adapt.

Learn and Adapt is part of the same basic process that all organisms follow (even the simplest bacteria learn from their interactions with the environment and adapt). It is part of continuous improvement, although it is really the continuous *search* for improvement that is important. Improvements tend to come in bursts, not continuously.

Learn and Adapt raises two core performance questions:

- How can we learn from our experiences and our world?
- How can we apply that learning to help us adapt to and shape our world?

Our Performance Model needs to address issues such as where and when learning best occurs. It must also embrace evolution as a part of the adaptive process and find a place for action learning and debriefing.

Learning is about feedback, gathered through experience, observation and from performance data. Performance environments offer rich sources of feedback (if we are geared up to receive them). The Performance Model must address the importance of feedback and how to generate, capture and use it. This is fundamental to creating a high-performance program.

Achieve Results

The final element of the Performance Model recognizes the end of the performance cycle. For an athlete, that might be the end of a game or the end of a career; for a surgeon, it might be the conclusion of surgery; and for the mountain climber it might be reaching a landmark on the way to the summit. Each represents a success.

Achieve Results reminds us that success is one of the most common triggers of the zone. As we celebrate milestones and the achievement of goals, we build confidence in our ability to influence and shape the world.

Unfortunately, in the global game people often fail to recognize their wins. They miss the chance to capitalize on this wonderful opportunity to build confidence. Success does little for us if our Performance Model causes us to ignore it or take it for granted.

Achieve Results means knowing the meaning of success and knowing which scoreboards are relevant. Is it the end result, a milestone or a process? Certainly we need a Performance Model that does more than take the narrow view that success is just the financial end result. Success in evolving organizations is much richer than the "bottom line" and includes the social, environmental, employee and customer successes that fall into the popular notion of the balanced scorecard. As noted in *CFO, Architect of the Corporation's Future,* "The best executives link value targets, through corporate objectives and strategies, to development of a balanced scorecard."[4]

In summary, we know that success builds confidence and triggers the dynamic zone. No Performance Model could be complete without an element that defines success and celebrates the results of all our efforts.

THE PERFORMANCE MODEL

The Performance Model is the template that you will use as a framework to design your high-performance program. It is outlined in its simplest form in Figure 9.2 and will help you to answer the central performance question: how can we build an organization that can achieve and sustain high performance under the conditions of the global game?

Throughout Section Four we explore each of the seven elements in detail and consider which aspects of each you might want to make a feature of your program.

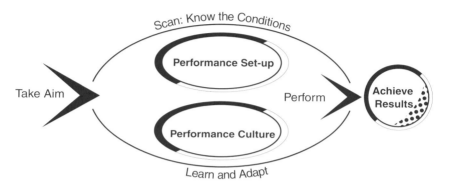

FIGURE 9.2 The Performance Model

WORKING WITH THE PERFORMANCE MODEL

The remainder of Section Three focuses on the essential Performance Leadership skills that you will need to create and refine your Performance Model.

Section Four then guides you to develop and implement the Performance Model for your high-performance program. Using the insights and skills gathered in the previous sections, the aim is to build a model with the resilience and agility needed to succeed in the global game. Importantly, the model, tools and techniques will give you a way to integrate many of your existing practices and some new ones to capture maximum value and performance.

Performance Leadership as a Competitive Advantage

Multiple leadership is the paradigm for the global game. Formal roles, such as that of CEO, are essential, but you also need acts of leadership from people right across the organization. The game is too fast and complex to rely on anointed leaders in every situation. Agility comes from leadership skills at the front line as much as it does from further up the hierarchy. As Sue Vardon, CEO of Centrelink says, "We are looking for leaders everywhere".[1]

We are at a point in history where we need a dynamic model of leadership that makes as much sense to the CEO as it does to the frontline staff member dealing with a customer's complaint. That model is Performance Leadership.

This chapter explores what Performance Leadership means for the formal leadership role and then expands that into a dynamic model that everyone in your program/organization can use to guide their acts of leadership and to bring the Performance Model to life.

CHALLENGE FIRST, COMPETENCIES SECOND

Conversations about leadership often start with discussion about the behaviors or competencies. Good leaders are expected to articulate vision, inspire creativity and empower their people, while bad leaders lack vision, stifle creativity and hang onto control.

Many organizations use this competency approach to design leadership models to guide their leadership recruitment and development.

Focusing on competencies is a useful way to understand leadership but many organizations do it without first looking at the challenges of leadership. For example, if you want to climb Everest, you look first at the challenge and then at the competencies. You study the mountain, its characteristics and its climbing history. You explore current technologies, acquire all manner of knowledge and start to form a strategy and a holistic picture of the physical, mental and technical challenges that the strategy presents. From those challenges the competencies become clear. Challenge first, competencies second.

Duncan Chessell reinforces this point with his view that the most important element in putting together his Everest expedition was knowing what challenges the mountain could present and then gathering the right experience and team to meet those challenges.[2]

First principle: Define the leadership challenges inherent in your business direction.

WHAT IS PERFORMANCE LEADERSHIP?

Performance Leadership is shaping, growing, influencing and making a positive difference to the performance of people, teams, organizations and communities. It is everything from executive leadership positions to the leadership that is so vital amongst the teams and other units that make up a high-performance program. Performance Leaders cross or remove boundaries, bring people and resources together, grow, prune and nurture. They invest to create value for the future and bring order, structure and function to extract value from the present. Sometimes, they lead people directly by their actions and, in other circumstances, they can be the thought leaders who create the new paradigms.

As described in Figure 10.1, Performance Leaders must be masters of the "and" because few things in the global game are one-dimensional.

FIGURE 10.1 Masters of the "and"

Short term	and	Long term
Leadership	and	Management
Hard	and	Soft
Strategic	and	Opportunistic
Order	and	Chaos
Complexity	and	Simplicity
People	and	Processes

A PERFORMANCE LEADERSHIP MODEL

To help leaders to get a clear perspective on the competencies of Performance Leadership, a leadership model has been designed, refined and tested in a variety of settings.

This competency model addresses five dimensions that are the core to most effective leadership models that are currently in use in business and in sport. Three of the dimensions — Strategic Leadership, Performance Coaching and Development Coaching — are fundamental roles in our High Performance Programmes. The other two dimensions — Performance Relationships and Personal Leadership — are part of the fabric of any organization that aspires to create and sustain high performance. We use the notions of coach and leader to remind ourselves that leaders can only produce results through changing the behavior of other people. Coaches are Performance Leaders who change behaviors.

These five dimensions are easily understood and provide you and your fellow leaders with a simple framework for looking at Performance Leadership and how it can give you a competitive advantage. In addition, if you already have a leadership model or set of leadership competencies, then you will invariably find that it fits into these five dimensions.

These five dimensions are defined as:

- Strategic Leadership — creating and mobilizing vision and strategy
- Performance Coaching — lifting and sustaining business performance

- Development Coaching — developing the capabilities of the business and its people
- Performance Relationships — creating and sustaining relationships
- Personal Leadership — leading by example.

FIGURE 10.2   The five dimensions of Performance Leadership

Each of these five dimensions makes a specific and combined contribution and impact on the organization. Figure 10.3 describes the key contributions and impact of each of these dimensions.

FIGURE 10.3 Contributions and impact of Performance Leadership

	Key contributions	Impact
Strategic Leadership	• Big-picture perspective • Stimulates strategic conversations • Creates/upholds charter • Challenges the status quo	Positioned for future success — short- and long-term
Performance Coaching	• Goals — alignment • Deploy resources • Motivate • Performance feedback and consequences	Producing results and adding value
Development Coaching	• Sustain and enhance capabilities • Facilitate learning • Grow new competencies • Attract and retain talent	Capabilities and competencies suit the strategy
Performance Relationships	• Create trust • Form new relationships • Build networks • Reveal and resolve conflict	Network relationships adding value to the organization
Personal Leadership	• Acts of leadership • Uphold the values • Provide personal energy	Leading by example (Business Athlete)

Let's explore how each of these roles is part of creating and sustaining high-performance programs.

STRATEGIC LEADERSHIP

The Olympic strategy described in Chapter 2 evolved from people who spent time thinking and conversing about the Olympics. It's a simple concept, yet strategic thinking and strategic conversations are surprisingly hard to find in business organizations. Consider the situation in your organization. Do you see and hear meaningful strategic conversations or is everyone spinning around the day-to-day issues and rarely looking beyond the immediate horizon?

Strategic Leadership brings the strategic perspective that is essential for high performance. Without this contribution the focus becomes performance activity instead of performance value. No one is really looking outwards or ahead.

Strategic Leaders pose questions and points of view that challenge people to think deeply about their program and the world in which it operates. Such questions might include:

- Why do we exist? (What is our charter?)
- What is our future?
- What is our value-proposition to customers?
- What are our values?
- How might we reinvent ourselves?
- Who will be our new customers?
- How will the world economy affect our supply chain?
- What opportunities can we exploit in the medium to long term?
- How can we position ourselves to manage the risks of new technologies?

Strategic Leadership is essential at the top of the hierarchy and no less important in the Performance Units where the same questions must be asked. Professor Bill Ford has recounted his experiences in large corporate organizations where "leadership is not just about leadership at the top" but about using action learning at a team level. He particularly advocates the use of what he calls "concept teams" who are coached to tackle an issue that requires strategic leadership to "develop and deliver outcomes".[3]

When Strategic Leadership is missing, Performance Units risk decay or destruction. When it is visible and effective, the whole program chooses its best future.

Excite people about their potential

To be a Strategic Leader, work with the big picture and, instead of using the "vision" word, talk about "potential". When Martin Luther King had "a dream", he spoke passionately of the potential of society. President John F. Kennedy excited the United States about the potential to set foot on the moon. Great Strategic Leaders lift people above their current levels by showing their potential.

Excite and engage people in shaping the future of your program by encouraging them to talk about potential, not just vision. Vision often limits us to a sort of pseudo goal-setting, whereas potential embraces the truly strategic questions of how to make the most of what we have. What more important role is there for a leader, whether that leader is a parent, coach, teacher or manager, than to inspire people to go in search of their potential?

Potential: Question from the coach

Over the next few days ponder this question: "What is my potential as a Performance Leader?" This is a question that can open up so many more ideas and options than seeking a destination in the future that might be called a vision.

Make the future today's business

Apart, maybe, from the annual two-day retreat, most of the time Bosses talk tactics, not strategy. Few engage each other and their stakeholders in truly strategic conversations. The mantra of "shareholder returns" and "next-quarter results" drives a short-term, tactical mindset that leaves organizations vulnerable. It is the battle between efficiency and effectiveness that has been waged for years. We see it often in our daily lives as we tackle the incoming task, fighting today's "bushfire", often wishing but rarely taking the time to make strategic conversations a priority.

How ironic that one of the casualties of the frenzied development and implementation of technology is the future. Of course, the current fashion is to speak of Internet years; of horizons of three or six months; and to think and plan accordingly. "If you cannot predict what will happen, then there is no point in planning for it" goes the logic of some and the behavior of many. This might be fine if you work in software development, but if you are in government or major infrastructure development and cannot think past the next year you are in trouble. And, equally importantly, let's not get caught in the trap of believing that strategic thinking and planning are the same thing.

Thinking or planning: Same thing?

Strategic thinking and strategic planning are not the same thing. The latter is important but hardly likely to give you a performance edge. It is the recording of your intentions and is a "must do" activity. Strategic thinking, on the other hand, and the dialogue of strategy offer a competitive edge because of the constant turning over of ideas. Without strategic thinking and dialogue the focus is "in" your business, not "on" the total system in which your business operates. Strategic thinking leads to great strategic planning — not the other way around.

To paraphrase Michael Gerber,[4] leaders who grow their organization devote time to working *on* their business instead of constantly working *in* the business. They position the organization for the future. This is the domain of Strategic Leaders and must happen at the executive or overall program level and in every Performance Unit under that umbrella.

Facilitate strategic understanding

Strategic conversations add a richness and diversity to your thinking that is difficult to gather by yourself. Even more, when you involve others in your strategic thinking it becomes theirs as much as yours. The argument for regular formal and informal strategic conversation is compelling in a rapidly changing environment. A High-Performance Leadership strategy that will help to create these conversations is to separate your regular information-sharing meetings from strategic-thinking sessions. Making time for meetings that address just one strategic issue gives people the opportunity to ask strategic questions and engage in strategic dialogue.

Challenge: When did you last grab a small group of people to tackle a genuine non-urgent strategic issue?

It is a legacy of the "leader-as-hero" leadership model that causes many Bosses to believe that it is a sign of weakness for them to engage others in helping to formulate and refine strategy. Are you trapped in the myths of heroic leadership by classical heroes like Ulysses, or are you openly engaging your organization and its broader networks in strategic conversations?

When people are engaged in strategic conversations, they understand what sits behind the strategy. This helps the Performance Coaches, teams and Business Athletes to translate that strategy into the actions that are needed to succeed on the front line. It is unimaginable that outfits like an Olympic team or a retrieval unit wouldn't engage in strategic conversations. It is the way of high-performance programs.

Principle: Get together everyone whom you can reasonably engage (subject to confidentiality issues) in strategic conversations. You will find gems of thinking from some unusual areas.

Scenario thinking for navigators

Scenario thinking and planning has been essential to explorers and navigators since mankind's earliest forays into the unknown.

Strategic Leaders are navigators and they think in scenarios. They are chess players who shift the "pieces" in their minds, weighing up how their actions might affect other elements within the system. They begin sentences with the words of the novelist: "What if...?". Duncan Chessell says that "on 'Summit Day' you have already programmed your responses to different scenarios".[5] Likewise for the Olympics and the global game.

You cannot plan for every eventuality, but if you are not at least asking the "What if?" questions and projecting scenarios for some horizons ahead then who is leading your program into the future?

Are you the leader of the future? Are you devoting a significant percentage of your time to strategic thinking and building strategic understanding into your organization or are day-to-day pressures putting you and your program at risk of being very efficient at doing something that is no longer relevant?

Principal challenges for the Strategic Leader

Five of the principal challenges of Strategic Leadership are to:
- Inspire and excite people about the potential for the future
- Design and sustain a clear charter (purpose and values)
- Design a strategy to fulfill the charter
- Engage commitment to the charter and strategy
- Continually review, revise and enhance the strategy.

These challenges, along with those from each of the other five dimensions of leadership, are built into a model that is outlined later in this chapter. This will enable you to assess your current Performance Leadership activities. Each challenge is as relevant to the CEO as to the team and unit leaders at all levels of your program. By creating the capabilities and practices of Strategic Leadership at all levels, you get people coming to work with what Shane Garland, formerly of Qantas, calls "the attitude of a General Manager".[6]

PERFORMANCE COACHING

The director of a drama production challenges, confronts, reassures, pushes and cajoles the students to bring their potential to life. This is Performance Coaching in action.

Performance Coaches stretch people far more than the traditional Boss ever did. They take risks, they engage in conversations that make people uncomfortable and they create a relationship in which people expect and want them to do exactly this. Would you sign up with a drama director who let you settle comfortably into mediocrity? A director who did not challenge you to bring out your potential, to show the world the brightness of your colors and who left you to perform on the stage of life as a dull and boring actor? And yet in business, too many managers shy away from the Performance Coaching role and people accept this because it is what they are used to. This paradigm of static, process-driven management is absurd and too many business schools keep churning out clones of this parody.

Performance Coaching is exciting and risky. It means taking full responsibility for bringing out the best in other people. You make judgments about people, take risks, expose yourself to criticism, experiment in search of new and better ways. You are alive and growing. People move quickly to you or quickly away from you. That's fine. This is the way of the high-performance world.

You are a Performance Coach when you:

- translate organization-wide vision, performance themes, imperatives and initiatives into actions

- deploy people into Performance Units that best suit the task and conditions
- build and relentlessly use measures/scoreboards to track performance
- develop teams that take leadership and produce better business results by themselves
- create a Performance Culture of high standards, high results and high consequences.

Commit to performance

Performance Coaches in past eras were usually of one style — autocratic, military-style leaders. But that has shifted as the expectations and capabilities of Business Athletes have increased. The best Performance Coaches are now flexible in style but always fiercely committed to performance; to realizing the potential of the individuals and teams they lead. Jon Westover, vice president of manufacturing for North America and Asia for lens manufacturer Sola Optical, sums up this approach with his advice to "give high visibility and focus to results and to their continual improvement" and "never accept excuses, underperformance and mediocrity".[7]

In every High Performance Leadership Programme, we develop Performance Coaches to have that commitment to high standards and direct consequences. Generally, the consequences for good performance will be rewards, such as promotion, salary bonuses, recognition and further development. For poor performance, there will be feedback and rapid attempts to develop, followed by either improvement or exit.

FIGURE 10.4 Performance coaching

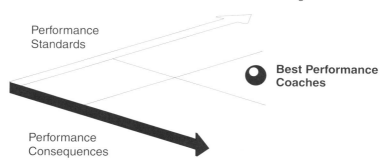

Performance
Standards

Best Performance
Coaches

Performance
Consequences

Champion of change

The Olympic coach would laugh at the curious business-world notion of "change leader". They would see it as a tautology. Leadership is about change: full stop, end of story. Performance Coaches are the ultimate change leaders, rarely using the "change" word and, instead, speaking of fulfilling potential, shifting strategies, building new structures, finding the performance edge. The Performance Coach uses the language of performance, not change. The latter is a given if you seek the former.

Reflection: Has "performance" been replaced by "change" in your organization?

Create a Performance Culture

One of the best descriptions that I have heard of the Performance Coach is one used by Australian rowing coaches who describe their role as "creating an environment in which success is inevitable". For the rowing program, this means an almost-obsessive focus on talent identification, teamwork, high-quality training and meticulous planning of the World Championship and Olympic campaigns. It means demanding high performance, measuring it constantly and providing all the support needed to stretch people to the next level and beyond.

Is this mindset different from the one that you see in managers in your business?

A Performance Culture is one in which athletes (sport or business) are powerful and confident. They have a high-performance ethic which comes from five elements that the performance coach instills into the environment — focus, discipline, achievement, leadership, and support.

It is in the role of Performance Coach that you place a relentless spotlight onto what is important about the task in particular teams and units and the values that underpin the total program. You bring and insist on a focus and discipline that leads to achievement and mastery. This builds confidence on a firm foundation. Your people will learn that they can be effective in this environment and, as with the child growing up, the discipline gives

FIGURE 10.5 Performance Coaches create Performance Cultures

a sense of certainty in a changing world. Importantly, the best Performance Coaches turn their Business Athletes into marketable commodities and that builds confidence and reduces career insecurity.

Build resilience

The Boss mentality creates and fosters reliance on itself, while the Performance Coach demonstrates leadership without creating dependency. The test of this is when people make decisions and create action without you. Business Athletes learn to exercise leadership when Performance Coaches give them space and opportunity to make their own decisions and control their own destiny. Offer support but do not rescue people. Build a resilience or toughness in your people that comes from taking risks in an environment where they know they are valued. Capture the learning that is gained from in-the-field experiences, and you will reduce the likelihood of mistakes being made or of re-inventing the wheel, and you will have a more confident, capable and agile workforce.

Stretch beyond current limits

People thrive in environments where they are stretched to use their skills and knowledge, and supported to continue learning and developing. The key to creating this type of environment is what I call "stretch coaching" and it becomes a core capability of organizations who make High-Performance Leadership a centerpiece of their culture.

Stretch coaching includes:

- Challenging your people to raise the bar on their aims and effort
- Pushing them to build and capitalize on strengths
- Guiding them to learn from their experiences.

Stretch coaching is a continual process. I have found that the best way to help managers develop these capabilities is for them to be coached. We do this in the High Performance Leadership Programme by linking the person's business and personal development objectives to quite a rigorous program of one-to-one stretch coaching and related business projects. In other words, we stretch coach to stretch coach!

Performance Leaders who are skilled in stretch coaching develop Business Athletes and teams with the capacity to respond to rapid changes in strategy and set-up.

Some of the strategies available to Performance Coaches are explained in the following table, which uses the Performance Model as the framework. Section Four elaborates on these strategies in considerable detail.

Principal challenges for the Performance Coach

Your five principal challenges as a Performance Coach are to:

- Achieve outcomes in line with the vision, values and strategy
- Maximize the performance of people
- Make decisions and manage risk
- Measure and monitor performance
- Build a Performance Culture.

The strategies to guide you in meeting these challenges are explained in Chapter 11 and in Section Four.

FIGURE 10.6 Stretch coaching and the Performance Model

Element of Performance Model	Action of Performance Coach
Take Aim	▶ Set stretch goals that exceed the public goals
Scan: Know the Conditions	▶ Show people examples of others who are performing better in service or speed, for example
Performance Set-up	▶ Expand job roles to stretch into new "risky" areas
Mindset/Culture	▶ Make performance standards and results public to create peer motivation
Perform	▶ Empower to make decisions
Learn and Adapt	▶ Facilitate detailed and tough debriefing sessions
Achieve Results	▶ Link results to consequences

DEVELOPMENT COACHING

Development Coaches teach, guide and facilitate the development of people, the overall program/organization and its community. From your earliest experiences at school you came across Development Coaches who probably taught all manner of things, from simple sports skills, like passing a basketball, to more complex mental and life skills, such as how to write prose or how to handle the disappointment of losing and the thrill of winning. Take a moment to reflect on those people who have coached you and built your skills. What did the best Development Coaches do that helped you to learn and refine your skills?

Development Coaches move from a teaching role to a true coaching role as the capabilities of their people increase. We find this in the experience of parenting, where our role shifts over the years from a disciplined teaching role to a coaching and facilitating role. Young children need to be taught disciplines and skills, but if the same process is used with teenagers the consequences can be horrific! Parents of teenagers get plenty of coaching practice, although the poor parents either abdicate the role or revert to a discipline model that does not work. If we get our coaching right, there are often mentoring and advisory roles to follow.

Development Coaches are essential in all areas of an organization so that you build and sustain the capability that is needed now and for the future. Too often and too easily the day-to-day pressures of the global game reduce the development work. This does not have to be the case, however, because like the Olympic coach you can use the high-performance environment to do on-the-job coaching of your Business Athletes.

Your program needs the Development Coaching role to embed

FIGURE 10.7 Coaching changes as capability develops

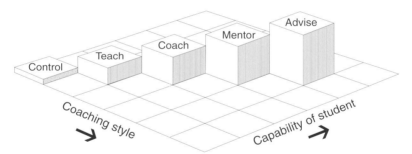

learning. However, unless this is linked to performance, the learning can seem disconnected rather than as a piece of the living jigsaw puzzle that leads to adaptation and evolution. Keeping this connection between learning and performance is an important element in High Performance Leadership Programmes.

You will know that Development Coaching is a part of the culture when:

- high-quality goods and services are delivered by Performance Units in all conditions
- individuals and teams produce real business improvement from their experience and learning

- Performance Leaders emerge at all levels across your program
- knowledge is converted into real value for the business
- individuals grow and are promoted
- people want to join your program
- ideas flow across the organization and adaptation is quick and effective.

The best Development Coaches are committed to the holistic development of people. In other words, they see the need not just to teach technical skills but also to develop the interpersonal skills and the self-understanding that leads to emotional balance and calmness under pressure. Would you have the courage to do what Phil Jackson (arguably the world's best basketball coach) did and train your Business Athletes in meditation? Or would you have the courage of Christine Charles, former CEO of the Human Services Department in South Australia, who took the CEOs of all government agencies on a visit to the Pitjinjara Aboriginal lands to meet, live with and learn from an indigenous community?

The traditional Boss adopts the view that training and development should only be funded if it links directly to the skills required in the organization. This is the same cost-focused mentality that weakens organizations and discourages high performers from joining.

Real Development Coaches invest in building relationships, guiding emotional development and fostering the development of broader thinking. They encourage people to develop as people, not just as mechanical devices for whom you add a new piece of software every so often. As Christine Charles suggests, "An intrinsic part of leading is actually helping people to reach their full potential".[8]

Performance Development, not management

Organizations have a habit of making a meal out of performance management/development processes. They build hugely complicated systems, with detailed paperwork or electronic systems, forgetting that performance management is fundamentally an ongoing dialogue between the Performance Leader/Coach and the individual(s) involved.

If your performance-management system does not make it easier for this dialogue to occur regularly and meaningfully, then throw it out and use the one-on-one agreement outlined in the next chapter.

Experts in medicine, sport and mountain climbing tell me that the aim is to develop people to the point where they are able to evaluate their own performance. As the person develops, the coach becomes the mentor and guide, providing expert advice and assistance in how to further develop the person's capabilities. Similar approaches have been used for hundreds of years in trades and professions.

In a professional football team, the players are physically, psychologically and technically profiled, and then each works with specialist Development Coaches to develop their skills. Responsibility for ensuring that development happens is shared between the player and the Development Coach. Who is responsible for this in your program?

A simple and pragmatic Performance Development system sets agreed goals for the business and the person; links development to those goals; and fosters regular review and fine-tuning of the development program. Suggestions for making Performance-Development a key part of your Performance Model are explained in Chapter 16.

Performance Development: Questions from the coach

Take a moment to reflect on whether you have an effective Performance Development system in place for your staff.

- Is performance management/development viewed as important?
- What value do you gain from your system?
- Is feedback and development continual or is it centered on a performance-management event?

Career coaching is essential to find and keep talent

Who is responsible for career management in the global game? There are many stakeholders in each person's career and, like most things in a complex system, there is not a single answer.

For example, one of our clients needs highly specialized engineers to work in their research center which manufactures specialist telecommunications equipment. Future success depends on attracting, developing and retaining these specialists and even on fostering their initial career choice. Accordingly, this organization, like many others, actively works with universities to encourage students to study this specialist discipline and, like sports teams, they have also become increasingly skilled at identifying potential talent well before they choose their courses at university. They also invest in upgrading the skills of their Performance Leaders in the basics of career coaching.

There are many reasons why building capability in career coaching will add to the toolkit of skills of your Performance Leaders and increase the viability of your business.

Once again the paradigm of sports coach is helpful here to understand the conversations that occur between coach and athlete. These are active and regular conversations about the athlete's abilities, aptitudes and interests. For example, swimming coaches help swimmers to choose what stroke or strokes they will specialize in, and team coaches guide players to understand and build on their strengths to fit the needs of the team. If a sports coach did not actively work with the athlete to plan their career development, then how could they possibly expect to build a high-performance program? Coaches also come across multi-talented athletes who can choose to either join another team, or even play another sport. Being able to articulate the career-development pathway is essential to finding and keeping this sort of talent. Can you articulate career-development pathways for your key people?

A client of mine refers to the three "As" of career coaching: Attitude, Aptitude and Ability. He uses the coaching skills gained through the High Performance Leadership Programme to guide his team members to:

- Scan the broadest options for their careers
- Make intelligent choices about career opportunities
- Maintain awareness of their strengths and build on these
- Manage their weaknesses realistically
- Keep motivated (by staying on the learning curve).

He is a talent scout, often aggressively seeking people to join his program even when there are no roles to fill. He has a reputation for giving people challenges that stretch them and help them grow. He introduces them to people in his network and makes sure that every one of his people keeps a portfolio that records their experiences and skills (in the form of a capability portfolio that you might expect of a consultant). Not surprisingly, his business is thriving.

Everyone is different

Career coaching must take into account the life-cycle of the person and also their capabilities in the three "As". Research[9] and experience shows that employees generally fall into three broad categories when it comes to defining their approach to their careers — proactive, passive and resistant.

Proactive people are committed to their careers, ambitious and fully immersed in a business persona. They center their lives around work and career, have high expectations of employers with regard to career-development opportunities and are very growth oriented. They take responsibility for their own career development and guard their skills and reputation carefully to ensure that they keep pace with shifts in the employment market. You should coach these people in what Louise Sauvage describes as a "partnership"[10] and in line with the needs of the business. They can consume a lot of resources but they are also likely to be your champions, so the investment is, more often than not, worthwhile.

Passive people expect advancement in their careers but they are not risk-takers in that regard. They participate in development but not to the extent that it has an impact on the rest of their lives. Their view of career is typically linear in that they see career planning in rational, step-by-step stages. Through career coaching you can have the biggest impact on this group. They are open to development but need your leadership. They are the gold mine that has yet to be fully exploited in most businesses.

Resistant people are often unhappy with their career and their environment but, paradoxically, resist doing much to change it. They see themselves as victims of the system and, based on their past experiences, that may be true. Some may not accept the victim tag and instead choose to rebel against the notion of career advancement as if it taints them in some way. I have found many of the latter in government agencies, where they have become bitter about the organization but still connected to the community cause. Career comes last in their priorities and the coach must therefore find a source of motivation, usually by working one-on-one with the person and connecting their work activities with the things that they enjoy in other parts of their lives. In such circumstances, many Development Coaches go back to basic psychology and look for ways to improve the physical work environment, to show these people that they are valued and to connect them even more to the community. They tend to learn best through experience, so you often need to take them to places where they can participate in new practices, and to see how others work together. However, avoid threatening them because low self-esteem is often a part of this group's characteristics and threats will only make things worse.

A fourth category, a composite of proactive and resistant which I will call "lifestylers", has emerged recently. These people are usually under 35, bright, skilled and not interested in playing by the traditional rules of the corporate world. They show up in start-up, entrepreneurial companies or in the fast lane of traditional organizations. Their motivation is lifestyle: their motto is "work to live" not "live to work".

Lifestylers are the most rapidly expanding group in the employment market and your challenge is to create a culture in which they can enjoy their work, achieve and still have a life. Attracting and retaining lifestylers is a potential source of competitive advantage.

Competencies and capabilities

Development Coaching is not just about building and protecting the competencies of people. There are also technologies, systems, infrastructure and processes that must be designed, built, purchased and implemented. Development Coaches play a critical role in this aspect because most technologies will succeed or fail based on the execution or implementation rather than on the hardware itself. This is discussed in more detail in Chapter 14.

Principal challenges for the Development Coach

The four principal challenges for you as a Development Coach are to:

- Attract people with the skills and values needed to achieve the vision
- Create the environment where people have opportunities to learn and develop
- Develop leaders in all areas
- Establish and utilize systems and processes to support the efficiency and effectiveness of the business.

In a corporate world, the Development Coaching role is also essential for translating the values into daily behaviors that can be reinforced by Performance Leaders.

PERFORMANCE RELATIONSHIPS

The Performance Relationship is the fourth dimension of Performance Leadership.

Performance Leadership is in itself a relationship between you and the people whom you lead. It is a relationship that empowers and strengthens those people to fulfill their potential and that of their teams, organizations and communities.

Nick Bolleteri, one of the world's most successful tennis coaches, commented that, "If you are half as good at building relationships as you are at teaching tennis, your student will be a winner".[11]

This is not to suggest that success is totally dependent on "warm and loving" relationships, because there are many examples of successful Performance Leaders who are task-oriented and very cold towards their charges.

Many good Performance Leaders are somewhat autocratic in their approach but are like good parents, who set boundaries and apply discipline. They respect the people whom they coach, although you may not always recognize this in their actions. Being nice to people is not necessarily good leadership. Most business coaching books overdo the "be nice to people" concept and forget that "tough love" isn't neat and nice but it can be exactly what is needed (and it is respectful).

Having worked with some very tough coaches and found myself querying their methods, I came to understand that the difference between the coach who loses the respect of athletes and the one who, despite what appears to be very directive behavior, is successful, is awareness and values. Autocrats who exert power for the sake of it and have little awareness of how this is affecting people are, typically, short-term successes at best. They drive out negative behaviors, bring a short-term focus to the program but quickly extinguish the initiative and spirit of all but the toughest of charges. Autocrats who are aware and have some capacity to modify their style know exactly what they are doing, and they can take the pressure off just enough when it is needed. "We love to hate him" was the expression used by athletes of an Olympic coach who fitted the latter criteria. He was uncompromising in his demands on his athletes but also gave them access to great support staff to help them through what was a toughening-up process. His athletes did not always like him but they respected him and they trusted him to make the most of their potential.

Tough coaching: Questions from the coach

Consider these questions or get your coach to probe your thinking:

- Do your Business Athletes trust you to make the most of their potential?
- How effectively do you balance the "toughness" with "respect"?
- Do you provide people with support so you can stretch them?

Too many organizations, particularly those where the performance standards are not clear, actually reinforce leadership styles that weaken people, and soften their ability to adapt to the world. In the short term, this might be comfortable but if you are in one of those organizations get out now. They are de-skilling you for the global game.

Develop relationships based on trust

Sustainable coaching requires relationships built on respect and trust. This is the fundamental point and High-Performance

Leadership therefore requires that you build respect and trust with other people. As Shane Garland reminds us, "People must feel they are trusted to do the right thing".[12]

Relationships generally evolve through stages ranging from indifference through negative states such as hate and fear, to respect and perhaps, ultimately, to genuine love. This suggests that trust is generated through competency, through the way you act (in accordance with values) and through communication. Your challenge above all else is to have an awareness about your relationships and the impact that your behavior has on others. To build this awareness use 360-degree feedback instruments, talk to people, observe the impact of your actions or do whatever is needed in your unique environment.

Bring conflict to the surface

Performance Leaders generate conflict from time to time because it is necessary. They challenge and confront and in so doing bring to the surface conflicts that Bosses often leave to fester, untouched. When Bosses allow this to happen, they get too many individual agendas and it diminishes performance.

Principal challenges for Performance Relationships

Some of the principal relationship challenges for Performance Leaders include:

- Building relationships based on open communication, shared responsibility and trust
- Identifying and challenging inequity
- Bringing conflict to the surface and resolving it
- Capturing opportunities for bringing people together.

PERSONAL LEADERSHIP

The fifth and final dimension of Performance Leadership is Personal Leadership, which means practicing and demonstrating the mindset and behaviors of the Business Athlete that were covered in Section Two.

Because Development Coaching is about transferring knowledge and building skills through demonstration, it is to be expected that people learn about leadership through your demonstration of acts of leadership (or non-leadership). Your staff and the people you interact with are little different in that respect from soccer players who learn to dribble and pass the ball through observing their coaches and fellow players and then practicing the skills.

Every time you confront a difficult issue, the people in your program see how you deal with it. They see your behavior, attitude and emotions and this shapes their own behavior.

The role of Performance Leader can be daunting and personally demanding. The Performance Model tells us that, at the very least, the Performance Leader generates the strategic vision and objectives, communicates this vision and responsibilities to team members, builds team culture and values, challenges Business Athletes to lift their performance, designs game plans, reviews and debriefs on performance, and stimulates the development and integration of new approaches.

The demands of these activities are why you, as a Performance Leader, must first be a Business Athlete and then a leader. This equips you with the personal skills to handle the demands of your role, and also gives you a model for understanding how to manage others better. This is all about Personal Leadership.

Principal challenges for Personal Leadership

Some of the Personal Leadership challenges are:

- Maintaining technical business know-how
- Acting in accordance with the values of your organization
- Managing the personal demands of leadership
- Sorting through many complex and ambiguous issues to identify and act on the important
- Taking responsibility and accountability.

PERFORMANCE LEADERSHIP COMPETENCY MODEL

The competencies from the five dimensions of Performance Leadership are summarized in Figure 10.8. These competencies are used as the foundation on which we build 360-degree feedback processes for organizations undertaking the High Performance Leadership Programme. Further details of this model and process are available on our website.

FIGURE 10.8 Performance Leadership Challenges

Relationships
- Build relationships based on open communication, shared responsibility and trust
- Identify and challenge inequity
- Reveal and resolve conflict
- Capture opportunities for bringing people together

Performance Coaching
- Achieve outcomes in line with the vision, values and strategy
- Maximize the performance of people
- Make decisions and manage risk
- Measure and monitor performance

Strategic Leadership
- Inspire and excite people about the potential for the future
- Design and sustain a clear charter (purpose and values)
- Design a strategy to fulfill the charter
- Engage commitment to the charter and strategy
- Continually review, revise and enhance the strategy

Personal Leadership
- Maintain technical/ business know-how
- Act in accordance with the values of your organization
- Manage the personal demands of leadership
- Sort through many complex and ambiguous issues to identify and act on the important
- Take responsibility and accountability

Development Coaching
- Attract people with the skills and values needed to achieve the vision
- Create the environment where people have opportunities to learn and develop
- Develop leaders
- Establish and utilize systems and processes to support the efficiency and effectiveness of the business

Summary

As a Performance Leader, you are the coach of strategy, development and performance. You are also a performer in your own right, as you meet the demands of leadership and model Business Athlete behaviors to others. Finally, as we saw in Figure 10.2, all of this happens within a field of relationships.

In Section Four, we bring each of these roles to life as you build and implement your Performance Model. However, before doing so, the following chapter explains some of the fundamental Performance Leadership tools and techniques that have been used to bring the Performance Model to life in High Performance Leadership Programmes.

Performance Leadership Skills

It is impossible to overestimate the importance of communication and relationship skills for Performance Leaders. Every one of the five areas of competency discussed in the previous chapter requires self-awareness about your interpersonal style and impact on other people; the Performance Model itself will only come to life through the communication skills of all the people in your program.

For these reasons, I want to introduce you to three foundation skills of Performance Leadership that will help you to engage your people in designing, implementing and owning the Performance Model. These are generic skills that we always introduce into organizations as part of High Performance Leadership Programmes and they are:

- Performance Leadership conversations
- Generating high-performance confidence
- Coaching the poor performer.

Each of these topics could itself fill a book but they are important for you to consider at a basic level at this time.

PERFORMANCE LEADERSHIP CONVERSATIONS

Conversations are one of your most powerful tools to shape and influence others. The techniques that follow will help you to generate high-quality performance conversations with other leaders, teams and stakeholders. It is through those conversations that you will build your Performance Model and bring it to life. Be mindful, however, that the techniques require practice before they will be fully effective, particularly in challenging conditions where there is pressure and conflict.

Performance conversations are characterized by two dimensions — presenting a point of view and probing another's.

Learning-organization theory calls these dimensions "advocacy" and "inquiry" and the relationship between the two is summarized in Figure 11.1.

FIGURE 11.1 Dimensions of conversation

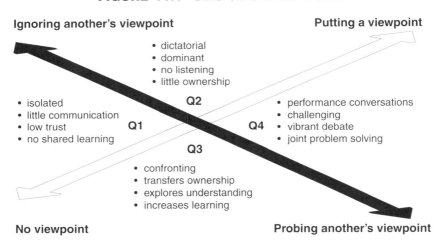

The value that comes from developing strong conversational skills along both dimensions is evident from looking at the impact on learning and performance in each quadrant (when leaders operate from that quadrant).

For example, in Q1 there is little conversation and little cross-exchange of learning. Performance is at risk as people hold on to their own knowledge. This is typical of low-trust environments and the impact on performance is obvious. Q2 describes a typical "command-control" leadership style. Information and ideas come from only one source and performance over time often diminishes as people tire of the one point of view. Q3 can be very confronting but it is a style that many coaches use effectively. They influence and shape through the power of their questioning and lead people to greater understanding. It can also be done very sensitively in the manner of a counselor who inquires into concerns. Q4 features a balance between presenting a point of view and probing the viewpoints of others. The best Performance Leaders and teams spend more time in Q4, engaging in a very dynamic style of conversation that features open debate and robust challenges of each other's viewpoints.

One of the indicators that the techniques and models of High Performance Leadership are becoming embedded in the culture is when conversations become more open, with clearer, deeper viewpoints and increased probing. Teams and other units that operate in this way have a distinct performance advantage because they test and expand each other's thinking in ways that are essential in high-performance environments.

Many Bosses mistakenly believe that they have already created a culture in which strong dialogue prevails. Instead, what you see are individuals expressing and defending their point of view very strongly but with little exposure of those viewpoints to critical review. Their body language and tone also suggest that their point of view is superior and beyond the need for critiquing. For example, many Bosses use anger and signs of impending anger to forestall the investigation of any other views.

While most leaders are generally quite good at presenting their viewpoint in a strong and definite manner, this skill is a double-edged sword. It ensures that the leader has the capacity to push a point of view but, in a complex environment, more is needed than the single view of the leader. Accordingly, the communication skills of advocating/putting a viewpoint and inquiring/probing into others' viewpoints are essential.

Proactive listening — a reminder of what you already know

We need a better model of communication than the traditional sender–receiver model (Figure 11.2). Far more important than putting emphasis on the sender is understanding what is important to the receiver and being a good receiver. Good communication sees the roles virtually reversed because the sender is open to receiving. This means checking if the message has been received and being alert to messages that are being sent by tone of voice, body language and the spaces in between words. Unfortunately, the skills of observation and listening are underrated in business organizations. One reason for this, as Arthur Battram suggests, might be that "Managers don't usually get promoted for listening to people".[1]

FIGURE 11.2 Outdated model of communication

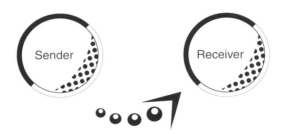

There is power in listening and not just because you will hear things that are useful. When leaders are poor listeners, other people pick this up very quickly and it affects how they communicate.

Even in the heat of competition, the coach looks the player in the eye, gives them total attention and draws out their key thoughts. The coach shows interest and the player responds.

Louise Sauvage believes communication with her coach is absolutely critical. "I can't train and compete at my best," she says, "when I'm not able to tell the coach how I'm going."[2]

Imagine that you are at a reception where a large crowd is gathered, milling in small groups. You begin a conversation but the other person is distracted. It's easy to tell, of course; their eyes and body language reveal that they are not focused on you. Their "ummm" and "uhh huh" responses give little encouragement that they are following what you are saying. You say something to get a response but there is none. You start to shut down, giving less and less information — shallow comments and observations — hoping to end the charade. Bosses unwittingly send lots of these "I'm not listening" messages and then get frustrated when people don't perform the way they want.

You don't hear what they don't say

Of course it is difficult to listen attentively amidst the distractions of the business world, and of course you do hear what people are saying even though you are doing something else. But when people see that you are distracted, they stop sharing their thoughts and ideas. You cannot hear what they do not say.

Listening: Question from the coach

Picture yourself at work. How often do you stop and look the person in the eye, rather than shuffling papers, checking e-mails or gathering things together ready to dash to the next meeting?

Proactive listening

To become an effective Performance Leader, you must be an excellent listener, but not the passive, "counseling" listener. Performance Leaders are generally proactive listeners, encouraging, checking, questioning and confirming what is being said. There is an urgency to their listening because they have got a lot of things to do; however, when the other person is emotional, for example, they are able to blend with the moment and the style of the speaker.

Adopt a more proactive listening style and, now and again, ask other people what they really think about your listening skills and practices. Take a few moments to really listen to their response.

LEADERSHIP CONVERSATIONS: THE TOOLS AND TECHNIQUES

We have developed two very practical techniques that can be used by leaders to:

- Probe the viewpoint of others (Inquiry)
- Put a viewpoint (Advocacy).

Experiment with each of these, but make sure that you adapt them to your personal style, and that you practice them. Like any new skill, it takes practice and we usually find that coaching is needed to get the probing skills honed.

THE SKILL OF PROBING

Performance Leaders are avid users of questioning techniques to influence others. This is more powerful than just telling people where they are going and then expecting them to follow.

Research and practical experience in sport and business coaching has shown that people actually learn more quickly and effectively when their coach asks performance questions and actively listens to/observes their responses.

Questioning leads to better learning and development because it makes people personalize and process the issue. When a Performance Leader/Coach asks questions to check your understanding and encourage you to solve your own problems, you are immediately more engaged and more likely to own the action plan that emerges from the conversation.

Common structure

When Performance Leaders use the skills of inquiry to probe another person's thinking, a common question structure emerges. This is embodied in the following six questions:

- What is your purpose (or problem)?
- What do you know for real (evidence, data)?
- What are your options?
- What is your best option?
- What should we expect of each other?
- What are you going to do next?

These six questions are introduced during High Performance Leadership Programmes using the acronym PROBED, to highlight the six points — Purpose, Real, Options, Best, Expect and Do.

You can use this framework in all manner of situations, ranging from discussing a person's career, to resolving a performance problem or a team conflict. Other common business situations where Performance Leaders use PROBED include coaching an individual in how to solve a problem, planning the strategy for a new campaign or creating a personal development plan. Let's look in detail at each of the six elements.

FIGURE 11.3 Elements in the probing technique

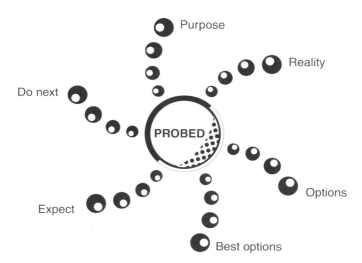

Purpose

As with the Performance Model, the first element is the purpose or the Aim. We start with purpose because all else follows. The Olympic coach probes to establish whether the athlete knows where they are heading, what the issue is, their direction and focus. Anything else risks waste of valuable resources.

Whether facing a problem, chasing an opportunity or refining a plan, Business Athletes benefit from the probing of Performance Leaders who help them to define the purpose or the problem. This avoids having to waste time solving problems that have not been defined, or expend energy without direction. Too often, we all get drawn into brainstorming the options without defining the problem or identifying the goal. "P" reminds us to clarify what it is that needs to be addressed or resolved.

When using PROBED, ask questions that inquire, push, lead and guide the other person to clarify the purpose. These questions might include:

- What is the problem/opportunity?
- What is the purpose?
- What do you want to achieve/what is your goal?

- At the end, when you look back, what do you want to have accomplished?
- What would success look like?

Use the structure of PROBED to remind you and people in your program to get clear about the purpose of what you are doing, and to define problems *before* trying to solve them.

Real

As the Performance Model suggests, high performance requires not only clear direction but also a pragmatic understanding of the conditions. That means knowing what the real situation is, ideally in terms of data or facts. Blind faith, optimism and wishful thinking have no place in high-performance environments.

For example, the R&D director wants extra resources to explore new technology. The CEO, a skilled Performance Leader, will use the PROBED technique to ascertain the real situation with questions such as:

- What is the market/the need/the opportunity/the risk-return ratio?
- Why is this the right time?
- Who else is pursuing this?
- What capabilities do we have to exploit the technology?

In performance environments, it is vital to ensure that people have taken into account all conditions before choices are made. Wherever possible, apply the principles of "everything being open to challenge", and "evidence-based decision-making" to understand what is the real situation.

Emotions can run high in the global game, causing people to underestimate or overestimate the risks and rewards in a situation and this leads to poor decision-making. Encourage people in your program to take notice of what is real, to describe the evidence and, wherever possible, to deal in fact. One of your most important roles as Development Coach is to enhance people's judgment and decision-making skills. Getting them to focus on the "R" is part of that coaching process.

"R" questions include:

- What do you know and what don't you know?
- What are the facts?
- Do you have data? What does it say?
- What are the constraints?
- What resources do you have?
- What are the risks?

More specific questions will come to mind as you apply the PROBED technique to your business issues. One of my clients, lens manufacturer Sola Optical, has posters around its manufacturing plant that simply say, "I value your opinion but show me the data". This reminds people not to just make decisions based on data but also to challenge the data and to refine and interpret it.

Options

In a fast global game you face a multitude of choices; however, there is always the risk of taking the first available option and ignoring other alternatives. Certainly you need speed of decision-making but, by using the discipline of PROBED, people learn that they can make decisions at speed but according to a disciplined process. "O" means canvassing your options before making choices: it is developing a range of choices before deciding on the best option.

Use your questioning, probing and brainstorming skills to coach this into all your Performance Units and make it a feature of the culture of your program.

"O" questions include:

- What do you see as your alternatives?
- What are the solutions?
- Give me another option ... and another?
- What if you do nothing?
- Is there another way to approach this?

Resist the temptation to take the first option; instead, encourage fast brainstorming as part of the Performance Set-up for your high-performance program.

Best

With a range of options, the next stage of PROBED is to develop the criteria by which you or others make the decision. For Performance Leaders, this requires patience and a preparedness to work with other people in a way that strengthens their decision-making skills. Avoid giving your opinion until people have demonstrated their capacity to analyze the merits of the options.

Help the less-experienced person to develop a process or template for choosing between the options. With the more-experienced, push them to evaluate the options thoroughly, particularly if they are under time pressure.

"B" questions include:

- What is your best option?
- How will you choose the best approach?
- What is the risk and reward?
- What does the evidence/data suggest?
- How do you rank your options?
- Is that really the best choice? Why?

Good coaches probe deeply and persistently at this stage because this is the pivotal point in the PROBED process.

Expect

Performance Leaders must have a fierce resolve to stay connected with the person until the job is done. Accordingly, the final two stages in PROBED are agreeing the expectations of each person and of the progress anticipated. This is similar to the one-on-one agreement that is explained later in this chapter.

At the "E" stage, the Performance Leader asks questions such as:

- What progress can we expect to see as your chosen option is implemented?
- What is your commitment? How will we see it?
- What do you need from me?
- When should we meet to monitor this?
- What milestones and timetable can we use to monitor progress?
- What resources do you need?

These questions help to reinforce the partnership between you and your Business Athletes, while ensuring that both parties are clear about what is expected.

Do

The final question is the call to action: "What are you going to do next?" This is the essential question to effect the move from analysis and decision to action.

"D" questions include:

- What are you going to do next?
- When are you going to do it?
- How are you going to do it?
- What will you do after that?

The "D" only takes a moment but it reinforces the importance of action.

PROBED summary

Avoid telling your Business Athletes and teams what to do (unless it is a short-term crisis). Instead, probe and prompt them to make their own choices.

Questioning (as a method of influencing) is a fundamental skill for Performance Leaders. It is a more effective method than simply telling or directing, because it generates greater ownership and, therefore, commitment. It develops the person's problem-solving and planning skills. It builds a coaching relationship and increases the speed and capability of the organization.

As people become used to the PROBED approach, we find that it becomes a useful tool for teams to use for any planning or problem-solving approach. It is a technique that you should definitely build into your Performance Model.

PROBED frees you to lead

PROBED gives you an ideal framework for coaching and leading through the power of questioning.

It can help you ensure that choices are made in accordance with values, the purpose and the current conditions while strengthening the capacity of your people to solve their own problems and to develop strategies. It is a key tool in moving you further away from day-to-day management and more into the Strategic Leadership realm.

THE SKILL OF "PUT"

Figure 11.1 reminds us that PROBED is only half of the leadership conversation. The other half is an advocacy technique called "PUT".

PUT is a simple technique to help you to present or advocate a point of view. When combined with PROBED, it helps to generate the sort of conversations that create and sustain high performance.

There are effective and ineffective ways to advocate a point of view. Presenting a point of view features three phases or components that are summarized in the word "PUT". When used effectively, they lead to a clear and strong presentation of viewpoints. The three points are:

P = present your point of view, including facts, data and assumptions

U = upshot — explain the effects, the impacts

T = test, explore — open up your thinking to PROBED.

FIGURE 11.4 Elements in the advocacy technique

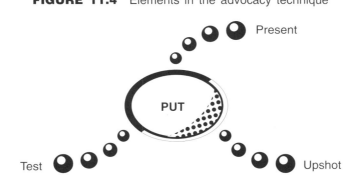

Have you ever worked for a Boss who was poor at putting their viewpoint? The following example shows how applying the PUT technique can help resolve the difficulties that arise in such circumstances.

Mary, a Call Center manager, had worked very hard to get to a leadership role. She read and practiced assertiveness until she reached the point where she believed that her point of view was clearly understood by everyone. Unfortunately, a typical point of view from Mary was just a blunt statement containing little information on the assumptions that sat behind her thinking. It rarely acknowledged the impact and certainly did not encourage any probing. Mary mistook assertion for good dialogue and, in doing so, created an environment in which people just listened passively to what she had to say and then often implemented it wrongly because they did not understand the reasons behind her expressions.

When 360-degree feedback revealed this problem, Mary was coached in how to use the PUT technique and very quickly opened the lines of communication with her staff. With the application of this technique, staff were able to understand the reasons behind her thinking and enjoyed the opportunity to add their thoughts and experiences. Several employee-led improvements were generated in the six months after Mary began using the PUT technique.

Let's now explore a little further what sits behind the three elements of PUT.

Present

Performance Leaders, particularly those in senior roles, influence people strongly through the point of view that they take on issues. While there are rare instances where a leader might need to say, "I can't explain the background; just trust me", they will be more successful in leading people when they present their point of view with supporting data, assumptions and reasons.

For example, assume that you believe that a different approach to customer service is needed in your program. A poor "P" might be, "I think we're on the slide and it's time to spend more time with our bigger accounts". Anyone listening could make any number of assumptions about the reasons behind your thinking.

A more effective "P" might be, "We're spending more time on small accounts than ever before and they are not giving us the same return as the bigger accounts (*data/reason*). My belief (*assumption*) is that it is time to focus more time and effort on where we are going to get a return, and that means the medium-sized accounts that have the potential to grow."

When you explain your reasons (ideally, supported by evidence) and assumptions, the level of understanding is much greater. On those occasions when you do not have the evidence, or perhaps cannot share it for reasons of confidentiality, people are also much more likely to trust you.

Upshot

The effective "P" can be made even more so by explaining the impact of the action that is to be taken: "We will need to manage the move away from the small accounts to ensure that we don't generate poor PR. However, if we do that well, then the returns from spending more time with the larger accounts should add somewhere between 20–30% to our gross revenues without any extra costs."

Including both the reasons behind your point of view and the impact that you expect, has the double benefit of causing you to think through those impacts, and explains further to others why the viewpoint is strong.

Listen in meetings and you will hear that a lot of conversation, and sometimes conflict, is generated as people try to get others to consider the impacts of their viewpoints on issues. Good Performance Leaders are vitally interested in the impact of their plans: they articulate them clearly and thoroughly, often going into scenarios rather than simply suggesting one impact.

Test

Of all the areas in PROBED and PUT, the "T" is the least used. Few people ask others to challenge their thinking and yet when members of teams do develop the confidence to PUT their viewpoints, they generate a robust debate that adds enormously to the quality of discussions. This is a genuine Performance Culture.

Imagine if all corporate boards were skilled at PUT. If board members encouraged their colleagues to test their thinking, and they did so using PROBED, how much better would be the decisions they made?

Leadership conversations: Questions from the coach

Reflect for a moment on your leadership conversations.

- Do you actively encourage people to test your thinking, to explore that the assumptions are valid and that you have considered the likely upshot of your intended actions?
- Are you actively coaching people to use the PROBED and PUT approach?
- What values will you gain by making effective leadership conversations a feature of your program?

When Performance Leaders use the PROBED and PUT techniques they encourage people to hold exactly the type of performance conversations that are so essential in the unpredictable global game. As Professor Bill Ford reminds us, "The willingness to question — the confidence to challenge — is absolutely critical".[3]

Reflection: Can you use your PROBED skills to encourage others to PUT their viewpoints?

The One-on-One Agreement

Sports coaches make a particular point of ensuring that their athletes know what is important (values, goals, priorities), what is expected of them (outputs, results and behaviors) and what the coach and/or program will do for them.

This approach suggests a simple and very practical technique for structuring leadership conversations. That technique we call the One-on-One Agreement.

Whenever you are entering into a performance environment with someone (employee, partner, manager), have a conversation using the format in Figure 11.5. Make it a feature of your program.

Performance Leaders use this style of conversation to ensure that activities start in synch, and they check against the agreement as things progress. The level of formality required (for example, putting the agreement in writing) depends on the situation.

GENERATING PERFORMANCE CONFIDENCE

Confidence and performance go hand in glove.

Economists measure consumer confidence and share-market confidence. Teachers aim to develop the confidence of their

FIGURE 11.5 One-on-One Agreement

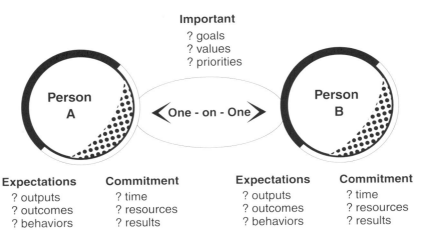

Important
? goals
? values
? priorities

Expectations	Commitment	Expectations	Commitment
? outputs	? time	? outputs	? time
? outcomes	? resources	? outcomes	? resources
? behaviors	? results	? behaviors	? results

students; parents want their children to be confident; and coaches develop confident athletes.

As a psychologist and coach, I have found the following four elements to be an excellent guide to the things that build and sustain confidence in individuals, teams and organizations:

- Achieve success
- Move towards or attain mastery
- Foster personal power
- Create a values-based environment.

When you focus on building confidence, people do extraordinary things when they have confidence in themselves and their organization. It is therefore worthwhile to consider these four elements before you begin building your Performance Model.

Achieve success

Success breeds confidence.

When athletes go into an Olympics, you want them to be confident. That confidence will have come from multiple "little wins" that have each boosted the feelings of confidence. Olympic medallist Louise Sauvage describes this as "having stepping stones so that talented people can see their progress and build their confidence and motivation".[4]

Wise coaches set up the goals and programs so that athletes experience lots of success along the way to their big goals. Success gives feedback that tells you that you are winning. And yet in business I rarely get a simple, clear answer from teams to the question, "How do you know you're winning?".

If people in your program do not know that they are winning, how can you expect to generate the momentum, the creativity, the boldness and leadership that come with confidence?

Work with your people to clarify their goals, get them to set lots of small goals or milestones and be prepared to lower the goals to build confidence for higher achievement in the future. Forget the macho notion that setting low goals is weak. If people are highly skilled and motivated, of course, you don't set low goals. But when confidence is low, there is every reason to get the ball rolling by setting goals that encourage a sense of achievement. What is your things-to-do list if not a set of goals, many of which are achievable?

When I start coaching a team, we usually set a series of achievable goals for one month and three months. These short-term goals build the foundation of confidence from which big things can happen.

When you want to really stretch people who are already motivated, try using the three-level goal-setting process that was covered briefly in Chapter 4 and that we discuss again in Chapter 12.

The level-one goal or "target" is the publicized level; level two is the stretch goal (not publicized); and the level-three goal, to use Tom Peters' term, is the "wow goal".[5]

FIGURE 11.6 Three-tiered goals

Goal Level	Characteristics	Value
Target	• Achievable with effort • "Publicly" known • Agreed	• Provides focus • Boosts confidence
Stretch	• A level above • Sets a new dimension • Agreed in-house as the target	• Motivational • Challenges the good performers
"Wow"	• Unachievable with current practices • Well above all stakeholders' expectations	• Encourages breakthrough thinking

The upside of this strategy is that people get the value of the boost in confidence from achieving the target. Publicizing it within the organization (or more broadly) increases its motivational value. Stretch goals appeal to people's achievement motivation, while "wow" goals lift people outside of current assumptions: they break paradigms. Stretch goals are best kept in-house so that people don't feel pressured. "Wow" goals cannot be achieved doing things the current way and are also for internal viewing only.

A simple example of a "wow" goal that we have used successfully with sales people during High Performance Leadership Programmes is to assume that for three months they will double the price of their goods or services. Doubling your price means that you have to find a way to double the value that the customer perceives from your product. After some initial resistance, this exercise always generates new ideas about service strategies that challenge the status quo.

Use the "wow" process whenever you want people to step out of their current assumptions (but do not use it when people are in the middle of executing their strategies or you risk distracting them unnecessarily).

By using three-tier goal-setting, you can build the confidence that comes from reaching targets while also stretching people to new levels.

Move towards or attain mastery

High performers are in a constant search for improvement towards mastery. As mastery is achieved at one level, they move towards higher-level skills. Confidence and pure enjoyment grow from this process of mastery. The sense of being in the zone is closely connected to mastery and confidence. This sense was once described by the actor Laurence Olivier as, "an overwhelming feeling [of] complete confidence".

While Bosses tend to take a one-dimensional view of mastery — seeing it solely as a case of building technical skills, such as financial skills or project-management skills — the Performance Leader develops the person not the "machine". Physical, mental, emotional and interpersonal skills are all part of the pathway to mastery.

When sports coaches take the one-dimensional approach, their athletes usually hit a brick wall in their improvement. Technical skills can only take you so far; the performance edge comes from improvement in areas such as judgment, emotional control, leadership and relationships.

The best Performance Leaders create a culture of mastery, where all participants in the system (athletes, coaches, managers, support staff) are fully involved in the search for mastery in their areas and in mastering the total system. Each person has a development plan, receives regular feedback on their progress and updates their plan.

Build confidence in the people whom you lead/coach through applying the principles of mastery:

- Emphasize holistic development (professional, personal)
- Invest in developing people in non-traditional areas (interpersonal, self-mastery)
- Create specific multi-dimensional development plans for every person
- Make people accountable for their own development (agree targets).

Obviously, the improvements get smaller as people approach mastery. So, as Shane Gould suggests, the challenge is to continue to find and see the improvement in your people, and to foster the notion of growth in all areas.

Foster personal power

When we don't feel powerful, we can't find the zone and struggle to produce a confident performance. This perception of power is an important factor in high-performance environments.

Good Performance Leaders highlight those things that make you feel powerful and they help you to be aware of what you do that weakens you. In particular, they help you to recognize how the conditioning from parents, teachers, managers and others has led you into patterns of behavior that reduce your personal power and affect your decision-making and performance. Consider the following example.

Jenny, a senior manager with a service organization, realized through a coaching process that there was a pattern to the way she dealt with situations where she did better than other people. After applying for and being appointed to her current role she had some of the former contenders for her position reporting to her. These people treated her well and she made a major effort to consult with them. Unfortunately, she made too big an effort and it was not long before people became disenchanted with her. They wanted more direction from the leader. On exploring the pattern, Jenny was able to recall a number of situations in her life going back to school days where she disempowered herself when placed in a position in preference to others. She recognized it as a feeing of guilt and her pattern was to try to almost recompense the other people by underplaying her power. Through coaching, Jenny developed her leadership skills to create a balance between direction and consultation. Her confidence is now much greater as she has come both to understand the patterning and learned skills to go past it.

You can empower people by giving them increasing control over decisions at a local level and encouraging participation in developing strategy and tactics. Share information and decision-making as a way of fostering greater self-worth and involvement/ownership in the total program. Even when things are going badly, people will feel more confident and empowered when they can see the decision-making process. As Stephen Covey puts it, "Involvement is the key to implementing change and increasing commitment."[6]

Provide support

Olympic coaches know that when they provide support for athletes, they can demand and expect more from the athletes. Unfortunately, too many Bosses see support as a sign of weakness.

People report greater levels of confidence when they feel supported and cared for by those around them. Though this goes against the notion of the survival of the fittest, the support teams of leading athletes are a stark reminder that if we want people to perform at their best, then support is an important part of the equation.

Performance Leaders do not hand out care and support like some form of welfare. It is conditional on people putting in an effort and doing the things that are consistent with the overall plan and the values of the organization.

As discussed in the previous chapter, you can stretch people further when they have support networks.

Make sure that people in your program understand that support is not about providing sympathy. It is showing understanding of the person's reaction and helping them to be stronger from the experience. For example, if a member of your team gets chewed out unfairly by a customer, don't sympathize: instead, counsel and even challenge them to learn something positive. Learning how to deal with the "customer from hell" is a good survival skill!

Create a values-based environment

A Performance Culture is built on implicit or explicit values that can be seen in everything that happens. This assures people how decisions will be made and generates a higher level of confidence.

As a Performance Leader, you are a custodian of the values of the organization. You define them and reinforce them through your acts of leadership.

When you adopt the perspective of Performance Leader (Coach) rather than Boss, you bring with you implicit values. Coaches tend to value performance, growth, honesty, passion, focus and teamwork. Bosses typically embody control, authority, adherence to rules and discipline.

Your high-performance program must have defined values and it is these values that help to build the confidence of your people. Once the values are defined, they will be true values when they:

- genuinely reflect the behavior of people
- are rarely, if ever, violated
- stand the test of time
- are difficult to question/challenge
- guide decision-making across the organization
- are applied consistently and predictably.

While traditional Bosses simply develop a list of values, Performance Leaders use values to guide their decisions and actions and build a Performance Culture. Catherine Livingstone sums it up: "As CEO, you need to walk the talk of culture and lead it all day, every day."[7]

Chapter 12 offers suggestions on how to make values a central part of your Performance Model.

Make confidence a feature of your program

Confidence is intangible, and yet it is definitely one of the keys to high performance. Tap into the four sources of confidence outlined in Figure 11.7 to build the foundation from which your people move towards fulfilling their potential in even the most demanding of conditions.

FIGURE 11.7   Generating high-performance confidence

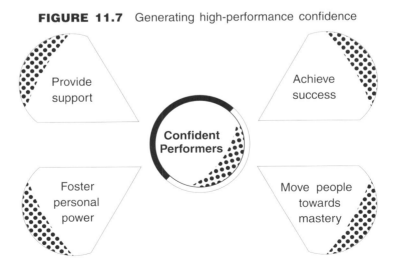

COACHING THE POOR PERFORMER

The way that you and other leaders address issues of poor performance will set the tone for the Performance Culture. To coach the poor performer requires a combination of analytical skills, patience to push past the inevitable performance blocks, and a pragmatism to know when enough is enough. High performance organizations do give people a second chance but rarely a third.

Bosses are inclined to take an emotional, and sometimes aggressive, stance to the poor performer: Performance Leaders are analytical. Bosses see it as the person's problem and react to the symptom: Performance Leaders take responsibility to find the root cause but do not let the person abdicate personal responsibility. They are very active participants in either resolving the performance problem or moving the person out of the team or program.

The Performance Leader works through the four stages described in Figure 11.8.

FIGURE 11.8 Coaching the poor performer

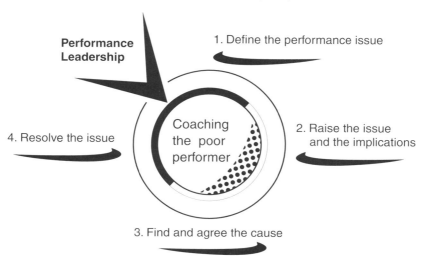

Define the performance issue

Except in the most dire of circumstances, gather your facts before you confront the person. Give yourself the best chance of a positive resolution by preparing the process and the environment in advance. Bosses march into people's space and confront them: Performance Leaders only do this in an emergency; otherwise they deal with facts, in a calm, firm and controlled manner at the right time in the right place.

Bosses reduce the chances of resolution in the cause of showing just how powerful they can be. Performance Leaders know the risks of giving feedback when they are angry and try to limit the damage.

Strategy to define the issue

Begin with the following questions to help define the performance issue and record the output on a balance sheet like that shown in Figure 11.9.

- What is the performance gap (results and process)?
- What are the potential causes (skill gap, motivation)?
- What evidence supports the situation?

FIGURE 11.9 Performance balance sheet

Expected results	Actual results
Develop presentation format ready for key presentations	Last two presentations not completed
Provide all team members with complete kit ready for rehearsal	Rehearsal kits incomplete and with errors in layout
Expected processes/style	**Actual processes/style**
Report any likelihood of not being able to deliver on time	No communication until last minute when asked for the kit
Proof check and be available to make any final corrections	Many errors and not available for corrections when needed

The balance sheet will help you to gather evidence of the performance itself and of the processes and standards. Importantly, it deals with behaviors and facts.

Look for positives to acknowledge what the person does well and engage them in any improvement (or exit) process. If you confront people with only the negatives, you reduce the chances of a positive resolution.

Performance Leaders are under more pressure to keep records of the process of dealing with poor performers because of industrial relations issues that can arise if termination of employment is the ultimate result. Accordingly, keep records of what happens at each stage.

Raise the issues and the implications

It is most effective to engage two heads in resolving the problem; so try to find a quiet venue and invite the person to discuss and own the issue. Avoid surprises and making things public.

Don't beat up on people and make the situation worse. Only chew people out when you believe that it is the best strategy for that person and this issue. Otherwise, apply the three golden rules that are part of the training of sports coaches:

Stay calm and reasoned — a calm and reasoned approach will reduce the defensiveness of the other person and ensure that you stay in control.

Focus on the issues and evidence — state specifically what the issue is. Don't jump into labeling people as "lazy", "weak" or "slack"; instead, start by detailing the evidence, not your interpretation of why this is happening.

Explain your concerns — explain the implications and consequences of the person's performance. This is far more powerful than trying to interpret why it happened. Let the Boss call the presentation "a shambles" and the person "a bad team player": the Performance Leader/Coach explains firmly how the presentation fell short of what is expected and what the consequences are. Bosses generate child-like responses from people: Performance Leaders have a greater chance of dealing with adults because that is the way they treat people.

Find and agree the cause

Dealing with poor performance relies on the same principles and tools of problem-solving that you apply to any other business issue.

Yes ... this is hard to do when you desperately want to tell the person what you really feel!! But, as the wise old coach constantly reminds the young boxer in Bryce Courtenay's novel *The Power of One*, the best approach is "First with the head, then with the heart!"[8]

As a Performance Leader/Coach you are a detective, gathering the facts and working with the person to discover why there is a gap between performance and expectations and what can be done to fill that gap. The Boss tends to diagnose from a distance and deal with symptoms.

Get to the root of the problem by using a mix of open and clarifying questions, together with good listening and observation skills. Use the PROBED process as a structure that gives the person every opportunity to participate as an equal partner in defining the cause of the problem.

Resolve the issue

When you work with a person to analyze a problem it is more likely that they will acknowledge that there is a problem and that they have a role in resolving it.

Resolution of poor performance is, of course, not always easy but the Performance Leader/Coach makes it goal-oriented, sets specific targets, shows empathy (not sympathy) and guides the person to resolve it.

Resolution requires management; so, do what an Olympic coach always does and agree to a monitoring process, including meetings and milestones. Sometimes, this will lead to the person moving on and, at others, to a performance breakthrough. In either case you will do better than the Boss because you leave the person's self-respect intact and deal with the root cause of the issue.

This is just one more reason to be the Coach, not the Boss.

SUMMARY

This chapter has addressed three key issues — leadership conversations, confidence and coaching poor performers. We now move on to apply your Business Athlete and Performance Leadership skills to building your Performance Model.

Section Four

Creating the Performance Model

Reference

Section Four deals exclusively with how to create and bring your Performance Model to life. The framework for that Model was explained in Chapter Nine and is outlined again below for your reference.

Each Chapter from twelve through to eighteen covers one element of the Performance Model in detail:

Chapter Twelve   : Take Aim: The Winning Strategy
Chapter Thirteen   : Scan: Know The Conditions
Chapter Fourteen   : Preparation: The Performance Set-Up
Chapter Fifteen   : Perform: It's All About Execution
Chapter Sixteen   : Learn and Adapt
Chapter Seventeen : Achieve Results
Chapter Eighteen   : Creating A Performance Culture

You may find it useful to refer back to this page from time-to-time to review the Model and to keep a perspective on your progress as you create your own Performance Model.

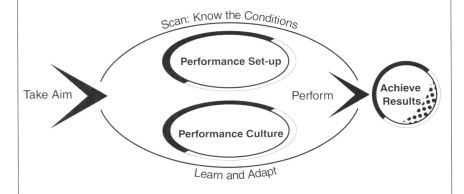

Take Aim: The Winning Strategy

In 1953, Sir Edmund Hillary mounted what was to become the first ascent of Mt Everest. He turned his vision of climbing the world's highest mountain into a mission that others joined and, together, as a team, they climbed step-by-step from base camp until Hillary and the Sherpa, Tenzing, reached the summit.

Binding the team together was Hillary's leadership, each individual's personal commitment to the quest and the shared values of honoring the mountain, and respect for each other.

Performance Leaders are the Hillarys of business. They walk, climb and clamber around the world of mission, vision, shared values and fierce focus. While Bosses talk the words, or even scoff about "the vision thing", Performance Leaders are honing their vision, framing the mission, gathering together people with like values and ambition, and leading through the challenges. They are Don Talbot taking Australian swimming to its summit, Richard Branson energizing the smiling Business Athletes of Virgin, and Tony Blair moving Israel and Palestine towards what seems an impossible peace. In history, they are Genghis Khan, Columbus, Luther King and Mandela.

They are masters of Take Aim, the first element of the Performance Model. Creating a vision, forging a mission, engaging people of like values in that mission and then building and sustaining the focus and resolve to keep going. They are what we hope for in our leaders.

Are you ready to build the first element of your Performance Model?

Where's the mountain?

Have you ever been so busy doing something that you lost sight of the original purpose? Or maybe reacted to a challenge only to find your overworked team halfway up a mountain of some kind asking "What is it that we are actually trying to achieve here?"

Organizations, particularly those in Western cultures, are programmed for activity. In fact, in many organizations it can be downright dangerous for your career to be seen sitting around thinking or planning. Bosses don't pay people to think; they pay them to do!

Reflection: How does the culture of your organization balance the need for action with the need to be clear about the purpose of that action?

"Busy" is a bad word

The programming begins when we start work, with simple comments like, "Just keep delivering results and you'll get on in this place"; "Look at Jenkins — always flat out"; "Make sure you look busy"; or "Karen can't be very busy, she's been sitting there for the last hour doing nothing".

Ask 10 business colleagues, "How's work?" and I'll bet nine will reply "Busy". Mostly we don't even ask the question, we just give people the answer: "How are you doing, Fred? Busy?" If Fred replies, "No, actually things are pretty quiet because I'm taking time to just reflect and plan", you'll be looking for the men in the white coats!

"Busy" has become code for "successful". All the trendy business magazines and websites preach "fast and furious", "busy" and, of course, "successful".

People who worship the god of "busyness" get promoted into leadership roles. From the position of power, they generate all sorts of busyness and mayhem amongst their people, consume huge amounts of resources, turn over staff and create a general fuss that others watch and admire. But it is not smart and it is not sustainable.

The global game is busy, too busy to be sensible and that is why you are going to break the mold, challenge the assumptions and be less busy and more productive. To do that, you need a way to Take Aim that suits the speed of the global game but doesn't suck you into the old cycles of boringly slow strategic planning that most organizations still follow.

From Railway Tracks to Oceans

Many Bosses believe that doing a strategic plan will solve their "too busy" problems, get everyone organized and let them move on with making money, getting promoted or whatever turns them on. However, quite the opposite usually happens, because they are so busy that the planning process happens in the blink of an eye, leaving no time to communicate, review and update the plan. Soon the business is working to an outdated map and getting itself into more trouble than just allowing each unit to do what it thinks is best.

The bad news is that most strategic plans are wrong the month after they are written.

Pre-global-game leadership used to be like choosing a suitable railway track, hooking up your engine and wagons and then just accelerating or braking as needed. Now it's more like sending out a fleet of yachts of all shapes and sizes.

Ironically, it is far more important for the fleet to have a plan than for the railway because of the volatile environment. The difference is in the need to allow for local variation and even total rewriting of the strategy if extreme conditions arise. That is why "Leadership, culture and strategy are more important in a downturn," according to Karl Sundstrom, CEO of Ericsson Australia, who also notes that "In uptimes you could be a follower and succeed — in growth times, most companies will succeed."[1]

So what does this mean if you are in a senior position where market analysts, the board and a host of others want the certainty of a great strategic plan? The answer lies in a far more dynamic direction-setting process that is relevant for a fleet and for each individual boat (Performance Unit). It is one that allows for tinkering with the plan, challenging its assumptions and making strategic and tactical decisions that can be communicated quickly to all participants.

WHO LOSES FOCUS, LOSES

Performance Leaders work to a direction or aim; Bosses to a strict plan. For many Bosses the world is like a project with clear specifications, neat boundaries, stable structures and a clear timetable of activities and responsibilities. Performance Leaders know what is and isn't a project; they deal in uncertainty, complexity and humanity. They always seek clarity of aim because they know that there is much merit in the saying: "Who loses focus, loses". They do not, however, expect the world to line up neatly with their plans. Clarity of aim is not always a plan; rather, it is a mix of purpose and targets.

Reflection: How are strategic and business plans created and used in your organization?

A key principle of the High Performance Leadership Programme is to start your Performance Model with Take Aim and be mindful that it is a dynamic and continual process because the world is changing and also because others in your fleet may find other aims along the way.

ALIGNMENT/COORDINATION

Every level of your business operations (program) needs an aim that is in synch with every other but is not the same aim. I see Performance Leaders constantly working on that alignment or coordination, while Bosses write it in the plan and then spend the year beating up people for not being perfectly aligned to the plan. Have you been there?

I am not convinced about the merit of leaders using "alignment" as a key word in their Performance Model. This is discussed further in Chapter 15 but, in brief, high-performance programs seem to focus much more on coordination and integration rather than alignment. For that reason, and the more detailed reasons explained later, I will use the combination of alignment and coordination at this stage.

There are two aspects of alignment/coordination of Take Aim: firstly, keeping the big aims aligned/coordinated to the real world and, secondly, keeping the in-house team and business unit plans aligned/coordinated with that. Slow organizations do the second part and often forget about the first.

FIGURE 12.1 Alignment/coordination

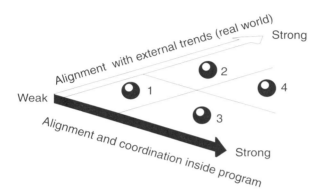

1.
- Disconnected
- Vulnerable to environment
- Low sustainable performance

3.
- Disciplined internally
- Potentially at risk from external factors
- May be slow to respond to industry change

2.
- Adaptable to environment
- Loose structure and/or discipline
- Potential to duplicate or have gaps

4.
- Adaptable
- Able to capture opportunities and move quickly to mitigate risk

The imperative to Take Aim

When I started coordinating the first High Performance Leadership Programmes, I assumed that most organizations would be clear about where they were going. They had detailed strategies that were refined into plans, with mission statements, key performance indicators and the like. But, when speaking to people across these organizations, I found very few could explain the direction, the priorities and their part in the big picture.

This made me realize that right across the world there is a major breakdown in communication of Take Aim from senior leaders of business organizations, governments and the community.

People do not connect to the big picture and it costs plenty in frustration and lost opportunities.

I assumed, wrongly, that Bosses who spent thousands of dollars on strategic planning processes and, in some cases, who had entire departments devoted to strategic planning would be able to instill focus and purpose in their business. Instead, I saw such contrasts to the Olympic programs, in which everyone was engaged, committed and focused on the next important thing. The connection to the bigger (Olympic) picture was vivid and it helped the focus on the present.

This taught me an important lesson: that the focus and sense of purpose in an organization bears no relation to the sophistication of the planning processes, or to the advice from Bosses that "people know the vision and the priorities".

To generate high performance, people need to focus on the next important thing. And if you can't create a sense of vision or purpose, then why is anyone going to focus on what you want them to do? They'll be focusing on the busiest piece of activity that rolls across their screen or maybe even on their next career move. On Everest, you die with that sort of focus, or perhaps, if you're lucky, you don't even get past base camp.

Create a common language

Part of the process of Take Aim is to create a language for performance, because you will not create consistent performance with an inconsistent performance language.

Can you imagine the potential for disaster if surgery teams, airline cockpit crews and SAS units did not have a common language? Discipline of language is essential in high-performance environments. Dr Bill Griggs' medical retrieval system has invested many hours in making sure that the communication systems between medical, police, fire and ambulance services are seamless and rapid. This means, of course, that a common language is an essential part of their Performance Model.

It doesn't much matter what words you use as long as the Performance Units in your program plan, perform and debrief using a common set of terms. This will assist your people to move between teams, to plan quickly, compare and align/coordinate plans and adjust quickly to shifts in conditions. You can increase the agility of your organization through this one simple strategy of creating a common performance language. Creating that language is a key task for the Performance Leader.

Let me now introduce you to three simple tools. The first two, the Everest-scape and the 10.10 Model, will help you to create a common performance language and an understanding of the elements of Take Aim. The third, the Clipboard Plan, will enable fast and effective alignment and realignment across your Performance Units. All three are in use in a broad variety of organizations in sport, business and government. They work equally well in large multinationals and small professional firms.

THE EVEREST-SCAPE

Do you have a clear and consistent performance language for your high-performance program (team, performance units, organization)? If not, the Everest-scape will guide you to set that language and help others to understand the main Take Aim elements of your Performance Model.

When taking aim, ensure that every one of your Performance Units addresses the six key elements outlined in Figure 12.2.

FIGURE 12.2 Six Take Aim elements

Element	Definition	Everest example
Vision	Ideal future	Stand atop Everest
Mission	The unique purpose	Make a successful ascent of Everest
Values	Guiding principles	Honor the mountain, the people of Nepal and each other
Goals	Targets	Assemble the best team, reach base camp by Day 5
Key Tasks	Actions to achieve the goals	Purchase oxygen equipment
Measures	Scores, metrics	Wind speed, meters from summit

The relationship of each element to the other is shown in the Everest-scape (Figure 12.3) in a format that can be communicated to people at all levels of your organization. We have also developed other scapes for expeditions and specific business situations that are used in High Performance Leadership Programmes. The value of

FIGURE 12.3   Everest-scape

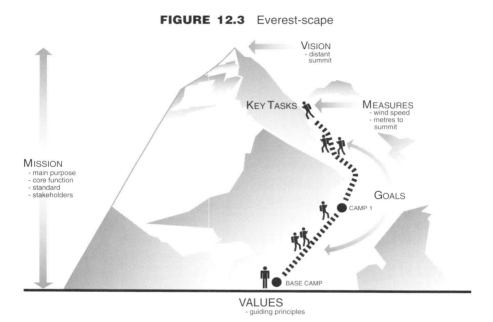

these is to create a way of making sure that everyone on the "corporate expedition" understands the performance language.

The Everest-scape illustrates the common language for the six key Take Aim elements. The main point here is not the terms but the use of *common terms*. Too many organizations variously use goals, objectives, aims and strategic objectives to describe the same thing. They confuse mission (purpose/why they exist) with vision (ideal future), often missing the point that the two are different.

Take a look at your current planning literature and see what terms get used for each of these six elements. If you do have common terms, then stick with them; if not, then get agreement about common language.

THE 10.10 MODEL

The 10.10 Model (which gets its name from the notion that world-class performance requires a "10" on achieving goals and a "10" on tasks/process) is used in two ways; firstly, to display the six Take Aim elements in a graphical form and, secondly, to plot performance. It highlights that world-class **Vision** (to be in the top five Olympic nations, for example) will only come from setting and achieving world class **Goals** (to win 15 gold medals in Athens), which in turn comes from doing the **Key Tasks** at world-class level (to build world-class-performance coaching programs). The **Mission** (to become a dominant Olympic nation) leads to the vision and is supported by **Values** (Olympic ideals, for example) and **Measures** (results at World Championships, perhaps).

Senior leaders often prefer the 10.10 Model to the Everest-scape because it shows performance levels and linkages in a form more akin to corporate reporting.

FIGURE 12.4   The 10.10 Model

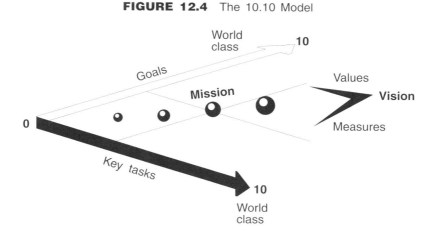

We have also developed detailed 10.10 Models that are used as assessment devices to plot performance. These assist Performance Units to discuss current performance levels (results and measures), to identify which goals need to be at world-class (or equivalent) level and which key tasks must support them.

Aim-at-a-Glance: the Clipboard Plan

After you agree your terms for the six Take Aim elements, the next step is to build them into what we call a "Clipboard Plan". This is a simple pro forma for use in the field, in the same manner as a basketball coach uses a magnetic whiteboard to plot the positioning of players.

Performers need a quick reference for Take Aim when they are preparing and in the field performing. You see it in motor racing when teams hold up placards and in football when the coach puts the game plan on the whiteboard. Likewise, the fighter pilot has the aim on a computerized control panel. What have you got to display your Aim-at-a-Glance?

An example of a mock Clipboard Plan is shown in Figure 12.5. You will notice that it gives a practical, straightforward, one-glance format for the six Take Aim elements. Clipboard Plans are an important part of the Performance Model in high-performance programs.

When every Performance Unit put its plans onto the Clipboard, the benefits are that it:

- focuses them on the direction they will take
- can be changed quickly when needed
- facilitates quick communication to other individuals and teams
- provides a standard pro forma for all teams, which means fast planning and better execution.

Sitting behind the Clipboard Plan is a single sheet for each goal that defines the goal statement, the key tasks (we call them "KTs"), risks and other issues, the owner/sponsor, who is tasked to do it and the timeframes. An example of the standard format for how a Goal Plan is used is outlined Figure 12.6.

FIGURE 12.5 Standard format for a Clipboard Plan

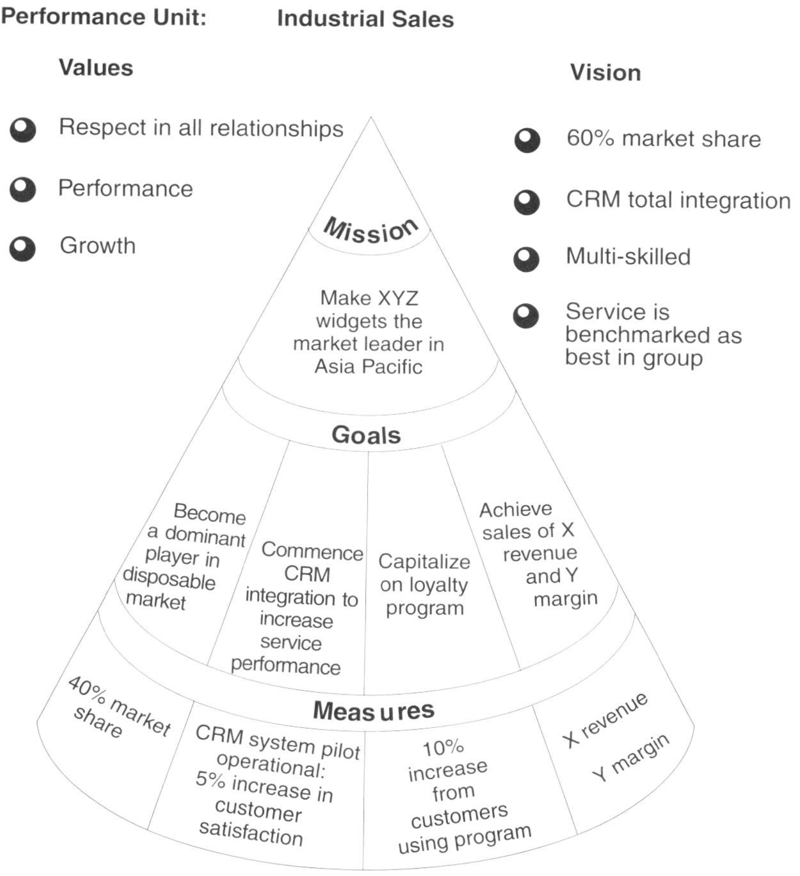

Performance Unit: **Industrial Sales**

Values

- Respect in all relationships
- Performance
- Growth

Vision

- 60% market share
- CRM total integration
- Multi-skilled
- Service is benchmarked as best in group

Mission

Make XYZ widgets the market leader in Asia Pacific

Goals

Become a dominant player in disposable market

Commence CRM integration to increase service performance

Capitalize on loyalty program

Achieve sales of X revenue and Y margin

Measures

40% market share

CRM system pilot operational: 5% increase in customer satisfaction

10% increase from customers using program

X revenue Y margin

FIGURE 12.6 Standard format for a Goal Plan

Goal 1	Increase customer-satisfaction levels by 5%				
Key tasks	**Issues/risks**	**Owner**	**Tasked**	**Start**	**Finish**
1. Commence CRM implementation	Ensure project plan structure is robust	JB	JB/LM	1/3	30/6
2. Assess impact of pilot program	Benchmark, include customer satisfaction	RB	SM/RB	30/6	31/8
3. Plan for roll out	Ensure commitment	JS	JS	1/9	1/11

Organizations that use Clipboard Plans or similar formats have a definite performance advantage over those with bulky plans because the Performance Leaders and the Business Athletes in each unit have clear sight of their direction and the broader context. We have developed various types of Clipboards for clients and there are also planning processes that give you a summary plan that are available commercially. The key is to build something that is simple, clear and relevant for your unit and others in the overall program.

How to Build your Clipboard Plan

When building your Clipboard Plan, remember that the intention is to create a clear aim that is easily understood by all stakeholders and capable of being changed if necessary. That means the process that you use is very important.

Ask yourself:

- Who should I involve in creating the Clipboard Plan?
- What research is needed to build a robust plan?
- Who can challenge and check it?

Think of the Clipboard Plan as one of the ways for you to free up your time from day-to-day management by giving people a clear focus and giving you a direct line back to check that they are heading in the right direction.

My experience is that when leaders use the Everest-scape to create a common performance language and then instill the discipline of using Clipboard and Goal Plans for all Performance Units (from the total company to the smallest cross-functional team), it adds agility and focus and gives the Performance Leader more time to focus on creating the future. That is what people want from their leaders and I suggest that every Performance Leader in your organization be coached in how to create a Clipboard Plan.

Facilitation process

From experience (facilitating many organizations to build their Clipboard Plans), the best approach is for each unit to allocate either one or two full days to the task, while allowing time for preparation of materials. Assuming a one-day forum, the day is divided into three segments:

- Segment one deals with context and features presentations by a Senior Leader on the overall corporate direction, core values and the challenges that lie ahead. When facilitating executive teams we ask the chairperson or the CEO to make the presentation. This session lasts no more than one hour, including questions and discussion.
- Segment two extends over a number of hours and involves building the various pieces of the Clipboard Plan. Pre-work will have been done by individuals and sub-groups.
- Segment three involves presenting the draft Clipboard Plan and supporting materials to the Senior Leader and at least one other person who has a clear perspective on the team and its mission (an internal customer is ideal). Robust probing leads to further refinement by the end of the long but productive day.

The unit members then further refine the Clipboard Plan ready for final presentation at a meeting within the following two weeks.

Let's now look at how you can lead your Performance Unit(s) to build each element of their Clipboard Plan.

Before you define your mission

While literally hundreds of business books, business leaders and consultants argue the case for mission and vision, they regularly jumble the meaning, replace one with the other and create confusion.

In performance environments there is enough confusion without creating more through your own planning efforts. Therefore, my proposition is that you accept that mission and vision are interlinked: that sometimes the vision is the mission (for example, win an Olympic gold medal); that sometimes the idea of vision comes before the mission (for example, to stand on top of Mt Everest); and at other times the mission is the vision (for example, to participate in an expedititon for its own sake). Confused? Fine, let's agree a simple approach and get on with it.

I propose that the energy source, the cause, the reason for you and others getting involved in the business, the community, the sport or whatever is the mission. This will undoubtedly include some vision but I suggest that "vision" be used to refer only to distant summits. Make vision an end goal or a very distant one, such as your three-year goal for a business or the 20-year view for government. Make it over the horizon, make it big, put it into the mission if you like, but see it as the end of a cycle or event.

Mission statement or symbol?

Unfortunately, missions and mission statements have a bad name in business. This is unfortunate because without a statement or symbol of core purpose or mission, how can anyone really know where they are heading, or be encouraged to join? Each of the high-performance programs in the Australian Olympic sport system has a mission and within these programs the sub-units (such as rowing crews) also have their own. The gold-medal-winning women's hockey team had a mission that the coach would read out to them when times got tough. It was a mission that concluded with "We choose to do this thing, not because it is easy but because it is hard".[2]

For speed, agility and high performance, ignore the doubters and take time to develop a clear statement or symbol of the mission of your program (team and organization). High performers are attracted and will dedicate themselves to a mission. Demand that every Performance Unit has its mission sitting proudly at the top of its Clipboard Plan.

Powerful missions generally contain three interlinked criteria:

- Unique function or cause
- Fundamental relationships
- Standard of the challenge.

FIGURE 12.7 Characteristics of powerful missions

Characteristic	Everest example	Business example
Unique cause/function	Climb Everest	Invent new technologies to deliver competitive edge
Standard	World's highest mountain	Global standard
Relationships	For God, country and team	For XYZ corporation

Examples of mission statements

Our unique mission is to turn ideas and innovations into commercial products that give us a competitive edge in global markets.
Development team in multinational business

To advance and communicate scientific knowledge and understanding of the Earth, the solar system, and the universe. To advance human exploration, use, and development of space. To research, develop, verify, and transfer advanced aeronautics and space technologies.
NASA[3]

If your mission is as clear and precise as "Climb Everest", then consider using a symbol to define and communicate it. For example, a picture of Everest might be far more powerful than a written statement. The principle is the same as developing an identifiable logo that conveys all the meaning of your brand. Sporting teams use past trophies, R&D outfits keep prototypes and hospitals show pictures of patients: each reminds people of the mission.

Hot teams have a unique mission

While Bosses look to mission for conformity and control, Performance Leaders search for the uniqueness. People are attracted to freshness and uniqueness. If your mission has originality and energy, people will come. It's even more exciting if they come and find their own mission.

Hot teams have an energy, an identity, a mission that oozes energy. You can foster this by giving them space and freedom to find a mission that is a unique expression of themselves. A good example of this is an in-house IT services team that met to define its Clipboard Plan. Circumstances were tough, retrenchments were in the air and the thought of an exciting mission seemed impossible. Over some hours of probing, the team arrived at: *"We will make knowledge central to the competitive advantage of this company".*

Mission: Questions from the coach

Try these probing questions on your unit/program:

- What special combination of skills, talents and experiences do we possess?
- How is our position and perspective unique?
- If we weren't here, what wouldn't happen?
- How can we use that uniqueness to make a difference to the world?
- How does our history make us different from others who might see themselves as the same?
- If we all got into the zone all the time, what could we do?
- What is our potential?

Use the questions above to help the people whom you lead to find new potential, freshness and uniqueness. When they find that sense of purpose, they will sign up with all of the passion that we spoke about in the earlier sections of this book.

Refine the mission into a statement, a set of bullet points or a symbol to put on the Clipboard. With the mission defined, the goals and key tasks will follow naturally. Before doing that, let's explore the elements of values and vision.

EMBED THE VALUES

At my first Olympic team managers' meeting, John Coates, President of the Australian Olympic Committee and Chef de Mission, gave a very clear and compelling message that stuck in my mind and assisted me over four Olympiads to make what I believe to be the right decisions in a vast array of situations.

John told us that we were selected on the Olympic team for one reason and one reason only, and that was to support the athletes in their quest to be the best that they could be. Time and again, he emphasized the core value "Athletes first".

"The Australian Olympic Committee aims to maximize the potential of Olympians and Olympic-caliber athletes by providing them with support and opportunity, reinforcing their positive role in Australian society as a whole. The AOC is committed to helping Australia's athletes achieve their dreams at all Olympic Games."[4]

Living to the value "Athletes first" meant that nothing would compromise doing everything possible to make each athlete's experience the most positive possible. John Coates also personalized the value and instilled confidence by reminding us that we had been chosen because of our skills and experience. We were members of one of the world's best teams.

Convert values into principles and behaviors

Ask any Olympic coach about their program and they will talk about their philosophy and the importance of embedding that philosophy into their program. To the sports coach, the core philosophy is sacred. It comprises their beliefs about the way the game should be played, how to gain competitive advantage and how to set up an organization that can win. Some elements of that philosophy will evolve over time, while the core values will likely remain in place for a lifetime.

They convert values into principles, calling them "team principles", "team rules" or "behaviors". Pat Riley, the renowned basketball coach, calls them "core covenants".[5] The language of values and team principles is an essential foundation for high performance and leads to behaviors that are consistent with the values. Sue Vardon, CEO of Centrelink, illustrates this approach: "The behaviors required in the new Centrelink culture are solving problems, listening, mutual respect, exploring, behaving ethically. Centrelink measures people's performance against these behaviors and their individual learning plans are linked to these behaviors as well."[6]

Real or spoken values

Most High Performance Leaders work to a short, practical set of values and principles. They define them in behaviors (as in the Centrelink example) and use them relentlessly by constantly feeding back to players the effectiveness of the decisions that they are making and how they relate to the values and principles of the program.

Bosses often fall into four traps when trying to capture the power that we all know comes from values-driven organizations. These are explained in Figure 12.8 and contrasted with the practices of Performance Leaders.

FIGURE 12.8 Creating a values-driven culture

Bosses	Performance Leaders
Ignore people and just set the values and issue a list	Engage people in debating, defining and agreeing the values
Select too many values or principles	Select a maximum of 2–5 values/ principles
Use one-word descriptions that make the values vague and confusing	Define the values in behaviors
Don't use the values or violate them	Act according to the values and use them to guide decisions

Well-selected, clearly defined and meaningful values enable people to make decisions about how to align their actions to the broader purpose. For example, an organization that I coach has "customer service" as a value. One of its units has converted it into a set of principles, including one that they call "No surprises". This means always letting a customer know if their order is going to be delayed or in anyway different from what is expected.

Values-driven organizations also have a performance advantage because of the common language and dialogue that facilitates the creation of a Performance Culture. As Catherine Livingstone says of the values-integration program in Cochlear, it has provided "a way of talking to each other" and a "framework for defining culture".[7]

Beware the emerging values of your stakeholders

The values of the workforce and community are changing and many of the emerging values are coming from the impacts of the global game. It is important to ensure that your program is in synch with the values of stakeholders such as employees, customers and shareholders. Three emerging values to be aware of are:

- Sustainability
- Lifestyle
- Security.

Sustainability

The trends are moving strongly against the selfish, resource-stripping values of the traditional corporation. Just as athletes are expected to be role models (not just winners), so too are corporations increasingly expected to add value to the community and environment in which they operate. And there is economic value, too. Fuji-Xerox Australia opened an Eco Manufacturing Plant in Australia as part of its strategy to position itself as an environmentally friendly company. The company's CEO, Philip Chambers, reports $25-million savings just in cost reductions, without even taking into account the increased service life of products.[8]

Lifestyle

Generations X and Y are not interested in corporate loyalty. They have seen their parents as slaves to corporations and watched wave after wave of downsizing. For them, work is increasingly about meaning and lifestyle. Corporations and leaders that can't relate to that are going to struggle to find talent. As author and leadership consultant Doug Stace observes, "I see a difference coming from the younger generation. They are not as beholden to the lure of the career ladder of the large corporation. They tend to be more autonomous people, having greater confidence in themselves."[9]

Security

The events of September 11, economic uncertainty and rising social problems linked to unemployment all add to people's unease. Security has become more important and, when combined with people's demands for lifestyle, adds to the woes of corporations that want to create a mobile, global workforce. How might increasing needs for security amongst your stakeholders affect the performance of your program?

Coaching the values

One of the project activities in the High Performance Leadership Programme is for each Performance Leader to identify a core value and build a coaching plan that they implement over a one-month period. At the end of the month, they make a presentation of the evidence that they have changed the behaviors of others through their coaching. During the project, they are helped to use the practices of the sports coach to embed the values and principles into their program.

Values are essential in your Performance Model because in performance environments the values and principles provide points of certainty, and a basis for making decisions. They build confidence and generate focus and commitment. Take time to understand the real values, to define the values that you want and then use the team principles and reinforcement to coach the values into your organization.

VISION — FEEL THE POWER

As already agreed, our definition of "vision" is "distant summits". That means that in some cases the vision is the driving force, where in others it is the mission. For example, eliminating terrorism from the world is much more a mission than a vision; while Greenpeace motivates people around a cause, a mission that centers on valuing the environment. For many Olympians, however, the vision of a gold medal is the energy source.

My advice is to use the combined power of vision and mission. When it comes to building the Clipboard Plan and engaging people in the mission and vision, the key is to create a view of the future that is at least over the current horizon. That may be six months, a year, 10 years ahead, depending on the lifecycles of products, projects and initiatives in your industry.

Use vision to help people to see beyond the current horizon. Lift their sights above the present situation to see the bigger picture or landscape and its patterns. Of course, this is the great advantage of sporting organizations where the size of the Performance Unit(s) and the clear visibility of results makes it relatively easy to use vision as a motivating factor.

On the Clipboard Plan, the vision should be specific, and written as a long-term goal or goals that people can identify. This will also ensure that there is a link between the current goals and the future summit.

To Find the Vision, Look to Challenges and Potential

"Vision" is a word that is used more often in business than probably any other field. In sport, the two words that you hear in conversations about distant summits are "challenge" and "potential". You will have a greater chance of finding and engaging people in a bigger picture if you use these words in your performance conversations. Let me explain.

Global and personal challenges

Performance Leaders find vision by looking for the greatest challenges.

These challenges can be global or personal. Global challenges are world's-best standard. Mt Everest, the Olympic Games, a Pulitzer prize and the like are global challenges. Personal challenges are simply the personal equivalent of Mt Everest. Getting to a single-figure handicap in golf, climbing to Everest base camp or getting a novel published are examples of personal challenges.

It is a characteristic of the sport landscape that coaches and athletes know what is the greatest challenge. For a track and field athlete such as 400-meter champion Cathy Freeman, the global challenges are Olympic gold medal, World Championship and World Record. In the business world, fund managers can get the best returns for their clients in a global market; sales people the trophy for most sales revenue; and cities can win the World Expo. Performance Leaders use these types of global challenges as rallying points to generate a high-energy vision. People respond to a challenge because it is specific, whereas vision, as someone once said, is something you can see and other people can't. Is there a global challenge that can be a distant summit for you?

Global challenge: Questions from the coach

Consider these questions as you seek or refine the vision for your performance program.

- What is the biggest global challenge that your program can tackle?
- What is best practice in your industry?

- What will be the benchmark in two or three years' time?
- Is there a challenge for you to shape your industry?

Mike Heard described the central "vision" question for Codan as "How will the world communicate in three years' time?" Great question.

The second type of challenge is the personal challenge. These apply to individuals and to teams. The famed Jamaican bobsled team had little chance of reaching the global challenge but they could set the personal challenge to get to the Games and be competitive. Charlie Walsh, for many years the head coach for Australian Cycling, constantly instilled in his athletes the desire to always be competitive. He believed that the global challenges would come if athletes set their own challenges and met these.

Personal challenges are about crossing the gap between current performance and the next level. Probe your Performance Units to find challenges that they want to take on. Hot teams are hungry for challenges, and it builds a confidence and motivation when there is a quest to get to a distant summit. Coach your people to have their own personal challenges and link these to the challenges of the performance program. Why not get your people together and brainstorm the following question: "What's the biggest challenge that we could take on?" In that brainstorm can lie the power of a vision.

Personal challenge: Questions from the coach

Consider these questions to further identify and refine your program vision.

- What is the next performance level for your Performance Unit(s)?
- What challenge can we take on?
- What is each Business Athlete's personal challenge?
- What is the next level for you as a Performance Leader in making Take Aim a strong feature of your Performance Model?

Performance Leaders use both global and personal challenges to find a vision. Frank Williams, founder of the Williams Formula One Team, instills both challenges into his team by reminding them that "there is no constant supremacy".[10]

Get people excited about potential

There are few more exciting things that our coach, manager, mentor, colleague or team mate can say to us than that we have huge potential. Potential hints at the possibilities that are out there to explore; it invites us to expand our thinking in ways that are never going to be seen if we talk in the dull, boring, left-brain language of strategic planning.

Bosses scoff at potential and see little past the obvious challenges of the day. Performance Leaders think and act in the language of potential and challenge. They engage their Business Athletes in discussions about the business, its markets, and its processes and systems. Performance Leaders excite others about potential. Like Hillary, they create programs that tackle the highest mountains.

How to engage the whole system in the vision

While Bosses think that they have to deliver the vision, Performance Leaders increasingly use their whole community of stakeholders to develop the vision and related strategy. Employing the methodologies of large-group design forums they minimize the resistance and slowness of traditional vision-planning activities, and gain real commitment to moving forward.

We use facilitated large-group design sessions with many High Performance Leadership clients to help them to develop visions and solutions to major issues. These are large gatherings (sometimes in the hundreds) in which a variety of members of the total system (customers, stakeholders, suppliers, employees, management) are brought together to work through a series of structured exercises aimed at designing an ideal future and various scenarios. Marvin Weisbord and Sandra Janoff[11] and Barbara Benedict-Bunker and Billie T. Alban[12] suggest excellent methodologies to work with these types of approaches and I encourage you to read their work.

For example, in a recent assignment for a government agency seeking to design a five-year vision for passenger transport across rural communities, we engaged 70 people in an innovative and exciting activity that drew many great ideas and a high level of energy from the participants.

Large-group design sessions also strengthen the link from vision to implementation, as highlighted by Bunker and Alban: " ... when everyone gets on board through these large group methods, less time is needed for implementation, and the implementation is more likely to be successful."[13]

Four ways to articulate your vision

Performance Leaders are always promoting the vision (and mission) to their team and other stakeholders. Large-group design sessions are one of four effective ways that we coach Performance Leaders to do this within business organizations. These methods have developed from experience in many different settings, from the performing arts to sport. The other three comprise:

- Miniatures
- Stories and symbols
- Prototypes and models.

Consider using a variety of these techniques (which are outlined below) to suit the different learning styles of your people.

Use the power of miniatures

The power of a message is, to a great extent, inversely proportional to the length of the message. In other words, sports coaches give short, sharp instructions because they will be remembered, and advertisers use quick "grabs" to impart a message.

If this is the case, then why do so many Bosses insist on sitting people through lengthy slide presentations that a colleague of mine calls "death by PowerPoint"?

The global game is fast and changing rapidly, and people's attention span just isn't what it used to be. So you need something more powerful than outdated, oversized presentations of business plans that put people to sleep.

Think about the Nike swoosh or the slogan of a favorite company, a poem, a photograph or a scale model of a building. They all have one thing in common. They are *powerful miniatures* that communicate a bigger message. Noted author and Jungian analyst James Hillman acknowledges the liking for size and expansion within the U.S. culture that has pervaded much of the global game, and yet argues that power lies in intensification or miniaturization. He writes, "A poem miniaturizes. It is like a computer chip or an optic fiber that carries many messages simultaneously."[14]

Performance Leaders create short, powerful miniature presentations that capture the passion and excitement of the vision. Think of it as being like creating a travel brochure. If you capture the interest, then people will read the itinerary; usually, people don't read the itinerary first.

In a High Performance Leadership Programme, each leader is coached to design a powerful miniature of the vision (or mission) of their team/organization. We challenge them to take some risks in the content and style and to present it to a group of colleagues who provide coaching feedback and advice.

Effective miniatures contain a strong, clear theme. They are delivered in less than 10 minutes and start with the end (distant summit): "I have a dream of a place where ... " They include the assumptions, rationale and impact on people of this vision and sell the benefits. They are vivid in language, end strongly on the positive future and leave people wanting to know more. They are not a business plan.

FIGURE 12.9 Characteristics of a powerful miniature

Elements of miniature	Structure
Theme	Strong and clear e.g. *"Sustainability is the only option"*
Time	Maximum of 10 minutes
Structure	Start with the distant summit e.g. *"In three years we will have reshaped the landscape ... "* Include assumptions, rationale and impacts
Content	Vivid imagery and language e.g. *"We will forge new alliances ... "* Use symbols and pictures
Sell	Focus on linking features to benefits for the audience
Close	Reinforce the positives and leave people wanting more

Many Performance Leaders have a core miniature and a series of "bolt-ons" that they add to suit the audience. For example, if you are presenting to the board, the bolt-on might include financial data and projections and risk analysis, whereas for a group of operations staff you might bolt on details of career opportunities and the implications of changes in technology for the design of jobs. Each bolt-on is designed to sell the features and benefits that are suited to that audience. Who are the audiences for your pitch?

Stories and symbols

"He was an old man who fished alone in a skiff in the Gulf Stream and he had gone eighty-four days now without taking a fish."[15]

Everyone loves a story, and none more than the Performance Leader/Coach who scours the memory banks, books, magazines and their network looking for stories to sell their message. Stories are powerful and if you can weave a story into your vision then all the better. They can be inspirational life stories, such as Lance Armstrong's fight against cancer and his triumphs in the Tour de France, or 16-year-old Jesse Martin's solo voyage around the world. Can you trawl back into the legends of your organization to tell of the founder or a great character?

My first job after leaving university was with an insurance company that is now a part of the AXA Group. The sales training manager, Reg Davis, was a great influence on my life through his unique energy and irreverence to the managers who tried to control him. Reg's view was that performance was all about passion and being prepared to keep coming back no matter how many setbacks you received. I recall his story of John Hunter, the top sales agent in the company. Hunter was a man who sold relentlessly in his country region from Saturday to Thursday and then, every Friday, came to the head office to process the business. Hunter created mayhem on Fridays because he refused to take no for an answer from anyone. Reg told all new agents the story of Hunter being ejected, mid-sentence, through the front door of a house and reappearing a minute later through the back door, still in the same sentence. John Hunter had seen people to whom he could have sold insurance left in ruins because of lack of insurance when a family member died or was disabled. His vision and crusade was to never allow anyone to be in that position and he therefore hassled, bothered and cajoled anyone and everyone to buy insurance.

The story sold the message about passion and vision.

How to structure a story

Effective storytelling is an art and I encourage you to think about ways to weave interesting stories that either tell your vision or illustrate the themes.

At the 2000 Games, we made use of current and former World and Olympic Champions to build the confidence of our athletes and to lift their sights and confidence beyond what they thought was possible. People like world boxing champion Kostya Tszyu, America's Cup-winning skipper John Bertrand and undefeated 1500-meter Olympic gold medallist Herb Elliott each told their stories.

Storytelling: Questions from the coach

By answering the following questions, you can begin to construct an interesting story to sell the vision.

- Who is your audience?
- What is your main theme?
- Where and when did it all begin?
- Who was involved?
- What happened and why was it significant (to the theme)?
- How did it finish?
- What is the key message?

Sport gives very vivid examples but so does business, as people interact with customers, solve problems and achieve great things.

Prototypes and models

Vision is always about innovation, and that means using the power of prototypes and models to illustrate your point. For example, if your vision is to create a waste-recycling business in your community, then build a simple model that highlights the flows of waste and its conversion into materials that are used by industry, which then employs people.

Models, flow diagrams and prototypes give people a chance to sell the vision. Travel companies use this all the time to get you to spend time on idyllic tropical beaches. Can you make a picture that fits the vision?

Coaches often show their athletes an example of something that illustrates the vision or the values that underpin the program. I know of a football coach who took the whole team to a grand final so they could soak up the atmosphere and get a vivid experience of what it is like to reach and win the final. Pictures were taken and pasted around the walls of the change rooms to keep the vision in mind. Can you put examples of winning products around your offices and work spaces?

Study tours and visits by members of an organization can stimulate vision thinking. Lion Nathan CEO Gordon Cairns, for example, says that his organization "took a group of people across to the U.S. and visited the 30 most admired companies in the country. It was a life-changing experience for those who went."[16]

Choose industries outside your own that are really good at something that is akin to your vision. For example, take people to a restaurant that provides special service, or to innovation awards and introduce them to winners. To articulate the themes of your vision, make it real and vivid.

Five rules for selling vision

Why do leaders fail to excite other people to join in the cause, even when they go through the steps that I've just described? The answer often lies in five common errors of positioning the message. To counteract the errors, we have formulated five rules:

Rule #1: Make it relevant: Speak the language of your audience by putting yourself in their position and understanding their perspectives. Blend to their style and speak to their needs. Too many vision presentations are business plans that might be interesting to the senior management team but no one else. A basketball coach would soon be sacked for such a presentation and, in the global game, the same is happening to Bosses.

Rule #2: You need credibility: People buy credibility. Never underestimate the ability of people to remember what you did in the past. Visions that are inconsistent with your past performance will be hard to sell. If that is your problem, then before you unveil Everest point to nearby summits and get some results happening.

Rule #3: Give it substance: Performance Leaders think through the issues and possible scenarios to put together a well-designed case and emphasize the substance behind the direction. Bosses just hand out that old business plan. As Warren Bennis reminds us, "There must be consistent policies and procedures to give the vision credibility".[17]

Rule #4: Minimize the dilution: People will quickly decide whether you are deadly serious or suffering from "training program delusion" or some other altered state. Set deadlines, show commitment through action, get some runs on the board and people will join your cause. Be aware that under competitive pressure the message gets diluted. Minimize the dilution or focus will wander.

Rule #5: Get involved: Bosses pitch the vision and disappear. Performance Leaders are visible, involved and show support through giving people the best possible Performance Set-up. They take particular care of their high performers and work one-on-one to keep them connected to the vision.

GOALS AND KEY TASKS

While mission, vision and values are the foundation on which performance is built, it is in the performance goals and the key tasks that the action happens.

Organizations can operate at high-performance levels without a distant summit or explicit values, but I have seen few, if any, that can sustain performance without the link from mission to goals and key tasks.

This is not surprising either, given that the short-term goal is the most powerful psychological technique. You can capture this power by focusing people on short-term, specific performance goals (with deadlines) and building feedback processes and consequences around them.

Put six goals on the Clipboard

Facilitate every Performance Unit in your program to identify no more than six critical performance goals to be achieved over the period of an agreed performance cycle (usually 6–12 months).

Any more than six goals starts to dilute the focus; however, in larger teams you might go to eight as a maximum.

For each goal, use the Goal Plan outlined earlier in this chapter to record the key tasks, the timeframes, the "owner", the person responsible for doing the tasks, and the start and finish times.

Most business managers are very comfortable with the notion of goals and key tasks, so there is little difference here between Performance Leaders and Bosses. To get a balanced set of goals, ensure that there is at least one goal each for:

- process and systems development
- people development
- customer relationships
- performance results.

Check that the six goals on each Clipboard Plan are aligned to the overall mission and vision, and to other Performance Units. For example, if you have Clipboard Plans for operations teams and support teams, such as human resources, get the teams together to make sure that the goals and plans are in synch. Sports coaches take great care to align/coordinate the goals and plans for each section of the team (offense, center, defense). Are you linking and aligning your teams to get speed, agility and performance?

DEFINE YOUR MEASURES

Performance Leaders/Coaches are avid keepers of feedback data. Like good manufacturing managers, they want to understand the impact of variables on the performance processes, although they know that they can't control the world with the same precision as is possible on a production line.

Most organizations have a huge range of quantitative measures or metrics, ranging from financial to operational and customer information. Too many managers go overboard collecting numbers on everything, but how effectively do they use the data to really influence performance? In performance environments, you need a small number of powerful measures that allow you to learn and refine as you move through the landscape.

Building a process of performance feedback based on the right measures is one of the essential elements of the Performance Model and we will explore this in more detail over the coming chapters.

From clipboards to emotion

Using the Everest-scape, the 10.10 Model and the Clipboard Plan will speed up your planning processes and assist in maintaining the Aim in a fast-changing world. As we conclude this chapter, it is important to make a point about striking a balance between data and emotion in the Take Aim process.

Traditional Bosses are most comfortable in a world of data, fact and objectivity. Performance Leaders/Coaches work with emotion because they know that turning people into tick-tock robots is a great way to drive passion and initiative out of any organization.

If you can balance the need for objectivity with clever intuition and a genuine feel for customers, staff and others in your system, then you are in a much stronger position to generate high performance. Let me give you an example.

Robert is a sales executive with an international company that has its roots and culture in manufacturing high-quality products.

Frustration overflowed at a sales meeting when he asked who had made the decision to shift the manufacturing of one of their leading brands to a country with lower labor costs. "Production makes those decisions," was the answer. Robert retorted, "Well perhaps you might tell Production that the premium that customers paid for that product was because of where it was manufactured. Now I've got customers refusing to take product manufactured at the new site. If we don't get some understanding of emotion into this business and realize that people don't decide things the way production engineers measure them, then we're stuffed!"

Robert believes that the organization has lost its emotional ability to act and to take risks and to really connect with the customer. He sees the culture as too ordered and clinical for the shifting world.

How close are you to the edge?

Watch for the people in your program who avoid failure rather than seeking success. Such people take the conservative approach to performance, avoiding things that they don't know and staying away from the edges where mistakes are possible. They take few risks, their initiative is low and they fail to fulfill their potential.

Watch also for those with no regard for history, who believe that there is nothing in the global game that has ever happened before. They will take blind risks that can wreck value.

When you facilitate your Performance Units to build and refine their Clipboard Plans, be mindful of the risk profile of the group and adjust your actions accordingly.

As a general guide, avoid a totally clinical approach to setting strategy, but test your intuition. Get a balance of risk-takers, managers and avoiders on the strategy team, and don't let any side dominate the debate.

SUMMARY

Take Aim is the first element of the Performance Model. However, in a fast-moving global game, the other elements all feed into the Take Aim areas as you continually refine and adapt your model for the global game.

In the next chapter, we look at how to foster the scanning processes that are needed to sustain a Performance Model that is attuned to the shifting conditions of the global game.

Scan: Know the Conditions

The Sydney-to-Hobart Yacht Race is one of the world's great open-water classics. On Boxing Day every year, an armada of yachts glides majestically out of Sydney Harbour towards Tasmania and the port of Hobart. In 1998, the yachts left Sydney on a balmy midsummer day, unaware of the dangers that lay ahead.

While some private weather forecasters were already warning of dangerous conditions in the open waters of Bass Strait, the official forecast gave only a hint of the rough weather ahead.

Within two days, five yachts had sunk and six sailors had died. Through coronial and other investigations it emerged that few yachts were equipped for the vicious storm that struck the fleet. Similarly, the Weather Bureau lacked the capabilities to predict the full extent of the storm and to get an urgent message to skippers of yachts that were forging their way into some of the wildest weather conditions ever experienced in a race of this kind. It was only because the rescue services *were* prepared and capable of operating in the middle of the night in the most dangerous of conditions that many more lives were not lost. In all, 55 sailors were rescued from their stricken yachts.

What emerged as lessons from the tragedy were the need for improved capabilities to anticipate changes in conditions and to communicate those changes. There also had to be improvements in the capacity to prepare for extreme conditions and to respond quickly and correctly to them.

Figure 13.1 highlights how the tragedy of that race changed the thinking in these four areas. Notice how similar these shifts are to those from the pre-global to the global game.

FIGURE 13.1   Shifts in performance thinking

	Pre-tragedy	**Post-tragedy**
Prepare	Yachts prepared based largely on personal experience — did not envision extreme conditions	High standards of risk-readiness amongst yachts, organizers and meteorologists
Anticipate	Most relied on single sources of feedback	Scan using multiple sources of feedback on weather, race conditions
Communicate	At long intervals — bulletins from race organizers/weather forecasters	Continuously open channels to provide feedback on conditions and to report danger
Respond	Ill-equipped with knowledge to make informed judgments	Resilience of boats and crew, plus access to information, increases ability to respond to extreme changes

To create and sustain high performance in the global game, your organization needs the resilience of the ocean-yacht racer, and the capabilities to anticipate, communicate and respond to changes in conditions of the game. Those conditions will not be 60-foot waves but their equivalents in new, unseen competitors, multiple stakeholders with competing demands and rising costs of insurance and interest rates.

This chapter challenges you to build the capability to anticipate changes in performance conditions. This capability of "Scan: Know the Conditions" is essential to all other elements of your Performance Model. Unless you can scan and envisage the range of conditions and maintain a constant awareness of shifts, you risk being like those skippers in the Sydney-to-Hobart who aimed their yachts unknowingly and ill-equipped into the eye of the storm.

ANTICIPATE: WHO WATCHES YOUR WORLD?

Performance Leaders are acutely, even obsessively, aware of the world around them. They are outwardly focused. They recruit and develop people and teams who understand the conditions, because knowing the conditions gives them a chance to anticipate shifts, thereby minimizing threats to their program and maximizing opportunities.

One of the distinctions between the Performance Leader and the Boss is the search or scanning strategy that they employ. The Boss is stuck in pre-global-game space, scanning narrowly amongst customers, and for consumer-demand patterns and technologies. They see old patterns but lack the insight or awareness to spot the new patterns that are just emerging. As skippers of yachts, they perform in good conditions but are ill-equipped for extreme conditions.

Performance Leaders scan the environment for competitors, alliance partners and opportunities, encouraging a culture in which everyone is on the lookout for the knockout wave or the friendly wind shift. They don't just spend time with customers, they get to know consumers who are not their customers. They learn what their customers are thinking today and what consumers need now and in the future.

A graphic example of this capability to read consumer and customer behavior was the OSHKOSH B'GOSH clothing group, which shifted from being a supplier of basic work-wear for men to becoming the leading U.S. seller of branded children's clothing. Using children's overalls as the test vehicle, OSHKOSH B'GOSH (named after its Wisconsin hometown, Oshkosh) quickly gathered speed while, importantly, keeping the company's core value of quality. By 1996, an EquiTrends survey ranked it alongside Mercedes-Benz and Lego as one of the world's top ten brands in terms of world-standard quality. Perhaps the likes of K-Mart, Andersen's, Baring's and Gateway Computers may have performed better if they had had better capabilities for scanning the conditions?

What are the potential knockout waves and friendly wind shifts in your performance environment?

Scan beyond your current paradigm

It is essential to your program that you play the role of Strategic Leader and equip your people to scan well beyond current paradigms. Do this by creating scanning systems and encouraging and supporting people to engage in dialogue with others from outside the system.

For example, day-to-day conversations provide precious information that will tell you whether a key business relationship is really a form of partnership or whether it has developed the typical pattern where the customers or partners see that your system is more interested in doing business with itself. Organizations easily drop back into old habits or paradigms and they need a Performance Model that includes scanning as a capability of all Performance Units.

Outside the paradigm: Questions from the coach

To challenge people to scan outside their current view of the world, ask questions such as:

- Who has capabilities in other industries that could match ours?
- What would it be like if things were 50% worse than our current financial projections?
- What are the most potent trends in our industry and what could they mean for us?
- Which of our stakeholders is least like us?
- How can we separate ourselves from some of the impacts of our environment (for example, up-skilling, or relocating geographically to avoid coming difficulties)?

It is difficult to overestimate the importance of paradigms to performance in dynamic conditions. For example, there have been, and will continue to be, shifts in the paradigm of financial reporting after the demise of Enron in the U.S. This shift has the potential to influence many financial issues such as disclosure of risk and provision for bad debts. Astute business and government leaders scan these types of developments looking for potential patterns of impact.

It is not uncommon for sales and manufacturing units in a business to operate from what can be opposing paradigms. Sales see things through a market-driven paradigm, while many manufacturing areas come from a product-driven paradigm. Performance Leaders create the dialogue between the two areas so that there is understanding of each paradigm. The same applies in team sports between the defensive players and the offensive players.

FIGURE 13.2 Create dialogue between holders of different paradigms

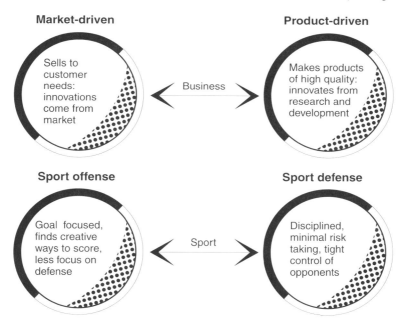

The top sporting teams have broken the paradigms of offense and defense; firstly, through making athletes aware of the value of both and, secondly, by incorporating more offense into the defense ("attack begins from defense") and vice versa. Leadership is often about breaking these paradigms and being prepared to look outside your paradigm.

Navigators must be continually connected to the conditions

Performance Leaders create organizations that are constantly connected to the environment. How else can those organizations accurately adjust strategies to meet the changing needs of customers and other stakeholders?

The Sydney-to-Hobart crews would have been better able to navigate the conditions if they had had continual connection with weather forecasters rather than occasional bulletins. In the time between bulletins, the conditions changed rapidly and beyond previous forecasts, leaving them at the mercy of the elements.

The rapid and unpredictable events experienced by the yacht crews are actually a predictable characteristic of all complex and chaotic environments. Small changes can create massive effects and many separate events can converge to create cataclysms.

For example, some of the events that converged in the Sydney-to-Hobart included the area of low pressure that strengthened unexpectedly in the entrance to Bass Strait. This is the location on the edge of the shelf at the foot of the Australian continent where it could whip up the largest possible waves. Add to that a fleet of yachts that would be in that position for only a few hours each year, the impending darkness and only private weather forecasters (who were providing information to just a small percentage of crews) warning of the danger.

The world's airline industry faced a similar convergence in late 2001 with the terrorist strikes, almost complete cessation of flights in the U.S. and the related fall in tourist and business travel.

The often-quoted "butterfly effect" of chaotic systems in which a butterfly in China can create the initial air disturbance that results in a hurricane on the other side of the world is just another example of the nature of chaotic and complex systems.

The key point is that you cannot predict exactly what will happen or when it will happen but, through envisioning a range of scenarios and continually scanning the world looking for emerging patterns and events, you are better placed to perform in these extreme conditions. Mick Keelty, the Commissioner of Australia's Federal Police, confirms the importance of building a scanning capability into the Performance Model: "We have done a lot of environmental scanning and scenario planning for some time. We need to build in flexibility as we will never be able to predict the future."[1]

Scouts see things early

Have you noticed that Bosses often react angrily and aggressively to changes and challenges from the environment because their lack of information (environment intelligence) means that they are taken by surprise?

There is high tension and pressure during Olympic Games and World Championships, so the coaching team includes scouts, assistant coaches and other tacticians. These people tend to be more detached and less emotional than the Performance Coach in a given situation. They can also lift their eyes from today's competition to see what is happening in the games of others. Information from scouts is essential to any high-performance program and the wise Performance Leader trusts these emotionally detached people to help them to navigate the organization through the next stage of the competition. Similarly, the athlete relies on the coach as part-navigator of their performance.

Challenge yourself and your team(s) to find out who can help you to know what is happening in your customers' and consumers' world today. For example, young employees will spot shifts and trends amongst their peers long before most market research will pick them up. Competitors might know about potential shifts in government legislation and consultants can tell you about emerging technologies in other industries. Inside large organizations and government, scouts can help find ways through the bureaucratic maze or understand the culture of other divisions.

Of course, when you put scouts all over the place, sooner or later they will bring information that challenges what you are doing. This is a test of emotional intelligence and leadership to be able to accept the information without shooting the messenger. I have seen many Bosses and some sports coaches let their egos get in the way, and reject otherwise-valuable information because they take an emotional view of the person who is bringing the message.

FIGURE 13.3 Use scouts to see things early

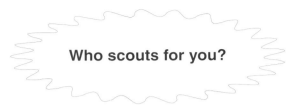

Who scouts for you?

One of the successful strategies used by the Australian Olympic Committee has been to send a delegation to the Olympic city as soon as construction of the village and major venues is under way. The delegation collects plans, videos and details on climate, travel and related issues and feeds this into the overall planning and to each high-performance sports unit. The early scouting process has also helped the Australian team to acquire a location in the village that allows for a team courtyard area, space for a medical center and a position not too far from the main transport hub and dining hall. Coaches use the scouting information on travel distances, timing of events and room-sharing arrangements to design simulations in advance of the Games.

Can you use a similar scouting and simulation or rehearsal strategy to prepare for major presentations, negotiations and forums?

Scouting is also a great way of cross-pollinating your business units, and corporations like 3M have built their reputations for creating and sustaining innovative and agile cultures through exactly these practices.

Interpreting the information

During a High Performance Leadership workshop, a support team in a postal-service business told us that their in-company customers were very pleased with the service that they provided. When asked to rank their performance on the 10.10 Model they suggested about 9.9. We doubted their assessment and decided that one of their projects in building their Performance Model would be to survey their customers on perceptions of service quality and the importance of various dimensions of service.

The data clearly showed that customers were happy with various dimensions of service quality, but on the highly important measures of speed (initiative and responsiveness) they rated quite poorly. In the analysis workshop that we facilitated with their customers, it emerged that the customers were considering outsourcing the service so they could get the level of responsiveness they needed.

Think of four or five of your major customers and ask yourself whether you really know what they are thinking about today. Do those customers believe that you are providing them with the quality they are looking for or do they feel frustrated and on the receiving end of things that you do?

Are you passionately and relentlessly connecting your organization to the customer? What have you got happening to connect with consumers who are not your customers? Challenge yourself and your team to make the commitment to "know what the customer is thinking today".

Coach the customer

Making the processes of environment scanning a strength of your Performance Model will give you feedback loops that can stimulate innovative ways to design and position your products and services.

A large home-appliances business undertaking a High Performance Leadership project discovered that many customers (and their competitors' customers) were frustrated with their products (washing machines, ovens) because they were not using them properly. It applied the principles of coaching to create a process that educated and coached its customers to operate appliances properly. Not surprisingly, the feedback was very positive and the business is reaping benefits from differentiating itself from competitors.

How many times have you bought a product and found that it doesn't work properly? On most occasions, the design of the product is fine but it is the coaching, the communication of how to use the product or service, that is missing. Providing only confusing instructions in small print on the throw-away packaging is a great way to lose a customer.

Feedback loops will help you to pick up on gaps in the market and in your service that suggest ways to make your business more effective and profitable.

KNOW YOUR POSITION

Trends in consumer behavior and attitudes and in technology are shifting at the speed of light and continually challenge you to align your organization with the emerging trends. For example, in the post-September 11 period the mood of markets and organizations and nations was to take a more risk-averse approach to business and activities. Customers trended towards security, and organizations that positioned themselves with these trends did well.

There are always a host of trends happening in a dynamic environment and there is a compelling argument for everyone taking a leadership role and responsibility for spotting patterns.

This type of positioning is fundamental to designing and executing a successful strategy. In the remainder of this chapter, we will explore some of the practical tools and techniques that you can build into your Performance Model to keep connected to shifts in conditions. While considering these, it is as important to remember about your own positioning as it is to understand what else is happening.

Foster regular facilitated customer and consumer workshops

One powerful strategy to extract immediate feedback for people is to conduct regular, facilitated workshops, in which customers (and people who chose not to use the service) are involved. With skilled facilitation, these can be very powerful sources of feedback for teams and organizations. Use them for units that have internal and external customers and you will reap the benefits of feedback.

If your organization already uses these types of workshops, keep them fresh and effective by changing the attendees, improving dialogue and quickening the implementation of ideas from the workshops.

Short-term SWOTs for every unit

The SWOT (strengths, weaknesses, opportunities, threats) analysis and its variations are a well-used and, in some cases, overused device in the business world. Nevertheless, one of the simplest and most practical strategies for ensuring that organizations keep in touch with their environment is having every Performance Unit produce its own Clipboard SWOT analysis every three months.

In the High Performance Leadership Programme we use a pro forma that fits onto one page, contains no more than five items in any category and identifies any changes over the three months. This monitors whether members of those units are fully aware of the environment in which they are operating, and alerts you to issues as they emerge.

Sports teams use simple variations of SWOTs in the lead-up to each game, thereby creating a common performance language and dialogue.

FIGURE 13.4 Clipboard SWOT analysis

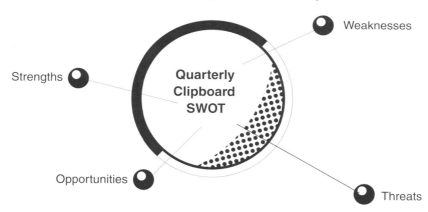

Scan the vital signs

There are few better examples of monitoring the environment than in the operating theater during surgery. Blood pressure, heart rate and other vital signs are monitored by the surgery team and they adjust their strategy accordingly. As Performance Leaders, the surgeon and anesthetist decide in advance what must be monitored and all members of the team constantly scan for any changes. The scan includes not just the patient but also the room environment (cleanliness, temperature) and the other team members.

The role of each person in this scanning process is important: if there is too much information, they will lose focus; if there's not enough, they make guesses. A high-performance unit can read the vital signs and each person is trusted to keep a constant check on these.

Apply the "vital signs challenge" to each unit in your program. Figure 13.5 shows some of the vital signs of traditional business and those of the global game.

FIGURE 13.5 Monitoring the vital signs

Operating theatre	Vital signs of traditional business	Vital signs of the global game
Heart beat	Cash flow	Customer perceptions
Blood pressure	Inventory	Productivity from implementing new technology
Blood loss	Debt	Alliance-partner relationships
Respiration	Staff turnover	Speed
Anesthetic	Capital expenditure	Potential disruptive technologies

Tactic: Appoint a person as "lookout" for each vital-sign area and have them provide regular, real-time information that is available to all team members. Make sure, however, that you employ people who genuinely know the field they are observing and the context. For example, if you want someone to monitor biotechnology patents, make sure they know the field and your current and future strategies.

Build the "know-why" and the "know-how"

I recently overheard a conversation in which a business leader lamented that his organization had "too much know-how and not enough know-why". In this simple statement lies a fundamental principle of high performance (and probably a commentary on the capabilities of the leader).

In small organizations and many sporting teams, there is enough informal contact between the strategists and the performers to ensure that the athletes know why a particular strategy is being used. As organizations grow and spread to different locations or into more specialized units, it is easy to lose the connection between strategy and execution.

You can address this through "state of the nation" addresses and discussions at workshops where Clipboard Plans and SWOTs are put together or reviewed. But, in many places, this is not enough.

The RAH retrieval team works in high-pressure environments, and has specialists in fire, air safety, policing, medicine and extracting people from car wrecks. It is essential that each member of the team knows the capabilities of the others.

If you are in a senior role, give people your e-mail address so they can contact you and comment on what is happening in your organization. One e-mail to a staff member will quickly spread the message.

Peter Bijur, Chairman and CEO of Texaco Inc., commented, "My own preference is for open-ended get-togethers with about a dozen employees at a time, to which managers are not invited."[2]

Dialogue again is the key.

The speed of play in the global game demands that your people have the capability, authority and understanding of context (conditions) to make decisions.

Make every meeting agenda customer focused

Do not allow any regular meetings to be held in your organization unless the agenda is clearly customer focused.

Figure 13.6 provides a useful checklist that you can apply to any meeting you attend.

FIGURE 13.6 Checklist for customer-focused meetings

Characteristics of meeting	Yes	No
Meeting objective was written in customer terms	☐	☐
Facilitator/chairperson linked every issue to the customer	☐	☐
Customer data, such as speed of response, was used to make decisions	☐	☐
Actions from meeting were customer oriented	☐	☐

Make the customer the centerpiece of your meetings and it will encourage better scanning of relationships and links to customers.

Think scenarios

Would you sail on an ocean-going yacht with a skipper who had not considered a range of scenarios that included major threats and opportunities? It's not very likely. Similarly no Performance Unit in your program should go into the global game without also running a series of scenarios. Make it a part of your Performance Model.

"What if?" sessions

All of our Olympic units do scenario planning in the lead-up to major competitions and tours by using what they call a "What if?" session. These sessions are facilitated to ensure that coaches, athletes and support staff take into account a range of the "What if?" situations that can affect performance. Some of the classic Olympic "What if?" questions for athletes include, "What if …

- the bus breaks down on the morning of competition?"
- our captain is injured?"
- there is a terrorist attack on the village?"
- we get off to a really bad start to the competition?"
- we get off to a really good start to the competition?"
- our toughest opponents create a completely new game strategy?"

"What if?" questions and dialogue help everyone to prepare for the range of situations and circumstances that occur in performance conditions.

You may find that some people view this as negative thinking, but it is no different from taking spare water and fuel on a trip across the desert.

Most agile businesses use "What if?" scenarios as a standard part of their strategic-planning processes because it reduces the potential impacts of unusual events and allows them to consider how variations, such as a 40% reduction in revenue, will affect the business.

In high-performance environments, "What if?" planning can be the determining factor in achieving success because it allows high performers to prepare to manage the events. As Gordon Cairns, CEO of Lion Nathan, notes, "When we looked at high-performing companies, external events had no impact on performance. They managed those events."[3]

Chess thinking: Getting your team to think two moves ahead

A major bank put 30 of its senior leaders through a High Performance Leadership Programme as part of the preparation to implement a new strategy. One of the activities in the program was Team Chess, in which teams of three bank leaders played simultaneously against a chess grandmaster. It created lots of interest and two teams even managed to scramble a stalemate in the time available.

During the debriefing, the grandmaster explained how he had developed the skill of building multiple scenarios for the future, and how each of the scenarios included not just his plans but also how he anticipated his opponents would react to those plans. He stressed the importance of thinking two moves ahead.

The executives found this chess strategy to be a useful metaphor when coaching their teams in planning scenarios. Many used chess games during scenario-planning workshops to give staff an experience of scenarios. Purdy and Koshnitsky, authors of the classic *Chess Made Easy*, remind us that many of the world's great leaders and thinkers — including Benjamin Franklin, Napoleon, Shakespeare and Lenin — enjoyed chess as a pastime.[4] Why not add a game of chess to your next strategy session?

Beware: Group mindsets can be dangerous

Meredith Belbin[5] helped the business world to understand that teams perform best when they have a blend of styles to cover all aspects of team activity, and include innovators, coordinators, planners, doers, completers and so on. As for teams, so for scanning. Too many Bosses recruit people of like mind, who sit around agreeing with each other. If, in your organization, innovation and breakthrough thinking come most often from pressure exerted from the outside (competitors, markets), then you are probably acting like a Boss.

Performance Leaders don't wait until competitive pressures force that sort of thinking. They constantly bring people with new views and opinions to their program. If they are engineering types they bring along the marketers and organization-development people, and if they are marketers they bring in customers and quality-systems people to stretch their thinking. This is the style of scanning and strategic thinking that makes organizations like IDEO world leaders in originating products and services.

Diversity: Questions from the coach

Who do you bring together to discuss the world? Have you got the variety of personality types, ages, gender, skills and capabilities that will generate a melting pot of ideas and perspectives from which you can genuinely choose the best? If you don't have a richness of perspectives, then bring others in from other parts of your organization, or from outside, and use them to stimulate your thinking.

SCANNING CAN CREATE "THE INDISPUTABLE NEED FOR CHANGE"

How do you generate higher performance from an organization that is already doing well by its own measures or standards?

Consider the example of Detmold Packaging, a manufacturer of paper packaging products with a good market share in Australia, a growing customer base and expanding presence in the manufacture and marketing of products throughout Asia.

Detmold's chief executive, John Cerini, is mindful of the need for this internationally growing business to adapt to changes in the market. He describes one of his most important tasks as being to create within the organization what he calls "the indisputable need for change". He believes that without this it is extremely difficult for organizations of any type to generate the groundswell of motivation to alter something that is already successful.[6]

Changing the behavior of people who believe they are already performers can certainly be very difficult. However, one of the most powerful strategies is to engage the ego of the other person. Specifically, show them how far off the pace they are. Be careful how you do this, but few things will get your people jumping higher than showing them other people clearing their high jump with ease. Of course, your challenge is to coach people to see the indisputable need for change and to make the required changes. Scanning is a powerful way to start the process.

Filter what comes in

As you build the capability to scan the performance environment, make sure that people can see where the conditions fit along the continuum from controllable to uncontrollable. High performers focus on what they can control and manage the impact of the things that they cannot fully control. Poor performers can sometimes become hyperaware of their environment and jump to control everything, or engage in endless philosophical debates about such things as globalization and monetary policy that are way out of their control.

Performance Leaders who retain a calmness when conditions are affecting performance are usually more effective leaders because they help people to focus on what they can control. Keep this in mind as you coach people in your program.

SCANNING IS A KEY ELEMENT IN YOUR PERFORMANCE MODEL

Each element of the Performance Model is essential. However, it is the *conditions* that weave themselves into every area, from Take Aim to Performance Set-up and Achieve Results. Figure 13.7 summarizes some of the tips and tactics for Scan: Know the Conditions that have been covered in the second part of this chapter.

FIGURE 13.7 Summary of scanning tips and tactics

Scanning strategies	To build a traditional business culture	To build a Performance Culture
Scenario planning	React to real-life issues and predictable "What ifs?"	Regularly run scenarios at 40–50% variation on what is expected
Capabilities	Foster know-how	Foster know-how and know-why
Style	Use formal scanning methods such as market research and focus groups	Set up dialogue across broad areas of consumers, industries and fields of knowledge
Meetings	Operate to a traditional business agenda	Work to a customer-focused agenda
SWOT analysis	Done mainly by senior teams at annual planning meeting	Use short-term Clipboard SWOTs for all units
Team membership	Recruit for operational capabilities	Sprinkle the technical mix with alternative views
Vital signs	Management does the scanning for vital signs	Make everyone responsible for scanning a vital sign
Generating change	Argue the case for change	Show your people how others do it better

Reflection: Take a few moments to recall the example of the Sydney-to-Hobart yacht race and the importance of the four elements highlighted there.

The four elements in Figure 13.8 are Performance Leadership rules to keep in mind as you continue refining your Performance Model.

FIGURE 13.8 Performing in global-game conditions

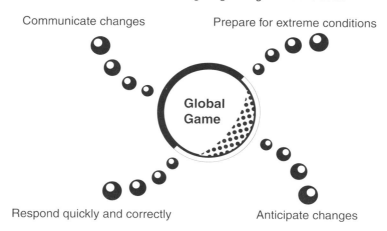

14

Preparation: The Performance Set-up

Olympic coaches use a simple questionnaire called the Profile of Mood States[1] (POMS) to measure an athlete's mindset a few hours before their event. By contrasting the positive mindset (vigor/energy) with negative mindset (confusion, anger, fatigue), the profile produced from the questionnaire is remarkably accurate in predicting performance.

The most poignant message in the effectiveness of the POMS is that the result of the athlete's performance is largely decided *before* they compete. In other words, their preparation has either provided the platform to succeed or to fall short of expectations.

Changes in two factors seem to have a direct impact on the POMS profile and, therefore, the performance. These are the climate/culture of the team/unit and the set-up (routines, resources, systems).

The experience of using the POMS has made sports coaches acutely aware of the direct link between high performance and the Performance Set-up and climate/culture that they create and foster. From that awareness have come some interesting ideas that business Performance Leaders can use to add to the agility and performance of their operations.

In this chapter, we look at Performance Set-up and challenge you to review and, where necessary, redesign the set-up of your

Performance Units as a key part of your Performance Model. The issues of climate and culture are then addressed in Chapter 18.

What is Performance Set-up?

Bosses have traditionally seen their Performance Set-up largely in terms of organization structure. The common view has been, and still remains in many businesses, that if you set the structure in concrete then all else will follow.

There is no arguing that structure is an essential element in Performance Set-up but there are at least seven other set-up elements that Performance Leaders consider in their Performance Model to shape the performance of the organization. These (along with structure/design) are explained in the following diagram.

FIGURE 14.1   Elements of Performance Set-up

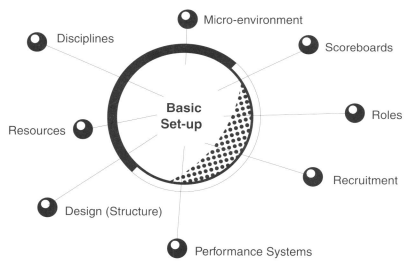

In the hierarchical (pyramid) structures of the pre-global game, roles, authority and information flow were tightly or rigidly prescribed. This made some sense in an era of relatively slow change, where Bosses were better educated and informed than staff, and cultural factors such as deference to authority, gender restrictions and promotion based on age were the accepted norm.

That, of course, is yesterday's thinking and it is time to get vitally interested in designing a Performance Set-up that fosters high performance and even attracts talented people to join.

Let's look at the eight areas identified in Figure 14.1. These are the elements that strongly influence the performance of people and, in turn, the speed and agility of your team or organization. This is not an exhaustive list but each of these elements requires attention and should get you thinking about the areas in which you plan to invest in your Performance Set-up.

DESIGN YOUR ORGANIZATION FOR FITNESS

Watch a field sport like soccer or hockey and many of the principles of organization design for the global game will unfold before your eyes. Small sub-teams emerge and "flock" together around the ball; others stay in their set roles ready to defend or attack; leaders issue instructions and reorganize from time to time; and specialist players come and go.

If you are a fan of field sports you will know that traditional set positions and roles have been largely replaced by a more flexible design in which athletes play various roles to suit the strategy and situation. Instead of working to a set structure, the team alters its design to fit the demands. This can be almost a moment-by-moment shift as conditions change and self-organization becomes the preferred design. Underpinning this will be a common set of performance principles but not everything will be predicted.

Instead of structure, the concept of "Designed for Fitness" is a characteristic of high-performance programs that has emerged in response to global-game conditions. This means developing a corporate structure that includes various designs to suit the niches in which the teams and divisions operate. It is a responsive organization of high-performance units that network together and share knowledge.

Of course, shifting the design of a hockey team is easier than redesigning a corporation. However, there are some interesting principles about Design for Fitness that you can use to test your current design and to refine it. As you consider these principles (set out below), it is important to recognize that any choice of organization design has its trade-offs and there is no perfect design.

As complexity increases move towards agility

Performance environments can range from the relatively ordered and stable, through the increasingly complex and uncertain, to the chaotic. As those conditions shift, so too does the preferred organization design. Because global-game conditions are generally complex, a design that mirrors the flexibility of the top sporting and medical emergency teams is desirable. Whereas the traditional model was rigid and was intended to minimize the impact of complexity, this design will allow your organization to engage with complexity and move among the opportunities.

Ralph Larsen, CEO of Johnson & Johnson, sees decentralization as essential to the growth of the business but highlights some of the trade-offs: "We recognize that decentralization is inherently disorderly. It demands a high tolerance for ambiguity and complexity. It demands, too, a willingness to bend and compromise."[2]

Design for Fitness means refining the form or shape of your enterprise to fit its mission and core strategies. When the mission changes, or the conditions change, you must redesign it again to be fit for the task. This is agility and its importance is neatly and powerfully captured by Francis Gouillart's statement, "strategic agility is more important than strategy".[3]

As you reflect on the process of redesign, consider to what extent you are prepared to allow your organization to design itself or, in the words of some complexity theorists, to flock around the opportunities and problems that emerge.

Minimize the set positions

Team athletes must have the capability to play in more than one position. The more specialist positions there are, the less agile will be the team; so this means organizing around a minimum of fixed positions. For example, making sales the responsibility of sales staff is yesterday's thinking. Everyone sells and is capable of selling in the modern organization. Similarly, developing capabilities in line and staff positions not only increases organizational agility but also develops better leaders.

Make teamwork an organizing principle

The business gurus talk a lot about teams and even the most traditional Boss is quick to catch on. Where Bosses and Performance Leaders differ is in seeing the distinction between teams and teamwork. Teams are an organizing structure, whereas teamwork is more about mindset and behavior. Bosses create organization charts with teams in the appropriate boxes; Performance Leaders create, foster and reinforce teamwork as an organizing principle.

Make fast-project-team formation a priority

The global game rewards organizations that develop the core capability of creating high-performance project teams. These teams form quickly around opportunities and threats, do their job and then disband. They are agile and around them there are individual champions (Business Athletes) and more permanent structures. Apple Computer has based much of its success on forming these types of flexible project teams. One of my long-term clients, SOLA Optical, the world's third-largest optical lens manufacturer, has made project teams a key source of performance advantage.

High-performance project teams (HPTs) can be alliances, partnerships, groups and all manner of different configurations. Most operate in some relationship to a broader entity/structure that is like the mother ship in science fiction movies. The mother ship provides resources in the form of capital, equipment, knowledge and networks while the HPTs focus on the task at hand.

As a general rule, when you want something done, give the responsibility to a Performance Leader/Coach and an HPT. When your organization gets bogged down in detailed, unnecessary discussions, consultation and all manner of doing business with itself, give an HPT the focus and space and support to get on with things that have to be done.

To make HPTs really effective, use the tools of High Performance Leadership. Combine the Clipboard Plan, PROBED and PUT with sound project-management principles to coach your teams to form fast and to get moving. Be aware, however, that you must allow time for teams to get their Clipboards and Project Plans in place so they don't waste a lot of unnecessary time and effort going back over things that should have been done properly the first time.

Never use structure as an excuse for anything

Are you bold enough to design what you need, and learn as you go, rather than be constrained by old structures?

Design and culture must be seen together. Some cultures need more structure than others; however, the less reliant an organization is on structure the faster it will be able to respond. Part of your role as a Performance Leader is to impart this understanding to people. Often it is the most senior leaders who struggle to give up their need for power, order and control and, therefore, impose or maintain structures that are past their use-by date. Take the lead from a client of mine who has made it very clear to every leader in his program that he never wants to hear anyone using structure as an excuse for anything. His successful strategy for eliminating those maddening boundaries and walls (sometimes known as "silos") that often exist inside organizations is refusing to allow people to act in that way.

Waiting for the perfect structure, or holding onto the existing structure, is a recipe for disaster. Complex environments reward those who adapt and evolve as they move along. This requires active leadership and coaching to help them to deal with the ambiguity and change. Remember to keep the "know-why" happening and use the debrief and learning processes set out in Chapter 15.

Flexibility can be a disaster if you don't have the right mix of skills and communication. At an emergency scene, this is illustrated vividly with the combination of specialist skills (medical, helicopter pilot, fire and police). As Dr Bill Griggs notes, "I don't have to know how to use the "jaws of life" to open a car wreck but I have to understand how it works. They have to know how our staff work as well. So it's a matter of specialist skills and communicating."[4]

USE THE FIVE-LEVEL DESIGN

While there will never be a perfect organization design, there is a five-level design that works well in many high-performance settings such as sports teams, franchises, the military and arts organizations. The key to the success of this design is the separation of responsibilities and the clear accountabilities at each level. I recommend that you consider this when trying to generate agility in your organization.

Figure 14.3 shows the five levels in professional sport and their business equivalents.

FIGURE 14.2 Six principles of organization design

Characteristics	Pre-Global Game	Global Game
Responsiveness	Maintain stability to minimize impact of complexity	As complexity increases move towards agility (to engage with complexity)
Roles	Maximize set positions	Minimize set positions: move towards self-organization
Organizing principle	Organize around teams	Make teamwork (not teams) an organizing principle
Team formation team	Control team formation through the usual hierarchy	Make fasts project-formation a priority: give them the tools
Use of structure	Rely on rigidity of structure	Never use structure as an excuse for anything
Right skill mix	Specialist skills with little communication/synergy	Communication between specialists: flexible and highly competent

FIGURE 14.3 Five-level design

Professional sport	Business
Owner	Owner/Sponsor — provides funding/space
Team/Program Chief	Responsible manager — oversees activity
Coaches	Team leaders — accountable for delivering results
Athletes	Staff — perform the operational tasks
Support crew	Support staff — enable operations to be performed

Systems that Generate Performance

Organizations have all manner of performance systems — quality assurance, safety, financial, maintenance, performance-management, enterprise-wide resource planning, and so on. Despite the huge investment in these systems, it is rare to hear leaders claiming that their systems genuinely deliver high performance.

The two most common reasons for this are poor implementation and the continual development of better systems, which means that what you just bought is outdated before you get it operating near to full capacity.

This presents you with two interesting challenges at an organizational and team level: which systems to invest in and how to implement those systems.

The first challenge can only be answered by a careful business-case consideration of your Aim, current and future Performance Conditions and Set-up.

Where the High Performance Leadership Programme can assist is in developing capabilities in implementing strategies. These strategies center on replacing Bosses with Performance Leaders/ Coaches who create a Performance Culture of scoreboards and fast-project teams, where the focus is on people rather than systems.

Invest in systems to send a message

The systems in which you choose to invest say a great deal about your values, leadership style and priorities to the rest of the organization. Equally, the implementation of these systems provides one of the best opportunities that you will get to coach your people to enhance performance.

For example, a newly appointed chief executive of an energy utility invested heavily in Occupational Health and Safety (OH&S) systems and practices. The strong message to the workforce was that people mattered. The results were outstanding, not just in reduced OH&S incidents and costs but also in speeding up the follow-on initiative of turning the culture from an inflexible, technical focus to a responsive customer-focused operation. Through the OH&S initiatives, leaders and teams started thinking about people, rather than just technical processes, and the CEO and his team used this as leverage to coach the whole organization to be much more oriented towards the customer.

This use of a performance theme, such as OH&S, that can be driven in a practical way right through the organization is a powerful way to generate consistent performance behaviors across an organization.

Emphasize performance, not systems

Ask a Boss about their business systems and there is a strong chance that they'll tell you about "the computer". For the traditional business-owner Boss, systems are expensive, intrusive and unreliable. They slow things down, put the wrong people in powerful positions and add unnecessary jargon and complexity to operations. For them, systems are to be avoided at all costs, unless competitors do it; in which case, you buy what they bought and then expect it all to work within seven days. Unless the business grows rapidly, such Bosses usually do OK because they use intuition and personal intervention (but that gets spread too thinly in times of growth). Their organization is person-centric and thus both at risk from loss of knowledge when key people leave, and highly vulnerable to competitors who offer customers better value (lower cost, speed of delivery, quality) as a consequence of better systems.

There are also "new-economy Bosses", for whom systems are a godsend, allowing them to retain control of the business through restrictive, data-intensive systems and processes. These Bosses are pedantic control freaks who can be far more dangerous than the old Boss. They usually lack the intuition of the business owner and often leave a trail of failed businesses with complex systems behind them.

A third category is the "hype-buyer", who is sold the latest "bells-and-whistles" system and invests hugely in its implementation and upgrade, never to gain the returns needed to justify even the initial outlays. For the hype-buyer, systems are about technology and it is through the technology that the business will benefit. It is not the traditional Boss who falls into this category but, unfortunately, a significant percentage of business leaders who have been led astray by an over-hyped technology sector.

What these three styles of leader have in common is poor understanding of the fundamental reasons for investing in systems and the principles of implementation.

FIGURE 14.4 Attitudes towards systems

Category	Beliefs about systems	Impact on organization
Traditional Boss	Too expensive and slow Puts power in the wrong hands Unnecessary complexity	At risk from competitors Person-centric — lose a lot of capability when people leave
New-Economy Boss	Everything can be systematized Information is power for the boss	Too reliant on interlinked systems Lose intuition and agility Restrictive "robotic" culture
Hype-buyer	Systems are about technology. Systems give competitive advantage New systems are best	Design and implementation errors are costly Performance drops; people blame the system Systems tend to be unstable
Performance Leader	Systems are essential for growth Implementation must be given top priority Systems are about people	Systems are designed for performance Implementation is effective People own the system because they are involved in its implementation

Effective systems are essential to growth. Well-implemented systems empower people, expand their productivity and reach, add quality to decision-making, reduce duplication and create performance environments in which people are more likely to be in the zone. Performance Leaders invest in systems that add to performance and they actively measure the impact of those systems. In particular, they take full responsibility for the implementation of a system. They see systems as an issue that concerns people, rather than simply being a matter of technology. This means that they invest in changing the behavior of people, rather than simply getting a machine or process to work consistently.

WHY SYSTEMS FAIL TO DELIVER AND WHAT TO DO ABOUT IT

Everyone wants to sell you a system these days. There is virtually nothing that a technology company cannot automate should you have the money and desire. And yet the statistics on the effectiveness of implementing new technologies are appalling.

Bosses make lots of mistakes in systems installation. Some of the most common include:

- buying off-the-shelf systems when customization is needed
- customizing when a simple off-the-shelf system would be fine
- using technicians to advise on what to buy
- excluding users from design decisions
- trying to build the whole thing instead of creating a successful prototype
- ignoring the impact of a new system on other areas of the business
- using compliance-based motivation, instead of building commitment.

Imagine how successful you would be as an international sports coach if you tried a similar approach. The equivalent decisions would be:

- buying a system from football and applying it to tennis
- getting a computer technician to design your statistics system
- tinkering with databases instead of leading a training session
- excluding senior players and assistant coaches from decisions on strategy and tactics
- implementing bold new strategies in big games without practicing them first
- telling only part of the team about a new strategy
- making the players comply with the new tactic without seeking their involvement and commitment.

Start with behavior questions

Performance Leaders look well beyond the system or process to think about how to engage people in its design and implementation. For example, a sports coach is always thinking about how to get the athletes to behave in a particular way. If we apply this mindset to installing a system for customer-relationship management, the Performance Leader will start by asking behavior questions such as:

- How do we want customers to be treated at the front line?
- How can we coach our frontline people to use the new information to add value for the customer?
- What might prevent people from acting in that way?
- How can we coach our customers to use more of our services?

For the Performance Leader/Coach, the system is part of the answer to these questions. However, for the Boss, many of these questions only emerge after they have decided to buy the system. Boss-type questions tend to be system-focused:

- What is the best technology?
- How can we get information to our frontline people?
- Can the system give us customer data in real time?

These questions are important, but they are secondary to behavior questions unless you plan to put in a system that totally replaces human beings. Systems implementation begins with questions about the effect of behavior on the field of performance. Only then should technology questions come into play.

Use coaches, not consultants

Systems implementation depends on the coaching capabilities of the consultants who assist you with implementation and the managers who are embedding it into the organization. If either are not good at coaching, then you can guarantee a poor implementation.

One of the innovations of the High Performance Leadership Programme has been to train systems consultants in coaching skills, including the use of the Performance Model as the framework to guide implementation. This helps them and their clients to gain higher commitment to the process and higher returns from the investment.

Demand speed with quality

Elite sports teams are quick to decide and quick to act. From competition decision-making in the coach's box to spotting and selecting new talent, speed is rewarded, provided that the decision-making is sound. Organization design, systems and training all add to speed with quality.

Spend a week with the coaching team of an Olympic hockey team. Specific information from games and training flows into the program through videotape, statistics and other intelligence collected by skilled observers. Members of the coaching team analyze the data, share it with the coach and players and convert it into new strategies and tactics to be practiced and then executed on the playing field by individual players and the whole team. There are two key points here. Firstly, the coaches have decided on what is critical information and, secondly, the right information goes to the right people. The intent is to speed up the organization and that means finding a balance between overloading the coaching staff and players, and withholding the data that will enable them to decide.

At a far more complex level, the same steps must occur within even the largest of corporations if performance is to flow. Once again, your role as Performance Leader is to add value by ensuring that the right information flows into the right place within your organization so that it can be analyzed effectively and then translated into new strategies and behaviors that are acted upon very quickly.

Mike Heard, CEO of Codan, believes that "gaining speed and not losing quality" is the number-one priority for his organization to remain world class in the future.[5] This has much to do with creating a Performance Model in which information flows quickly to Performance Leaders at all levels who are empowered to make decisions.

Look at even the largest organization as a series of high-performance units that must be able to act independently and interdependently, much like the players in the medical retrieval situation or an orchestra. This is the model for high performance.

Avoid the counter-culture reaction

Bosses hold the people who install the systems accountable for making sure that the systems work effectively. Performance Leaders, on the other hand, know that any new system or process has the potential to work against the existing culture. They therefore take steps to ensure that people are actively involved in the design and implementation of systems. This minimizes the counter-culture effect and increases accountability for execution and integration. This, in turn, results in changed behavior as well as new systems.

DESIGN AND USE THE RIGHT SCOREBOARDS

Scoreboards are an essential aspect of Performance Set-up. They tell you and others how various units are performing and they focus attention and discipline onto the critical processes at a given time. Be mindful, however, that the most obvious scoreboards can be the least useful when it comes to coaching teams and individuals. For example, the public scoreboard at the Olympic basketball stadium can be as helpful as looking out the rear-vision mirror of a car. It is a *results* scoreboard, which tells you where you have been and it can greatly under- or over-estimate what is currently happening on the court.

As we will discuss in Chapter 17, High Performance Leadership Programmes are highly results-focused and set high standards and consequences. Thus, the results scoreboard is important. But it is equally important to be multi-dimensional and practical when it comes to selecting scoreboards.

Ric Charlesworth, Australia's dual gold-medal-winning Olympic hockey coach, sums it up this way: "Analysis of performance is crucial to the team and coach. Both parties must soberly assess performance and progress. A focus merely on the score can pitch a team into depression or reinforce self-delusion. Neither of these outcomes is useful or desirable."[6]

Traditional business scoreboards have had a narrow focus on financial results such as achieving budget or reaching the sales target. Concepts such as the Balanced Scorecard (one that the corporate world uses to measure financial, customer, employee and operational performance) and the Triple Bottom Line (often used by governments as a financial/economic, social and environmental measure, to which they then add, of course, political factors) have helped leaders to make big strides in understanding that things other than direct results are also important and there is not a direct correlation between results and performance.

Selecting the Right Scoreboards

To retain focus in complex performance environments, use fewer scoreboards rather than more, keep them up to date and accept that not everything that matters can be measured.

Experiment with scoreboards

The search for scoreboards that give an accurate picture of performance will never end and is one of your most important tasks in Performance Leadership. When you find real-time, local scoreboards you will have a valuable tool for coaching your program. For example, one of the most practical advances in recent years has been the use of heart-rate monitors to assess an athlete's work rate during training. This allows the coach and athlete to optimize the training load, rather than relying just on intuition. Simple measures such as heart rate provide the linkage between the big picture (for example, winning an Olympic medal) and the daily actions (training load).

Reflection: What are the business equivalents of the heart-rate monitor for you?

Don't drown your champions

Most Bosses love data because it gives them a feeling of security and certainty in an unpredictable world. Unfortunately, many soon drown themselves and their organization in piles of measures that have to be reported against.

Drive out data that is drowning your people, and hone it down to a few critical scoreboards and pieces of information. The era of Bosses putting in more and more measures on the assumption that "if you measure it, it will happen" has passed. If your business hasn't refined its scoreboards in the past year, then you are probably a Boss.

New systems are great but they generate masses of data that encourages risk aversion and slows down decision making.

Let's now look more closely at scoreboards and how you might put them into your Performance Model.

Put scoreboards on your performance themes

If your most important performance theme is "speed", then make sure that you have scoreboards that tell you about speed, such as how quickly a customer's request is processed or the time needed to fill a vacant position.

Performance Leaders use scoreboards to focus attention on the theme and they are relentless in linking consequences to the performance.

Coaches feel it: Bosses refuse to believe it

While old-style entrepreneurs rely on hard-earned intuition, many new MBA graduates think that numbers are the only things that are real. Between these extremes lies the philosophy of Performance Leadership.

The art of Performance Leadership in the 21st-century is to combine measurable data with the intuition and experience of the wily entrepreneur as coach. For example, advances in the coding of videotape now provide athletes with almost immediate, specific feedback on their technique. The coach no longer has to rely on eyesight, and the athlete does not have to try to understand the

FIGURE 14.5 Performance theme and scoreboard

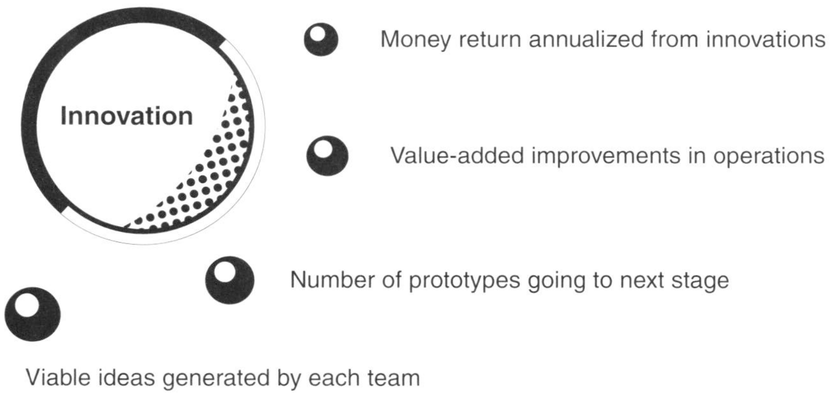

Money return annualized from innovations

Value-added improvements in operations

Number of prototypes going to next stage

Viable ideas generated by each team

coach's explanation of incredibly complicated movements to give them the mental picture of what is needed. The coach can combine personal experience and observation with external data. Similarly, in an interesting blend of the "mechanical" and the "creative", developments in sound recording now enable musicians to capture the talent and creativity from jam sessions and assess it piece by piece.

A particularly telling commentary on getting the right balance between data and intuition is provided by Dr Tony Kerns in his book on Cathay Pacific Airways' (CPA) automation policy: "It is the [company's] policy to regard automation as a tool to be used but not blindly relied upon. At all times flight crews must be aware what automation is doing and, if not understood or not requested, reversion to basic modes of operation should be made immediately without analysis or delay. Trainers must ensure that all CPA flight crews are taught with emphasis on how to quickly revert to basic modes when necessary. In the man — machine interface, man is in charge."[7]

Sometimes we get ahead of even the most up-to-date scoreboards. As a guide, the closer you are to the customer in business, or to the athlete in sport, the more likely that your intuition is actually ahead of the scoreboard. However, if you can combine up-to-date scoreboards (or dashboards, as they are referred to by some experts) with a willingness to back your own intuition, then you are in a Performance Leadership position.

Know your stakeholders' scoreboards

It is not just performance that counts in the global game of business and sport. For example, three factors have a major impact on the earnings of professional athletes and professional consultants: performance; selection for major events/assignments; and marketability/brand value. Performance is arguably the easy and obvious factor when it comes to scoreboards. Time, distance, goals and a multitude of statistics tell the tennis player about performance, while for the business consultant, client retention, time utilization and profitability are important.

Selection for major events is clear cut in some sports (based on objective performance criteria) but very subjective in others. For example, to make the U.S. track team for an Olympics you must finish first, second or third, but in soccer or basketball the coaches will have their own criteria, such as team chemistry and match-up with key opponents. For business consultants, selection means winning the best clients, being invited to pitch for interesting projects and getting the right alliance partners.

Marketability is the number-one criterion used by sponsors. Performance counts, but only to a point. This is the "Anna Kournikova effect" coming into play. You don't have to win if you have more to offer and, equally, winning an Olympic gold medal is rarely the pathway to riches that most athletes believe it to be. The IBM advertising program, "No one ever gets sacked for buying IBM", is an example of a company capitalizing on its brand value.

Aspiring high-performance businesses are well advised to factor the same three criteria into their scoreboards. "Performance" is an obvious choice here, but what about "selectors and marketability"?

Stakeholder scoreboards: Challenges from the coach

Does your program need to attract investors and partners to fund and enable growth? These groups are akin to selectors of the sports world and, quite reasonably, they are seeking to put together a team to take on the world. These selectors will be interested in future growth in value and may ask questions such as:

- Where will it come from?
- What is the strategy to achieve it?
- What will it cost and what are the risks involved?

If you are a business outfit, they will also want to know about how much cash you have available because, in the global game, cash gives the power to choose options and indicates manageable debt. Extracted value is another element, as is the margin that you get from your product or service.

Finally, your investor or partner will be interested in your exposure or, more specifically, how capable you are of dealing with the economic roller coaster. Be mindful of the scoreboards that others use and keep tabs on them yourself.

FIGURE 14.6 How stakeholders might keep score

Investors/Owners	Community/Government
Profitability	Environmental practices
Future earnings prospects	Corporate citizenship
Brand value	Growth in employment
Customers	**Employees**
Price	Development opportunities
Availability	Culture
Quality	Ethics

RECRUIT TALENT

Few things are more important in the global game than identifying and recruiting talent. As William Heinecke has pointed out, "You will never regret the time you put into developing and working with great talent. It is people such as this who will help to make you a more successful entrepreneur."[8]

The best sporting nations recognized many years ago that money and time spent in talent identification is an investment that is returned many times over. In high-performance programs the recruitment falls into three interlinked areas: attracting talent, identifying talent ("Talent I.D."), and recruiting talent.

Attracting talent

High-performance programs act like a magnet to the best graduates, developing athletes, musicians or whatever talent they need. Gordon Cairns says of this process that "to attract and motivate people is to have a high-performance culture. The best gravitates to the best."[9]

Identifying talent

Professional sports teams employ talent scouts to spot individuals who meet the required skills for the sport and the specific needs of the team. Olympic sports, particularly those with clear physiological requirements such as rowing and cycling, have made some startling progress in their talent-identification techniques and processes (athletes with no rowing experience are now reaching World and Olympic finals in less than two years).

High-performance programs must be constantly and actively seeking talent in the global game. Just filling positions when they become vacant is not enough. Apply this principle to recruiting people for your business and when you are looking for joint-venture partners or, indeed, anyone you need with you on the journey.

There is more to identifying talent than merely spotting technical capability. Factors such as self-awareness, motivation, concentration and interpersonal skills are keys to success in high-performance teams.

In the SAS, says Stuart Ellis, "selection is renowned for being physically tough but this is simply a tool to test the mental and character toughness of the individual."[10]

Recruiting talent

Three factors are particularly important to the recruitment process in the global game:

- recruiting for shared values
- trying before you buy
- finding and selecting leaders who can lead under pressure.

Recruiting for shared values

Apart from the obvious technical capabilities, any new recruit must demonstrate values that are compatible with your program's values. They don't have to be identical, but they should be close enough to coexist when under pressure. A misfit of values will just lead to frustration and under-performance.

There are three values that must always be probed very closely in a recruitment process: performance ethic, integrity and conflict preference. These are explained in the following table.

FIGURE 14.7 Three values to probe when recruiting

Value	Characteristics	Impact if not in synch
Performance ethic	Drive, the need to achieve, urgency, competitiveness	Disagreements over workload, contribution, motives for growth of business
Integrity	Honesty, openness to share, trustworthiness	Breakdown of trust, no delegation or teamwork
Conflict preference	How the person deals with conflict — do they avoid, seek to resolve, generate or confront? — and the level of conflict that they can work with	Breakdown of personal relationships under pressure, arguments or dissatisfaction with how conflict is managed

Fast teams and organizations need diversity and fit — a challenging combination, but not impossible when you go out and find people with passion and shared values.

Trying before you buy

One of the best recruitment strategies is the "try-out". The concept, which is becoming more popular among businesses and talented people, is to give the candidate a chance to work for a brief time within the organization and/or to undergo some training while they go through the selection process.

This "self-service recruitment" is mutually beneficial because both parties experience each other in as close to the real situation as possible. Try-outs are not always possible, particularly in executive roles, but even spending a morning attending a meeting or two, doing a presentation to a team, or solving a problem shows both parties what working together may be like. Likewise, doing some training and induction lets the person decide if your culture is something different from what they expected.

Of course, if none of this is possible, just go and play golf with them!

Finding and selecting leaders who can lead under pressure

In the Take Aim section of your Performance Model, you focused on defining the values that are important to the culture you want to create. The next step is to find people who have the capacity to lead and who share those values.

Old viewpoints and processes emerge under the pressure of performance environments. People go to their "default styles" of dealing with customer complaints, handling quality exceptions and making decisions. This sort of behavior can quickly take your organization backwards and out of the global game if you do not have leaders on site to coach people through these situations.

I've seen this in Olympic hockey, where players reverted to a style of play of passing off to their team mates rather than taking a risk and going for the goal. Coaches who have experienced this will put on-field leaders in place to challenge the behaviors and to model the right decisions.

In the SAS recruitment process, the mental and character toughness "are qualities that will develop into strong individual leadership qualities with significant flexibility", according to former SAS leader Stuart Ellis.[11]

When recruiting at all levels, reflect on whether you are creating a critical mass of people who make the right decisions under pressure. This is a fundamental principle of Performance Leadership.

ROLES, RESOURCES AND DISCIPLINES

Let's combine the next three elements of Performance Set-up, Roles, Resources and Disciplines, and address the most important issues in each area to consider for your Performance Model.

Roles

The global game, and the notion of creating agile organizations, has changed the nature of the roles that people actually play, as we saw when we looked at Design for Fitness earlier in the chapter. Reducing the number of set positions, using teamwork as an organizing principle, pushing responsibility towards the front line and encouraging flocking are all evidence of the flexibility needed by Business Athletes in the global game.

More leading and less doing

What has not been fully challenged up to this point is your role as a Performance Leader and how you set up that role to allocate time between:

- daily tasks (fixing problems, doing reports, attending meetings)
- vision/strategy (scouting the future, investigating options, thinking, visualizing)
- building capability (coaching people and teams, championing systems).

As organizations develop and move beyond issues of short-term survival, it is essential that their leaders spend more time on vision/strategy and building capability, while reducing their time on daily tasks. This can be personally challenging for many who are conditioned to being involved in the day-to-day running of the business and feel lost and out of touch when delegating it to others.

Reflection: What is the current balance between these three areas for you and other leaders in your program? What does the business need now and in the future?

Of course, the more skilled you and other leaders are as coaches, the more you are able to do the kind of day-to-day coaching that enables your people to develop the capabilities to take over some of your roles.

FIGURE 14.8 Allocating time to leadership

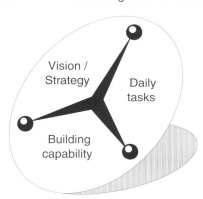

When new in the role, take the opportunity to make changes

Countless leaders have learned to their disadvantage that it becomes increasingly harder to make changes to the Performance Set-up once they have reached the end of their honeymoon period. Remember the saying, "You are only a new leader once" and act quickly and decisively to reconstruct the set-up. This is particularly important for the design of your leadership team.

Resources

Just prior to the reunification of Germany, I was fortunate to spend some time in East Germany visiting the Leipzig Sports Institute. This was home to much of the intellectual and political power of the East German sports system and a training base for many of their Olympic champions.

When invited to view their weight-training facility, I expected something like the Australian Institute of Sport, with gleaming weights and the latest resistance machines. Instead, there was just a gloomy room with high ceiling, broken floorboards and weights that looked like someone had got to them with paint stripper. My host smiled and said something to the effect that it was the weights that were important; everything else was just decoration.

Create a performance focus, not a conditions focus

One of the critical differences between the top performer and the also-ran is that the performer focuses outwards on the performance, while the also-ran looks to the conditions and resources (often as an excuse).

Sometimes we just need to take off the "corporate filter" and see that requests for offices, expenditure budgets, cars and information are about increasing or flaunting status and power, and not about increasing performance. High-performance programs are into performance, not ego.

Coles Myer, Australia's largest retailing group, created a plush executive headquarters in Melbourne which became known, somewhat derisively, as Battlestar Galactica. Recently, the group's new chief executive, John Fletcher, had the building refitted as part of his strategy to address what journalist Richard Gluyas called a "corrosively, inwardly focused culture". In the same article, Fletcher is quoted as saying, "I just can't lead an organization and say we're all one team and then go to work every day and sit in a place like that".[12]

By all means, get the resources you believe you need; but if you create a program that attracts talented people, then they'll find creative ways around a lack of resources. And, as we discussed earlier, most organizations are bad at implementing expensive systems, so you do not need the best of everything to compete successfully.

If performance was just about investment in resources then life would be much simpler. No doubt we need resources, such as finance, information and some bricks and mortar, but keep your focus on implementation and adding value. High performers get great value from all their resources, which means they don't carry a great load of overheads up the mountain.

Disruptive technologies: Answer the call to minimalize

Can you imagine the cost of establishing a bookshop in every city in the world? The oft-quoted example of Amazon.com has shown that this can be done at a micro-fraction of the cost of establishing a physical presence. Sure, we are yet to see this sort of disruptive technology cut a swathe through the traditional bookstore, but e-business offers new channels to your customers and it might not be anywhere near as expensive for them as your current set-up.

The call to action is to go back to the mission on your corporate Clipboard Plan and be really sure of what your program/ organization will and will not do. Be lean, though not necessarily mean, in deciding the resources that you need to compete, and always challenge whether new resources add to or take away from your agility.

Explore options such as shared service arrangements that can release overheads for use in core business activities; look at how technology is reshaping the value chains in other industries;

and keep your organization agile, so it can shift its strategies to cope with disruptive technologies.

Discipline: Going beyond controlling

Traditional Bosses see discipline as being about tight control and restriction. Narrow job descriptions, limited delegation of authority and many rules are the tools of the Boss. Performance Leaders, on the other hand, are acutely aware that organizations need discipline but they build disciplines and controls into the culture of the organization rather than exercising their own power or the power of the hierarchy.

Discipline has two interlinked meanings. First, there are the rituals such as reporting, meetings and other forums, and the tools and systems such as project management. Second, there is the culture of discipline that must be instilled if a program is to be successful. In the latter context, discipline comes from people caring about what they do and being willing to follow a method or system, often in a way that limits their desire for freedom.

Disciplines are the routine of the sportsperson. Every Olympic athlete and coach knows the importance of defining minimalist routines and sticking to them in all competitions. For teams, in particular, the athletes must have trust in what each other does. When disciplines are not followed, trust breaks down.

Create a culture of discipline or you are doomed

To create a culture of discipline ask yourself, "What is the single most important element of performance that we should focus upon?" This is not an easy question and it may take you considerable time and effort to find that point. In recent times, that point for many businesses has been margin. Margin can be measured. It is the tangible product of many things, such as capturing cost reductions through e-commerce and related initiatives, and maintaining price levels when other measures such as turnover can encourage price-cutting and longer-term trouble. The Performance Leader can build a case for margin, a reason for its importance, and people can be mobilized around it.

For medical teams, disciplines are built through relentless attention to standards. Maintaining this relentless attention and linking consequences to breaches are essential. When people breach the team disciplines, it is the Performance Leader and their peers who must act.

High performers are disciplined: they do the basic things consistently when under pressure. Your role as a Performance Leader is to keep the heat on the core disciplines. Without this, your program is doomed.

Flair or discipline?

Olympic coach Ric Charlesworth argues that flair is grossly overrated in sport. Success, he feels, comes from well-practiced skills that are executed effectively under pressure.[13]

Flair is great to watch and has its moments — a Tiger Woods sand shot or a Harry Kewell goal — but more often than not the player has practiced relentlessly and that is why they can produce it under pressure.

After working with many of my country's best athletes, I have come to the same view as Charlesworth, with the additional point that flair was perhaps a more valuable performance weapon a few years back. Standards are now much higher and moments of "out-of-the-box" brilliance are rare.

CREATE A MICRO-ENVIRONMENT

In Chapter 5, we looked at how Olympic athletes are able to create a micro-environment despite myriad distractions at the Games.

The global game has all the distractions of the Olympics and more, so look for ways to shelter your Business Athletes from the distractions and allow them to focus on those things that are most important to the task.

A few years back, we were asked to work with a special-projects team who were preparing a major tender that would either secure the future of the organization or possibly see it slide into oblivion. After facilitating the Scan and Take Aim parts of their Performance Model, we encouraged the team to create a micro-environment that sheltered them from the day-to-day distractions of the business and allowed them to focus on their very important task. The overall organization was in chaos and was definitely not a high-performance program. Their separate physical space helped the team to build the sense of teamwork and focus that was essential to their mission. They also developed their own name and created an on-line site where they could keep in touch with each other as they moved around the country. The ultimate success of this team in creating an excellent tender and winning the business was, to a large extent, a function of creating a micro-environment in which they could unleash their potential. Importantly, the team leader did not take on a lot of day-to-day responsibilities; instead, he did whatever was needed to provide his Business Athletes with the environment in which they could perform.

Many organizations are too under-resourced to give team leaders this role and yet this is such a valuable role and one that is just so obvious when you look at other high-performance environments. Can you imagine a coach playing in a World Cup soccer team, or a team manager driving in Formula One or a hospital CEO operating on patients?

Reflection: Do you value the importance of having people who can help to create the micro-environment around teams that allows them to perform, or do you chase efficiencies that actually reduce team performance?

SUMMARY: CHANGE THE AIM, CHANGE THE SET-UP

We have reviewed eight elements of Performance Set-up, each of which has its place in creating a high-performance program. Not every aspect must be at world-class level in your Performance Model, but top-performing organizations make a feature of the elements of their set-up that are consistent with their Aim and the Performance Conditions.

Be alert to Performance Set-up, particularly to those aspects that add to or detract from speed and quality. Within these eight elements, one message must prevail over all others: **"If you change the aim, then change the set-up."**

Bosses have a remarkable habit of changing their strategies or goals without adjusting the Performance Set-up, or changing structure without addressing elements such as new scoreboards, performance systems and roles. Performance Leaders make a strong Performance Set-up a key feature of their Performance Model.

Reflection: Do you have the Performance Set-up that is needed to achieve your Aim?

15

Perform: It's All About Execution

In a perfectly ordered world, you would Scan the Conditions, Take Aim, arrange your Performance Set-up and then Perform according to your strategy. But, of course, such linearity is not the stuff of the global game. Aim, set-up, adjustment of mindset and the like happen when they need to happen (not just at the start of our endeavors) — the pilot deals with an incident in the cabin, the IT director responds to a systems crash, the coach interrupts training to meet an important sponsor, and the theater director moves a prop in the spilt second before the curtain rises.

High-performance environments are mobile feasts of activity in which the challenge is to keep the connection with your overall strategy, while dealing with the performance issues that emerge every moment. As Duncan Chessell says of the Everest expedition, "You have to be constantly reassessing progress and be flexible enough to deal with the conditions.[1]"

While other elements of the Performance Model may be similar from one organization to another (everyone does a mission, builds a performance culture, debriefs performance), the Perform part of the model is unique to your business because it addresses how you execute your unique strategies.

However, what is important is that you and your Business Athletes execute the strategy brilliantly, because strategy execution is a distinctive feature of high-performance programs. The demise of Gateway Computers is just one example of an organization that was unable to execute a strategy as well as its competitor, Dell, on which it modeled its approach.

This chapter addresses the challenges of putting strategy execution into your Performance Model by bringing together five elements that have been discussed in various contexts earlier in the book. Those elements are outlined in Figure 15.1.

FIGURE 15.1 Brilliant strategy execution

Make strategy execution everyone's business

Align, coordinate and improve your Model

Create and foster fast teams

Encourage fast decisions

Demonstrate acts of leadership

Brilliant Strategy Execution

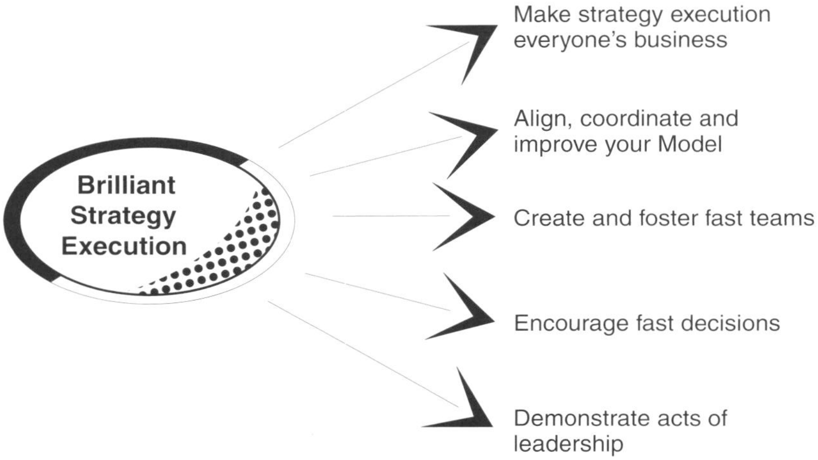

High-Performance Leadership is often used by organizations after the overall strategic blueprint has been decided to provide the common framework, language and practices needed to execute that strategy. The five elements outlined in Figure 15.1 are an integral part of that process.

MAKE STRATEGY EXECUTION EVERYONE'S BUSINESS

Watch a Wimbledon or U.S. Open singles final. Both players have strategies. The winner has the better package, one of physical, technical and mental strategies designed with their own strengths and limitations in mind, and an intimate understanding of the conditions and their opponent. Should it be any different in your business?

The answer is actually "Yes", because there is probably at least one critical difference. That is, in tennis the players are involved in designing and executing the strategy. In businesses of any size, relatively few people have much input into strategies for such areas as product selection, market segmentation, supply chain and the like. However, everyone *is* involved in executing their part of the strategy, which is why the best Performance Leaders make sure that people understand, interpret and act in alignment with the strategic directions.

Unfortunately, it is still standard practice in many organizations for Bosses to give people a little piece of the strategy without any context or understanding of how it fits into the total picture. This might be successful in times of short-term crisis (where command-control leadership has its place), but it is a recipe for losing the motivation, commitment and skills of the intelligent generation of the global game, who want to be empowered.

Devise, communicate and lead your strategy

I often meet business leaders who complain that people are not doing the things that need to be done to execute their strategies quickly and smoothly. My usual response is that in similar circumstances in sport it's the coach who is sacked, not the athlete. This usually doesn't get a smile but it does send the message, and the Performance Leadership principle, that even the best strategy will only be executed well under pressure when it is well communicated, coached and practiced.

Devising winning strategies for your program is only one-third of the job of a Performance Leader. You also have to communicate the strategy and build a passion and commitment amongst people for executing it brilliantly.

FIGURE 15.2 Devise, communicate and lead the strategy

- Devise the winning strategy
- Communicate the strategy
- Lead the execution

Bosses rarely get these three pieces happening together. Either they can't find the time to strategize or they do it behind closed doors and then circulate a boring planning document and call it communication. Or they miss the opportunity to engage people's hearts and minds in the execution of the strategy by going straight to the detail instead of starting with the big picture. Remember the "miniature" that was discussed in Chapter 12? Use this as part of your toolkit to engage people in executing strategy.

Strategy execution: Challenge from the coach

Consider the different characteristics of the Boss and Performance Leader in Figure 15.3 and challenge yourself as to which are most like you.

FIGURE 15.3 Linking strategy and execution

Boss	Performance Leader
Small executive team does an annual plan	Brings people together to strategize — refines this into a strategic blueprint
Reviews monthly plans in isolation from the strategy	Constantly checks and refines the strategy against current performance and conditions
Distributes copies of the plan through the hierarchy	Tells the story and uses tools such as Clipboard Plans and miniatures to embed the strategy
Reacts to day-to-day issues — loses sight of the big picture	Constantly monitors and talks about the link between performance and strategic blueprint

ALIGN, COORDINATE AND IMPROVE YOUR MODEL

Everyone talks about alignment, but I believe a more practical term in performance environments is "coordination". Alignment implies that everyone is hooked to the same engine; however, there is a lot more to coordinating the Performance Model of an organization than simply aligning plans and activities.

In talking about the evolution of the Royal Adelaide Hospital's emergency-retrieval model, Dr Bill Griggs has stressed the importance of coordination so that things happen "in parallel". He has contrasted this to the old paradigm, a slow, linear process that might have been aligned but certainly wasn't rapid and responsive. The RAH retrieval team is often called upon to deal with retrievals in the harsh Australian outback. For example, some years ago, at 4.30 one morning, in an outback region approximately six hours' drive from Adelaide, a family car left the road and rolled. The driver (the father) was killed, the mother and one child were trapped and unconscious, and the other child was in no condition to do much. It was 6.30 before the car was noticed. At 7.15, an ambulance crew arrived, extracted the injured from the wreck and, by 9.15, had arrived at a small country hospital. For the next hour, the local doctor worked to stabilize the two most seriously injured patients before finally calling the retrieval team at 10.30. By the time the team reached the site via the Flying Doctor service, more than eight hours had elapsed since the crash. Under the new system, the retrieval team would have arrived at the hospital before the patients.

The new coordinated system is built around a centralized communication system that relays information to all emergency services. Working to a set of criteria, the trauma system is then activated at some level. Coordination ensures that the ambulance communication staff activate the right resources — paramedics, retrieval team or local doctor — to get to the scene rapidly. Equally important, says Dr Griggs, is knowing when *not* to send resources such as helicopters because of the costs and risks involved. Importantly, more than 100 doctors living in rural and remote areas of South Australia have been coached in core skills such as how to manage patients at an accident scene and how to coordinate with ambulance, fire, police, paramedic and retrieval teams.

Creating this type of coordination has required leaders to operate in each of the three Performance Leadership roles:

- Strategic Leadership to create the overall communication and coordination system

- Development Coaching to ensure that people within the system have the knowledge and skills
- Performance Coaching to manage the activities as they unfold.

Maintaining coordination between Performance Units, and between the strategy and activities, is an essential role for Performance Leaders. Some of the High-Performance Leadership tools and techniques that are available to you to enhance that alignment and coordination are summarized in Figure 15.4.

FIGURE 15.4 Enhancing alignment and coordination

High Performance Leadership Tools/Principles	Impact on the organization
Clipboard Plans	Clear mission and goals for all units means quick, well-planned and coordinated action
Common and public scoreboards	Line of sight from aim to results means non-value-adding activities can be eliminated and the spotlight put onto the execution of the priority strategies
Communication	Creating common forums and shared information sites improves formal and informal coordination
Feedback	Good practices are reinforced and developed, while poor practices are eliminated
Rewards	Rewarding execution increases motivation and attracts high performers
Recruitment	Recruiting operations leaders who are passionate about implementation
Prototyping and simulation	Running pilot programs and building prototypes increases learning when strategies are fully rolled out: simulations also strengthen skills and common understanding
Miniature vision and strategy presentations	Every person hears a compelling message that links their job to the overall mission

High-performance programs sustain high performance because Performance Leaders in operational areas are passionate about executing strategy. They make it a key feature of their program. Are you using the principles and tools of the Performance Leader to make strategy execution a distinctive feature of your organization?

UNLEASH YOUR BUSINESS ATHLETES

In search of agility and responsiveness, organizations are recruiting agile high performers, but many managers are quite uncomfortable in dealing with high performers who expect to be given the freedom to roam and to choose their own pathways to performance.

A good friend and colleague of mine (who prefers anonymity) has a quirky approach to coaching high performers but one that does challenge you to think differently.

He suggests that coaching the "agile high performer" is like training a cat, and explained his thinking this way:

"Think of your high performers as being like agile and alert cats. Your challenge is to coach them enough so they don't become feral but not so much that you turn them into fat cats. Dogs will do what you want but you can't control a cat. All you can do is create the right conditions that will keep them agile and alert but not feral."

In this regard, my colleague suggests five tactics, which are explained in Figure 15.5 alongside the equivalent lessons for coaching the agile, high-performing Business Athlete.

Many Bosses struggle to deal with people who want to roam. They see this as a threat to their power and control. But CEOs like Gordon Cairns of Lion Nathan say you have to give people freedom with guidelines if you want to attract and retain highly talented people.[2]

FIGURE 15.5 Coaching the agile high performer

Training cats	Coaching the high performer
Make them slightly hungry	Reward them for excellence, not average performance
Open the door to let them roam but give them a home to come back to	Give them a support base but allow them mobility to cross boundaries
Allow natural instincts to emerge (assist a little with kittens), but not inside the house	Back their instincts for identifying opportunities
Give them the terrain that suits their natural agility	Give them your biggest challenges
Let them learn that dogs chase cats (but not until they are big enough to climb the fence)	Throw them in the deep end with a life belt that can be used if really needed

CREATE AND FOSTER FAST TEAMS

Individuals never win gold medals, climb Mt Everest or master the global game of business. Only individuals supported by teams stand a chance in high-performance conditions. No matter how good you are, the standard of performance is too high, the conditions too changeable and the complexity too great for you to do it entirely alone.

One of the most powerful competitive advantages that a business can have is the capability to form and disband teams rapidly as they develop and execute strategies in changing conditions. The matrix in Figure 15.6 illustrates the importance of fast teamwork in an emergency. People within and from each area may need to come together to form teams in many situations.

Creating teams that can execute strategy and implement other change rapidly and effectively is a core competency of Performance Leaders. When people like John Chambers, chairman of Cisco, tell the 2001 Davos forum that institutions must seek and capture a reduction in operating costs of 25–50% over three to four years through e-commerce, they are also issuing the challenge to implement change that can only come through Performance Leadership and Fast Teams.

FIGURE 15.6 High performance units sit in a large matrix

In the global game, goods must be handled faster and services provided instantly. Fast Teams implement the systems, coordinate the manufacturing and supply activities and give competitive advantage. Fast Teams are, indeed, a critical source of competitive advantage

One team

Unless you can get a team culture that makes the team more important than the ambitions and needs of individuals, Fast Team work is not going to operate to its full potential. Here, the trick for the great Performance Leader is to give people individual responsibility while showing them the rewards that come from being a member of the team.

When I walk into a sporting organization, it is pretty obvious straight away that this is a team. There are all manner of symbols that tell me immediately. On the wall there will be team photographs; in the foyer there will be something about the tradition and history of the team; and the players will be dressed in a way that identifies them with the team. When coaching business teams, I ask them to think of the same concept and find what reinforces the team ethic. Some of these questions are covered below.

Team ethic: Questions from the coach

What is it about your team that genuinely binds them together as a team? Is it ...

- personal relationships between the members?
- a common vision/mission?
- shared values?
- the physical environment/location?
- the type of work activities?
- the style of meetings and gatherings?

While the Boss talks about teamwork, the Performance Leader is actively coaching the team behaviors and building the symbols and processes of teamwork that generate faster and better results. They also tend to use more active training approaches to reduce what experiential-training expert Darren Williams calls "the big gap between knowledge and the ability to behave it".[3]

Everyone has plateaus

The quest for high performance is never a journey of continuous improvement, even though that term is very popular in business. Except in the early and fast-development stage of learning, improvements tend to come in short bursts separated by troughs, plateaus and sheer hard work.

Shane Gould sees it as essential that Performance Leaders help people to keep a perspective of where they are heading during tough times. She believes that the leader who takes a holistic view, and is keen to develop the life skills of their Business Athletes, is best equipped to guide people through these inevitable experiences.[4]

ENCOURAGE FAST DECISIONS

Decisions in high-performance environments have to be made with less-than-perfect information because if you wait for 100% certainty you'll be like the surfer who either misses the waves altogether or gets cleaned up by a very large wave (what surfers call "a close out set"). In Chapter 5, we discussed this concept and considered how Business Athletes make 80/20 decisions about the choices that they face in the global game.

The notion of 80/20 decisions is foreign to leaders who grew up in the pre-global game. It means engaging with risk and uncertainty that used to be a signal for deciding to do nothing. But, as Charles Handy reminds us, the most costly errors in the global game are often missed opportunities, not the traditional mistake.[5]

Most global-game decisions have risk and reward attached and little time in which to decide. Often the choices are between two good or two poor alternatives, with the rewards going to those who position themselves to grab the opportunities and minimize or manage the risks. No wonder that many organizations make sure that risk management is a core capability of Performance Leaders.

Use 80/20 to clear the little decisions

Agile Performance Leaders use the 80/20 mindset to ruthlessly prioritize what has to be done, and move on with the value-adding activities.

Scan the decision-making in your business and probe the decisions that you and your people hang onto and revisit time and again. They are chewing up organizational resources and probably adding little in the way of value or of minimizing risk.

At the next management meeting, challenge people to tell you about decisions they have made in the past month that are genuinely 80/20 in nature. If they can't think of any, what does this say about your leadership?

Quick decisions are often better decisions

For the big decisions, by all means take the time to study the risks and rewards and make measured decisions. But you will not have the time to consider the big issues if you are bogged down with analyzing every decision.

That is why Performance Leaders delegate and give people the freedom to make those decisions and encourage them to accept the consequences.

In High Performance Leadership projects, we find that placing emphasis on being quick to decide and quick to act leads to better decision-making, because people scan the environment more closely when they know that decisions have to be made quickly.

The global game has pushed a lot of decision-making onto teams at operational level. Therefore, your role in raising their skills to make rapid and accurate decisions is essential to sustaining your performance advantages. Once again, the skill of coaching people to solve their own problems is a core capability for Performance Leaders.

Stop doing business with yourself

Bureaucracies are brilliant at doing business with themselves. Layers are created to deal with the next layer. Rules and processes are designed to virtually ensure that a large percentage of the organization's time and energy is devoted to dealing with itself rather than with its customers, partners and other performance drivers.

Organizations that do business with themselves hold lots of meetings, pass decisions from one person to another, create departments that are isolated from customers and build complicated processes that drive customers mad. They cannot be agile and many of the great business turnarounds of the past two decades have involved pointing organizations outwards towards the market and the customer: that is, driving out what are currently called "non-value-adding activities".

Make it your passion to find and eliminate any tendency to do business with yourself.

DEMONSTRATE ACTS OF LEADERSHIP

In business, sport, politics and beyond, it is the acts of leadership that bring the organization's values to life, show people through action what the values mean, and create visible and powerful symbols which guide and inspire. This applies to fast strategy execution but also to every aspect of your Performance Model.

Have you noticed how the units that can be relied upon to perform in tough conditions are invariably those that have leaders who demonstrate the values through these acts of leadership? These leaders — such as Anita Roddick working with indigenous people to bring their handicrafts to market, and Jack Welch driving boundaries out of GE — show the values in action. Performance

Leaders see the opportunity to demonstrate leadership and have the courage to do it. For example, a retail executive we know invited ex-customers to a staff forum and encouraged a no-holds-barred critique of the responsiveness of the business. Her actions and openness to be criticized showed everyone that responsiveness and openness to feedback are essential (and more important than status and reputations).

As you would expect, it is values-driven leaders who more often demonstrate acts of leadership when crises occur, when decisions must be made and paradoxes must be handled. Values-driven leadership is an essential aspect of the Performance Model of organizations that are quick to execute strategy.

Opportunities for acts of leadership emerge when customers are dissatisfied, when decisions need to be made, when values are breached, when conflicts and divisions fester, and when unclaimed problems emerge. Where are the opportunities for you to demonstrate acts of leadership?

SUMMARY

Performance Leaders make it their business to ensure that what is needed gets done. Whether that is giving someone the information and authority to make a decision, or resolving a customer problem in a way that stops it from happening again, the leader gets it done. They instill an urgency through their acts of leadership that makes brilliant strategy execution by team and individuals a feature of the Performance Model.

16

Learn and Adapt

Do you remember the scene in the book (and the movie, of course) *Jurassic Park* when mathematician Dr Ian Malcolm explains why the animals will find a way to escape the controls of the park? "Life breaks free," he says. "Life expands to new territories. Painfully, perhaps even dangerously. But life finds a way.[1]" This is a simple and vivid example of how living organisms learn and adapt to changes in their environment.

Organizations, cultures and ecosystems all have this same capacity to learn and adapt. They are what complexity theorists call "complex adaptive systems", and they have the potential to gather feedback and use it to adapt themselves, to maintain fitness and, therefore, to survive and grow.

This capacity for self-organized change is built in to organizations. However, Performance Leaders can and must strengthen this capability because of the rapid change in the performance environment and the tendency for many organizational cultures to become settled and resistant to change.

Note, please, that I use the word "adapt" to include the process of evolution.

FIND THE DYNAMIC POSITION

In a high-performance environment, you have four possible options or combinations of options open to you: remain unchanged; adapt to the changing conditions; shape the conditions to suit your current capabilities; or shape and adapt.

These options are illustrated in Figure 16.1, along with some of the characteristics of programs/organizations that fit distinctly into one of the quadrants.

FIGURE 16.1 Options for adapting, shaping and changing

Adapt to the conditions (Adapter)	**Shape the conditions and adapt (Shaper/Adapter)**
• quick to learn and adapt	• entrepreneurial
• rapid followers of new technology	• future formers
• responsive to customer/market demand	• leverage use of knowledge
	• creative and innovative
Remain unchanged (Settler)	**Shape the conditions (Shaper)**
• slow and stable	• strategic
• poor at quick strategy execution	• powerful or well-leveraged
• averse to risk	• use alliances
• product- or technology-driven	• entrepreneurial

Let's explore the characteristics of organizations that operate predominantly in one of these quadrants and then look at strategies to increase the "adaptive intelligence" of your outfit.

Settler

Status-quo managers keep their organization in synch with their business plans and/or with the norms of the organization. These "settlers" tend to be slow followers of change, and are seriously at risk in a changing environment. Only choose to remain a settler if you are in a very protected environment where there are no rewards for change. Make sure also that your Performance Model is strong in the area of Scan: Know the Conditions as discussed in Chapter 13.

Adapter

Organizations such as British Airways, Qantas and Citicorp have built reputations as rapid adapters by changing service features to meet changes in customer demands.

To create a strong "adapter culture", it is essential to build the links in your Performance Model between Take Aim, Scan, and Learn and Adapt. Focus your scanning on the broad market and your customers and put in place systems and processes that allow you to respond quickly to changes in your environment. For example, build the capabilities of flocking and high-performance project teams, use real-time customer feedback scoreboards, and coach people in rapid prototyping.

Adaptability is closely linked to agility which, Matt English and David Robertson suggest, comes in part from organizations removing non-value-adding activities and having "the ability to view themselves through the eyes of their customers".[2]

Consider who are the players in your industry that are quick adapters. What benefits does this give them?

Shaper

In Chapter 1, we discussed James Carse's notion of finite and infinite games and suggested that the global game is increasingly becoming an infinite game with fuzzy boundaries, fewer rules and greater uncertainty. This is an environment that is likely to spawn "shapers" who, in effect, dismantle the finite games.

For example, the combination of Tiger Woods and golf technology is changing the nature of the game of golf (and potentially rendering the standard-length golf course obsolete). In business, some of the reshaping of the landscape that is taking place is coming from mergers which, in many industries (for example, wine), are threatening the survival of medium-sized businesses. Other shaping, such as the creation of shared services and supplier networks, is of course linked to technology.

Shapers do what humanity has always done: remodel the landscape to suit their needs better. This requires an understanding of the existing paradigms, and challenging and changing them. All high-performance programs have the potential to reshape their landscape, whether at an industry level (such as Amazon.com reshaping the book-selling industry) or inside an organization (such as creating a shared-services model).

The audit and risk-management division of a large telecommunications company used High Performance Leadership as a strategy to reshape its position inside the organization. Through creating new competencies and relationships, it moved from an auditing (end of the line) checking function to a key strategic advisory role. Its position, structure, relationships and role have all been re-shaped to better meet the company's needs.

Shaping: Questions from the coach

Consider these questions to assess the extent to which your program is a shaper.

- Who are the shapers in your system (industry, organization, profession)?
- How have they used shaping as a strategy to adapt to the performance conditions?
- What advantages has this given them?
- Are you a Performance Leader who fosters a shaping mindset?

Shaper/Adapter

The special military forces offer excellent examples of shaping and adapting. They train for fitness to the terrain, while also using physical and social engineering to rearrange the performance landscape. It could be argued that one reason for the quick success of the war against the Taliban and al-Qaeda in Afghanistan was the U.S. strategy of using Northern Alliance and other local forces, who were best adapted to that environment, for ground operations. This strategy was combined with the use of high technology and small commando units on the ground to prepare the best possible environment for the Alliance fighters; that is, they altered the terrain. Part of the U.S. strategy also included humanitarian aid in the form of food drops, and educating the population through a PR campaign of leaflets explaining their intentions.

Shapers/adapters in the business world include Dell, Amazon, IBM, Cisco and 3M, to name just a few. The challenge, as English and Robertson advise, is to "manage the balance and tension between leading change in some areas and adapting to change in others".[3]

In the remainder of this chapter, we will focus on practices for you to consider bringing into your Performance Model to develop these capabilities. These are practices that Performance Leaders employ to create future-forming capabilities.

It's all about Adaptive Intelligence

The market for your goods or services is a system (of which you are a part). It is constantly shifting under the influence of new ideas, technologies, products and information. If your organization is adaptively intelligent, it will have the capacity to appraise and adjust all elements of its Performance Model as it sees and/or visualizes what is happening in the market. In other words, it will rapidly and effectively:

- scan the environment (awareness/feedback)
- interact (testing ideas/observing effects)
- assimilate those ideas (dealing with feedback)
- adjust the elements of the model
- continue the loop from action, feedback and adaptation.

Even bacteria have adaptive intelligence and yet even a cursory look at organizations suggests that many are adaptively dumb. Let's explore some ways that you can make your organization adaptively smarter.

Porous Organizations are Smarter

Have you noticed how traditional hierarchical organizations stop ideas from floating to the surface? This is a great way to dumb-down your organization and make it a slow adapter and a non-shaper. But it doesn't have to be that way.

By listening, asking probing questions and installing processes, you can drill holes in your organization and unlock the pockets of ideas and opinions that are stuck in the system. When people can share ideas, you get what Sony CEO Nobuyuki Idei calls "emergent evolution". He describes this as innovation that emerges from the interaction of the business units and teams in Sony and believes that it is his personal challenge to create a business model that fosters such innovation.[4]

The four projects in High Performance Leadership Programmes that we have found to be most powerful in unblocking organizations are:

- Bringing the whole system together
- Capturing the power of the debrief
- Exposing people to the whole game
- Grabbing the coachable moments.

Give consideration to using projects of this type to make learning and adaptation a feature of your Performance Model.

Project one: Bring your system together

Performance Leaders regularly bring people together to learn, to solve problems and to discuss better ways to co-evolve. Accordingly, this project employs the techniques of the large-group design session that were discussed in Chapter 12 to engage a large group of people (30–300) in strategizing on problems and opportunities.

As a leadership project to open your organization to new ideas and to share perspectives, it is hard to beat the large-group design sessions, even though you may find resistance from Bosses, who typically see intelligence as residing solely with them.

When you bring the various players in a system together, there is huge potential to solve problems because there is greater brain power, and people come to understand and own the implementation of change. It is definitely a way to increase adaptive intelligence.

Project two: Capture the power of the performance debrief

When Karl Sundstrom, vice president and general manager, global services, of Ericsson Australia, says, "We analyze why we win deals and why we don't",[5] he is describing performance debriefing. The military has made an art form out of the debriefing session and some of the best sports teams have also made debriefing a real feature of their programs.

Unfortunately, this is done only infrequently in the vast majority of businesses. However, when it is introduced by leaders with good coaching skills, debriefing quickly becomes a source of performance advantage and one of the most important practices to include in your Performance Model.

Duncan Chessell credits much of his success in climbing Everest to a previous expedition to one of the world's highest peaks. He says that the expedition had the wrong performance model but he learned from it and, ultimately, created a model that put him on top of the world. The process of debriefing helped him to plan his preparation, goals, team roles and structure, and day-to-day strategies.[6]

The argument for regular and skilled debriefing is compelling; however, it is too often a casualty of the busyness of the corporate world. That is why we insist that High Performance Leadership participants do a debriefing project using this powerful technique. (In this project each participant is coached to debrief the performance of a unit that they do not lead.)

Reflection: When did you last get your team together to do a detailed debriefing that fully explored the task planning, the execution and the people issues?

Project details

There are three components to completing the debriefing project: design a debriefing pro forma; facilitate the debriefing; and write an implementation plan for applying the information to adapt and evolve.

The basic structure for debriefing should include an agenda, a list of attendees, a set of core questions, ground rules for the participants and facilitator, and an action planning sheet.

Some typical starting questions that you might use include:

- What did we set out to achieve and what was the result?
- What happened at each phase (describe the events in detail including people, places and quantities)?
- What was the gap between what we wanted and what eventuated?
- How did we plan and set up?
- How did we execute the plan?
- What helped and hindered our performance?
- In hindsight, what could we have done differently at each phase?
- What have we learned?

• How and where can we use this learning to perform better in future activities?

The framework of the Performance Model can also be useful to guide the debrief, and is used on assignments by many PwC Consultants to lead seamlessly from debriefing previous performance to developing the Performance Model for the next phase.

If the budget allows, engage an independent facilitator to manage the process. The facilitator's role is to involve everyone, to probe issues, to manage conflict and to ensure a thorough debriefing of all elements. If you do facilitate your own program, then be sure that you use a Development Coaching style to make it a positive experience.

A few traps for the unwary

A few of the common mistakes that reduce the value from performance debriefing include:

• Not doing it
• Excluding people who have an interesting perspective (e.g. contractors, customers)
• Only addressing the task (not people issues)
• Dry-cleaning the past (ignoring blemishes)
• Not projecting to future activities
• Allowing managers to dominate
• Failing to agree on how to adapt and evolve.

Build debriefing into your Performance Model by using it on a regular basis for key events and milestones and to review exceptional events, as described in Figure 16.2.

FIGURE 16.2   Choosing when to debrief

Basis for debriefing	Examples
Cycle-time	End of quarter, annual
Event/Milestone	Completion of project, mid-point in an event (e.g. a conference)
Exceptions	Crisis, major problem (e.g. loss of client, system crash)

The SAS approach to debriefing illustrates the importance of this aspect of the Performance Model. Stuart Ellis described it thus:

"After each operational activity/exercise, there is a very detailed debrief. It is not uncommon for patrols to take between three and six hours to be debriefed, and this usually occurs immediately on return from the operation. This is to ensure that all possible detail and accuracy is recalled and the learning to be gained is gathered as an absolute priority."[7]

Project three: Expose people to the whole game

When you involve them in the game (performance environment), people will see the need for adaptation and spot opportunities for change. For example, if you were to visit any store of one of Australia's largest supermarkets you will find that the range of branded goods has been reduced to make room for home-brand goods (which presumably offer higher margins). As you return unhappily to the checkout and comment on this to the assistants, they will immediately hand you a suggestion form and tell you to fill it out "because everyone's complaining and it's the only way that management might listen". That is what I call an adaptively dumb organization.

The purpose of this project is to create an adaptively intelligent organization by exposing people to the parts of your business and the supply chain that they don't usually see. That means getting management out of their offices, sales people into manufacturing and vice versa, getting finance people into operations and so on. Eliminate the barriers to understanding and increase the adaptive intelligence of your organization.

In the project, the participating Performance Leaders set a goal to expose a few people each month to other areas of the game. Not surprisingly, they soon start seeing the benefits in quicker response times from individuals and performance units.

Project four: Grab the coachable moments

Geoff pitched for the biggest account of his young career. He was 25 years of age and this one was the one he expected would lift him out of the pack of account managers and into the big league.

The organization had an unwritten policy of conducting rehearsals of important presentations but Geoff backed away from a suggestion that he do a rehearsal with his manager, Jenny, reassuring her that he had done the preparation.

On the day of the presentation, Geoff appeared to be confident and well prepared but he was quickly put off by some sharp, pointed questions about the history of his organization and hypothetical questions about how the account would be managed. It was a shaky performance and afterwards Geoff knew that he had missed a big chance and perhaps jeopardized future promotions.

For Jenny, this was a "coachable moment", an opportunity to help Geoff to learn from the experience and to be stronger for it.

Good coaches relish the coachable moments and have the skills to make the most of the opportunity. This project requires you to capture and report on two coachable moments over a one-month period. The report that we ask for in the High Performance Leadership Programme describes how the participant:

- recognized the coachable moment and the potential lessons
- engaged the person in a debrief of the situation
- directed the person towards the inherent lessons.

Coachable moments include losses, personal upsets, unique events and crises. The common point is that each event or situation shakes the person's existing beliefs and leaves them open to adaptation and evolution.

SMART ORGANIZATIONS SEVELOP LEADERS

Allan Moss, CEO of Macquarie Bank, acknowledges that "investment in culture change and leadership is on the agenda for CEOs".[8] In fact, one of the most important personal responsibilities of all Performance Leaders is to develop the leadership capabilities of their people. We have discussed numerous times how high-performing organizations have multiple leaders, so this raises the question: "how do you develop leadership throughout the organization?"

The answer is to focus on three interlinked strategies: structured training and development; corporate experience in a learning environment; and feedback. Each of these should be considered for inclusion in your Performance Model.

Structured training and development

Leadership development requires a process to introduce leadership concepts to your people in line with the leadership model for the business. Invest in a variety of learning methods, including seminars, individual and small-group coaching, mentoring and projects. Make a particular feature of using the leadership-development process to solve real business issues and to strengthen the culture. This emphasis on structured action learning is the model that prevails in all high-performance programs (sport, medical, expedition, special forces).

For example, our High Performance Leadership Programme is rolled out through organizations using the principles of reinforcement and action learning. Figure 16.3 shows a typical program outline, including needs analysis, agreement of the Leadership Model, feedback, development activities, and action-learning projects.

FIGURE 16.3 High Performance Leadership Programme

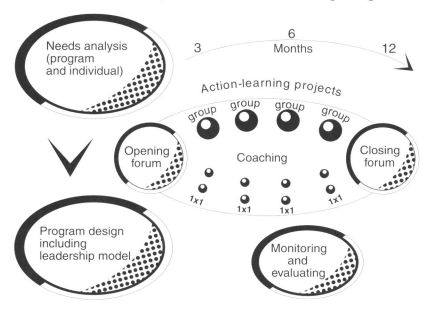

This type of structure is increasingly being used in business to capture the benefits of action learning. It usually requires a combination of internal and external coach/facilitators and a learning culture. It is what Professor Bill Ford describes as replacing the training mentality with a learning mentality.[9]

Corporate experience

Few effective leaders have taken the narrow road to the top. Instead, most have held many positions (operational, technical, corporate), faced tough challenges and had successes and failures. Similarly, in top-level sport a great many of the best coaches have been only average athletes, but they have learned how to maximize their abilities through confronting highs and lows.

Learning seems to come fastest and best from adventure. Your challenge is therefore two-fold: to find the best ways to give your people those adventures and to support their experiences so that they capture and apply the learning.

People learn from success, failure, setbacks, training, observation and challenges. Use your coaching skills and knowledge to give people the opportunity to learn according to their individual styles and preferences while, above all, keeping it active and relevant. In particular, keep in mind Duncan Chessell's observation that the key to benefiting from adventure activities is "learning how to analyze the situation and then applying those skills to other performance situations".[10]

A good Performance Leader/Coach helps people to make the connection between skills learned in one setting and how they can apply them in another.

My former manager at the Institute of Sport, Mike Nunan, trains race horses. To this, he brings a unique action-learning approach gained from his background in coaching at senior level in football and in managing a business.

He has found that traditional trainers have a huge amount of intuitive knowledge about the process of preparing a horse for competition: they are good observers of behavior. What Mike is now bringing to bear is the power of more structured questioning and documented observation. For example, he has the stable-hands record the behaviors of the horses in the days leading up to competition, and maps the workload of horses while they are grazing. He uses heart-rate monitors to measure training loads and prepare horses in the same manner as is used to prepare Olympic athletes in speed, endurance and field sports. Other trainers are now taking an interest in what he is doing and, while it is early days, he is already having enough success to have others adopting his mindset.

Mike is doing what Performance Leaders do in a global game — fostering a culture of learning, building the systems that allow for observation, testing hypotheses and adapting their operations as they learn more. (For more details on action learning, I recommend a book of that name by Krystyna Weinstein.[11])

Leadership feedback

The more senior you become in an organization, the more difficult it is to get accurate feedback. Yet chief executives and senior leaders need feedback just as much as everyone else if they are to improve. The use of 360-degree feedback has been a very good step in this direction, although it is a tool that is still not used well in many businesses.

The most effective 360-degree feedback systems are situated on the business intranet or in an easy-to-use modular format that encourages leaders to regularly seek feedback on elements of their performance. If you do not have a customized leadership model, then consider using the High-Performance Leadership Model (Chapter 10) as the framework to give you the information that you need to improve as a leader. (Details of a commercially available version can be found on our website.)

A version of the Leadership Model was used in the lead-up to the Sydney Olympics to provide feedback to team managers, and to help them refine their approaches.

Feedback is one of the essential elements in creating a high-performance program and it is as important in the development of leaders as to any other aspect of the program.

MAKE PERFORMANCE MANAGEMENT IRRELEVANT

Do you really want someone else to "manage" your performance? Probably not; yet organizations routinely brag about their "new performance-management system" as if it was some novel way to generate high performance. Interestingly, most of those that brag seem to be happier about the technology than the culture.

Let's be blunt. Performance management is a bad brand. For most people, it means appraisal, salary review and compliance. It is impersonal, rigid, bureaucratic, artificial and reeks of compliance. Bosses don't like it and do it badly or avoid it altogether.

An Olympic sport program needs athletes to accurately evaluate and adjust their own performance. The athletes want a seamless link between short-term performance and long-term development. They want performance development, not management. Theirs is the real learning organization in which the system provides performance data, regular performance debriefing, constant search for improvement and structured development processes.

Let's agree to start the improvement by using the term "performance development" rather than management.

Simple is best

Having seen literally hundreds of performance-development systems, we have found that the best, unquestionably, are the most simple. Typically, they contain four key elements: a disciplined process led by skilled coaches; a direct link from performance goals to development plans; frequent performance conversations; and a direct link between performance and consequences.

Test your performance-development system against these four elements:

Performance Leaders are committed and skilled

No career coach would contemplate running a program without a system for developing people for the future and maximizing their performance now. Similarly, no high-performance program could sustain itself without a process of disciplined performance feedback conducted by skilled Performance Leaders/Coaches. Do you have a simple, disciplined performance-development process led by skilled Performance Leaders/Coaches?

Every person has SMARTA goals linked to personal-development agreements

The last thing Business Athletes can afford is to be de-skilled. They want to participate in actively agreeing performance and development goals and plans. As always, these goals will be specific, measurable, achievable, relevant, time-framed and agreed (and summed up in our acronym SMARTA). The best performance-development systems feature clear development agreements, which the person and their manager/coach take joint responsibility for creating and monitoring. Do you coach your Business Athletes to set goals for performance and goals for personal and professional development? Do they each have a personal-development plan?

Hold frequent performance conversations to align expectations and performance

Performance Leaders hold regular performance conversations using a structure such as the One-on-One Agreement. If you're not doing this at least every quarter, you are too busy on day-to-day tasks or something else is wrong.

Show the clear link from action to reward

Top performers want to know what they have to do to get rewarded. The best systems do this by showing the clear line between action and reward. Importantly, the best systems also offer multiple rewards in the form of development opportunities and other incentives, and not just salary. When performance is not up to speed, make sure that you act quickly to coach and develop the person.

Figure 16.4 highlights the performance-development process.

Make self-coaching the goal

The aim of every Olympic coach is to develop the athlete to the point where they are capable of effectively analyzing their own performance. Without this skill, the athlete relies on the

FIGURE 16.4 The performance-development process.

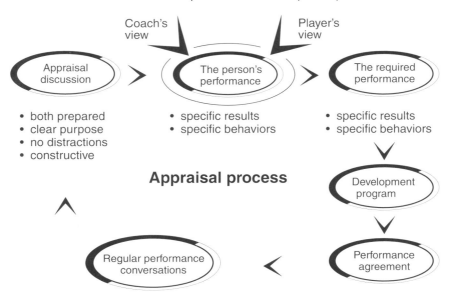

coach and cannot self-correct in the heat of competition or while traveling without the coach. Shane Gould has observed that one of the strengths of the Australian swimming program is that athletes learn to coach themselves, which means they sustain their performance level when their personal coach is not selected on the national team.[12]

Conventional business thinking says that managers appraise the performance of their people. This is too slow. Instead, why not coach your Business Athletes to seek feedback, to interpret it and to act on it themselves. Start this immediately through asking questions, rather than telling, at the next meeting you have with a team member. Use your PROBED technique and make feedback a centerpiece of your Performance Model.

USE YOUR SCOREBOARDS TO PROVIDE FEEDBACK

Manufacturing organizations display scoreboards for measures such as safety and yield on notice-boards and walkways. People see them as they move around the factory and they are usually in "dashboards" that can be quickly understood. For example, some companies use "temperature gauges" that register the current injury levels compared with previous cycles, or "speed gauges" that show speed of production cycles.

When you display feedback information publicly you increase the likelihood that your Business Athletes will act upon that information. In other words, they are more likely to Learn and Adapt, and thus increase performance. People do change behavior quickly when they are confronted by information that they perceive to threaten their survival, so using visible scoreboards is a powerful and yet underrated technique for lifting performance.

Intuitive scoreboards

Not all scoreboards are dashboards. Sometimes when you are driving your car you know that something is not quite right even though all the instruments look fine.

Performance Leaders take note when the numbers all look good but the people in the system think something is wrong. They use their listening skills to pick up on these pieces of information, while the Boss just keeps telling everyone that things are fine.

Howard Gardner's revolutionary work on intelligence reminds us that all intelligence doesn't reside just in the abilities to reason, communicate through language and do physical tasks.[13] These are the typical intelligences of business people, but there are also capabilities to navigate (spatial intelligence), to access inner feelings (intra-personal intelligence) and to relate to others (interpersonal intelligence).

Armed with this information, you can then gather data to support or refute the perceptions. Encourage people to use these talents by asking them how they feel things are going. Without devaluing data, you can get people to highlight issues such as changes in relationships with customers or shifts in market patterns that will not show up in standard scoreboards for some time.

While a total reliance on intuition might lead to chaos, as we saw in Chapter 14 there is wisdom in using your intuition and that of those around you. Many's the time a sports coach has told me that they should have ignored the data and gone with their "gut feel". You're the Performance Leader, so sometimes take the risk and back the intuition: it may have far more wisdom than the numbers.

FROM LEARNING TO ADAPTATION

There are three very practical tools or techniques that you might want to consider building into your Performance Model.

Franchise your best

Michael Gerber challenged the business world to capture the value of the franchise model or franchise prototype.[14] Many have done this in their business model but few have applied it to in-company agility.

For example, can you imagine how many businesses have people looking for solutions to problems that have already been solved in other departments? Such circumstances cry out for a franchising approach. Look around your own business. There are probably dozens of processes and systems that have been custom designed to solve a problem or capture an opportunity. How many of the training programs, record-keeping systems, sales strategies and performance-management systems are needed by others inside your own business? Instead of reinventing the wheel each time, why not franchise them?

Franchising inside the business saves a lot of extra effort, increases alignment between systems, enhances teamwork and makes great business sense. And, of course, once they are franchised, there might be commercial opportunities to sell your intellectual property outside of the organization.

One of the most powerful and value-producing projects in the High Performance Leadership Programme is the franchising project in which participants apply the franchising process to a process, system or product inside their program.

Find the right distance

Inside the corporate garden, we tend to see only the immediate landscape. Absorbed with the daily chores of weeding, watering and planting, we get little respite to look at the bigger picture. Settled in a pattern of busy activity, it is easy to forget that the original aim was to create a self-sustaining garden (enabling us to go on to other things).

Teams and organizations need distance to view the whole ecosystem and not just their little garden. What are you doing to get your teams and Business Athletes to step back from their own patch, to reflect on successes and failures, to understand their current position in the bigger system and to see what needs to be done to move further forward? Without distance, you run the risk of your program becoming just a blur of activity.

During my athletic career, the sports coaches who had the greatest impact on me were those who helped me to step back from time to time and take a look at the bigger picture. Their calmness under pressure helped everyone to deal with the challenge and to be faster to adapt. Somehow, by teaching and demonstrating the principle of distance, they seemed wiser, and we all follow wise leaders. Can you bring distance to your Performance Model?

Distance can mean facilitated review sessions, visiting other "patches", time for genuine reflection, and people sharing their knowledge of the wider world. It can also mean giving people the specific responsibility to scan at a distance, looking at both the organization and the world.

Bring discipline to your adaptations

Even the best plans will need to change in the global game. Anyone can change their plans, but the adaptively intelligent organization is quick to modify plans or change them totally, provided that it is done with discipline.

For example, the team leaders of a software-development company operating in three geographic markets hold weekly teleconferences with their leadership teams to evaluate if there is any need to modify the plans. Each regional team meets quarterly to conduct a more detailed review, and the whole company assesses progress together every six months. At this facilitated meeting, the successes and failures are analyzed and debated before adjusting the Clipboard Plans for the next six months and refining the 12-month plans. Speed is of the essence, so the Performance Model and common performance language give full value from Learn and Adapt sessions while not wasting time on a bureaucratic process.

RESISTANCE TO CHANGE IS NATURAL

In any given field, from sport to science to performing arts and business, there will be organizations that willingly adapt and some that resist. Resistance to change is a natural act of self-preservation for individuals and cultures.

It is particularly strong when people do not identify with the organization. They see themselves as separate from the organization, from management and from other individuals and teams in the organization.

This separation is often made worse by Bosses who hold onto information, issue commands and don't listen. Equally, it is lessened when Performance Leaders genuinely listen and observe in order to find ways to communicate with the audience.

"The trick," says acclaimed artistic director Robyn Archer, "is to introduce the notion of change without seeming to disenfranchise people who really love what is already there."[15]

Consider the following illustration.

A government agency introduced High Performance Leadership to its managers. One participant, Bruce, had an action-learning project to encourage a particularly change-resistant department to adapt to the "new world".

We encouraged Bruce to tune into the change resisters' needs for security and recognition. With this understanding, he framed the question facing him as, "How can I communicate to these people so they see the need to adapt or evolve?"

Bruce knew that simply telling the change resisters that customers wanted things faster was unlikely to get the response he wanted. Instead, he helped them to gather their own feedback on current response times and customer needs, and to publicize it alongside comparative information for other areas.

Bruce was amazed at the transformation. Speed of response increased almost overnight, thereby illustrating a very important principle of the psychology of adaptation.

When feedback on people's performance or related information is found by them and made public, the drive for self-preservation will push them towards adaptation. In other words, pride or embarrassment is a potent motivator. This will only work, however, if the data is plausible and public; so make sure of these two elements.

Summary

Adaptation and evolution are essential to sustaining your organization and this aspect of the Performance Model needs careful attention. Central to everything that has been covered is an almost-obsessive focus on feedback so that you know the reality of yourself and the organization. As Mike Heard of Codan observed, to stay at a genuinely world-class standard demands "savage doses of reality about oneself and one's organization".[16]

Many of the skills of Performance Leadership covered earlier, together with the other elements of the Performance Model, are relevant to Learn and Adapt; but more is needed if you are to make it a distinctive feature of your organization. It needs that dose of reality that only comes from a total commitment and openness to feedback and for Performance Leaders to act upon it.

◆ 17 ◆

Achieve Results

High-performance programs produce results. Full stop, end of story.

From Manchester United to NASA to Cirque du Soleil, results are the ultimate, tangible evidence of success.

It might sound obvious, but in high-performance programs people know what they mean by success. There are implied standards and a culture of accountability to deliver results. That does not mean that high-performance programs are obsessed with results to the exclusion of process. Rather, they only reward processes that are linked to achieving success. In other words, a rowing crew does not focus constantly on winning an Olympic medal; instead, their attention goes to the teamwork, technique and race plans needed to perform at gold-medal standard.

Accountability for results is part of the language of high performance. As Matt McGrath, Creative Director of George Patterson Bates, says of his company's approach, "All our creative ideas are merely things we use to improve a client's business. Their value solely depends on the outcome they produce for that business."[1]

The fields of business, sport, media, science, education and exploration understandably crave results and, whether they are seen as milestones or endings, results are an element in your Performance Model that is not negotiable.

A Focus on Results

There are noticeable differences in the ways that the average performer deals with Achieve Results as compared with high performers. You see this in the cauldron of the Olympics, where the best programs reveal three qualities that are built into their Performance Model. The first is an unconditional belief that only results can validate that they are high performers; the second is a commitment to very high standards or benchmarks; and the third is the way that they attach consequences to results. These are explained in the following table.

FIGURE 17.1 Differences in results-focus

Achieve Results	Average performers	High performers
Belief about results	Results are important	Results are the only true validation of success
Performance standard	Benchmark is standard for peer group (e.g. making the Olympic team) Tend to see performance in three levels — good, OK and poor	The benchmark is very high as compared with peers (e.g. making the Olympic final) See many different levels of result — excellent, very good, above expectations, expected, etc
Consequences for high performance	Differences in rewards between high and next level not as great	Very high rewards for exceptional performers as compared with the next level
Consequences for poor performance	Slower response to poor performance and acceptance of less-than-expected performance	Rapid response to less-than-expected performance: "develop or exit"

Being results-focused does not mean that winning is the only thing, in the sense that nothing else matters but the bottom line; quite the opposite. High performers put what *does* matter in the Take Aim part of their model. For example, if making a positive impact on the natural environment is important for a business, then this will be how they define success and its consequences, and what they focus on fanatically. The Body Shop is a well-known example of this, as the comments of its founder, Anita Roddick, illustrate: "The principle of environmental performance must be a major priority for every business, big or small, if for no other reason than it is impossible to make a more tangible stake in the future."[2]

The message is that when something gets into the Take Aim frame of high-performance programs, they don't just do the "talk-fests" and window dressing. Instead, the Performance Leaders hold themselves accountable for results that reflect what is important. This also reveals how the values chosen in Take Aim have a defining impact on what becomes the definition of success.

ONLY RESULTS VALIDATE HIGH PERFORMANCE

Taking your business to high levels of performance means challenging yourself and others to define success, to set up the systems that measure success and to know who will ultimately decide success. Each of these elements must be considered in your Performance Model.

Ask, ask, ask: "What does success mean?"

This is a great question, and one that is asked constantly by Performance Leaders. What does success mean to you, your team, this project, the customer, a stakeholder? Do you ask your Business Athletes that question a hundred times a month? If not, try it. You'll get people thinking. When your leaders initiate change, ask the question. When a new project starts, ask the question. When things are slowing down and getting confused, bring people back to what success means.

As I have said before, the advantage for sport, the performing arts and emergency medicine is the visibility of performance and results. This visibility makes planning and analysis more straightforward. However, inside the processes of government and major corporations it is so much more complex and difficult to be sure what we mean by success. Because of this, the best leaders are even more relentless in posing the question "What is success?"

They know that without an answer, or at least a clear point of view on this part of their Performance Model, they cannot take aim, set up or adapt.

Fuzzy goals lead to fuzzy performance. High-performance programs aren't about fuzziness.

Set up before you set off

Performance Leaders have numerous projects running throughout the organization. New customer-relationship management systems, training courses, customer-loyalty activities and new product development are all investments in the future.

Take a researcher's view of these projects in your organization and build in techniques that measure the return on investment or at least give you a guide as to the impact. For example, doing a survey of your employees before and after launching a Take Aim initiative can help you to monitor progress and judge effects on aspects such as leadership behavior, understanding of strategic priorities and career satisfaction. This data allows you to see which aspects of your communication and related processes are most effective and which need to be refined or dropped altogether.

In the speed of the global game, it is tempting to set off instead of setting up. However, time spent establishing the right measures and evaluation processes will pay off as your projects and activities unfold.

Know who defines success

Knowing what success means to you and your people is but one part of the equation. A further question is, "Who judges success?" *Karen, a divisional vice-president of retail products, and her management team believed that it had been a successful year. After acquiring and merging two new businesses, they made big progress in refining and integrating the cultures and business systems, and now feel that a platform has been built for future success. Her colleague, Brett, leads an adjoining division that handles industrial sales. His team has had a simpler year, focusing on existing brands and generating revenue in line with a tough budget by selling more products to growing customers.*

The board gathered recently for the annual review of business performance and expressed their concerns. Which part of the business caught their attention? Not surprisingly, it was Karen's division, because it had shown little growth in revenue and increases in expenditure. The board liked the cash flow that Brett's business was generating. They required the CEO to monitor Karen's performance closely and recommended that if it does not improve quickly, a change should be made.

This simple example reminds us that results are judged by people from their own perspective. Performance Leaders understand the perspective of their "judges" and they take responsibility to educate and coach those who make these judgments. Whether that means boards, staff or communities, a common understanding of success is vital.

Unfortunately, too few boards find a point of balance between the short term and the long term. Many lack the breadth of understanding of investment other than direct capital expenditure, or they bow to the short-term mindsets of market analysts. The high-performing boards are those who deal with the "and": that is, short-term results *and* long-term investment in future results.

Judging success: Questions from the coach

Consider these questions or have your coach probe your thinking:

- Who judges your results and decides your level of success?
- Where are the opportunities for you to shape their thinking?
- Is this a test of your coaching skills?

MAKE SUSTAINABILITY PART OF YOUR MODEL

We are on the cusp of a new paradigm in business but it is not clear how long it will take to fully emerge. This is the paradigm of sustainability that challenges organizations to see their results in a different way from the current model, in which share price and bottom line are king.

The criteria for defining success are shifting towards considering a net increase in value for the total system (community, industry, environment, employees) rather than just for the organization itself.

As a Performance Leader, you can expect people to challenge you in this regard and to question whether an organization can be considered to be high performing if it exploits and decimates a resource, such as a mineral or ecosystem.

We are seeing this debate being played out increasingly with ethical investors and through legislative change and community action.

My view is that any Performance Model that does not hold sustainability as a central value is ill-equipped to deal with the demands of multiple stakeholders. The negative impacts of excluding sustainability may include being unable to attract talent, a backlash from customers and an inability to obtain funding.

STANDARDS: PAR ISN'T GOOD ENOUGH

Figure 17.1 illustrated one of the key differences between the average and the high-performance program. That is, high performers set higher standards and tend to discriminate much more closely between different levels of performance. Golf provides an excellent analogy for this.

The good club golfer aims for par and typically evaluates performance on the basis that achieving better than par is excellent, near to par is good and anything else is poor.

For the PGA Tour professional, results are set higher (better than par/leading the tournament) and include much more detailed analysis of the score and data (the number of fairways and greens hit in regulation, up-and-down from around the greens, and mental errors). This data is assessed against the Tour statistics. Anything less than the expected high performance will be fully evaluated.

What we see in the professional is exactly what happens in high-performance programs. That is, they benchmark against the best and, irrespective of the score, also have a perspective on the elements of performance. They see many levels of performance ranging from the exceptional to the lower-than-expected, and all points in between.

In the world of medical retrieval, a system called TRISS (Trauma Injury Severity System) is used to benchmark the rate of deaths per thousand patients. Using a mathematical model validated in the U.S., it rates the severity of injuries and provides a benchmark for performance. The Royal Adelaide Hospital program uses TRISS to assess its performance against other services but, most importantly, says Dr Bill Griggs, it "can compare our current performance to past performance and it shows that we've got significantly better outcomes".[3]

Standards: Questions from the coach

As you review and refine your Performance Model, take a few moments to reflect on the standards that are applied to results in your organization.

* Are you using high-standard benchmarks and, if so, for what elements of performance?
* Is there a need for Performance Leaders to challenge the current standards by choosing new benchmark standards and new elements to consider?

HIGH PERFORMANCE MEANS HIGH CONSEQUENCES

Because high-performance environments are on the edge, they tend to be extreme in the consequences that they produce. In these environments, you need to be mindful that many of the rules of traditional salary and conditions are being replaced with a process more akin to the worlds of media, sport and the performing arts. In other words, you can expect exceptional rewards for exceptional performance and what might appear extremely negative consequences for less-than-exceptional performance.

Give exceptional rewards for exceptional people

The differences in rewards given to the different levels of performers in the global game are becoming extreme. For example, some chief executives are earning a base salary, performance bonuses and equity over 50-times the size of the income of average employees. In the media, too, the top radio and television stars command much more than studio executives. In sport, the best basketballers are on payments that are many times greater than those of their team mates.

Many people argue that these examples point to inequities and there are cases that support their point, particularly where corporate leaders receive huge payouts for what has clearly been substandard performance. Nevertheless, as a Performance Leader, you must deal with an environment that does reward the high performers exceptionally well, because if you don't you'll find yourself unable to find and keep talent.

You can only give exceptional rewards if you know what you mean by exceptional performance and you know what constitutes a reward.

Reflection: What does exceptional performance mean in your organization? In what areas do you need exceptional performance?

Figure 17.2 highlights the why, the what, the how and the who of rewards. Some guidelines for deciding rewards are explained in the next segment.

FIGURE 17.2   Exceptional rewards

Why	What	How	Who
To create a Performance Culture and to find and keep talent	Reward those who add exceptional value and/or are rare and important	Individualize the rewards to meet the needs of the person	Anyone, anywhere in the hierarchy: this is about value, not position

A few guidelines on rewards

- **Reward results**: Exceptional performance must always be linked to results, because when it isn't you get the sort of gold rush that happened in the dot-com bonanza. For example, in the media you will only be treated as a star if you produce a product that is commercially attractive to media outlets and sponsors.

- **Accept scarcity:** Some people are a commodity and some are not. For example, if you have an expertise in commercializing biotechnology, you are less of a commodity than if you just have experience in accounting. This is no different from in Formula One, where lots of guys can drive fast but only a few can put together the commercial package of sponsors that fund their chance at a drive. Drivers are a commodity; drivers with access to money are a special product. This is the global game.

- **Reward the future:** Too many bonus schemes for senior executives reward the short-term mentality, and actually provide the incentive for people to destroy future value to get the best result now. We all know of CEOs who walked away with great bonuses for stripping millions of dollars of value from the culture of an organization just to please the analysts who drive the direction of the share price. Make your bonuses payable in installments based on future earnings and use them as a retention tool, as Glaxo-SmithKline has done with the deferred bonus packages for its CEO and other senior executives. Remember, too, to have the board (not senior management) engage the remuneration consultant.

- **Individualize the rewards**: The best reward systems are those that include a variety of rewards (monetary, development, services, status) and are individualized to suit the needs of the people involved. Many management-designed incentive schemes are almost guaranteed to fail. Those in which people are involved in negotiations about performance levels and rewards are a better option.

Poor performance has direct consequences

Can you imagine an Olympic coach sitting idly by while an athlete continues to under-perform at training and in competition? Not likely, because Performance Leaders intervene quickly when performance is not up to standard.

The response depends on the context but it is always fast — fast to analyze the cause of the problem, fast to agree a solution and fast to implement that solution.

Reflection: What are the consequences of poor performance in your organization?

Here are a few guidelines for you to follow:

- **Act quickly**: Average organizations are slow to deal with performance problems because it is hard work. Instill in your people an expectation that poor performance will be addressed immediately, and give them the coaching skills needed to handle the sensitive issues. If you are slow in this area, get your coach to work with/on you.

- **Make development the first consequence**: Go quickly into Development Coaching when people fall short. Agree the development strategy, how it is going to be measured and the expectations. Use your One-on-One Agreement to structure the arrangements.
- **Be consistent**: Don't treat everyone exactly the same but stay consistent to the organization's values. For example, dealing respectfully with people through a termination or redundancy can be an opportunity to live and demonstrate the value of respect. Sports coaches are always cutting people from their programs and it never gets easier, but the ones who do it with humanity are the ones whose athletes dig deeper next time the coach is under pressure.
- **Resolve it**: There is a school of thought that suggests that we should give people a reasonable amount of time to correct deficiencies in performance. The toughness of high-performance environments now means that customers don't give you a third chance; so Performance Leaders only give people with very high potential (or special circumstances) more than two opportunities to get it right.

FIGURE 17.3 Summary of guidelines for consequences

Exceptional performance	Poor performance
Reward results or processes that lead to results	Act quickly to address the issue
Accept that scarcity raises the price	Make development the first consequence
Reward the future, not just the short-term focus	Be consistent with the organization's values
Individualize the rewards	Resolve it without third chances

CREATE THE CULTURE OF SUCCESS

The way that you structure the Achieve Results element of your Performance Model will have a significant effect on the culture that you create. Consider the following items as issues to include as part of the philosophy of your model.

Make success visible and celebrate it

When the Australian cricket team — the current World Champions — win a match, they gather together to sing a team song. Only one player is responsible for leading the singing, and this is a responsibility that is passed on to another by that player only when he leaves the team. The song is a celebration ritual that marks success and it has become a great source of team motivation and bonding.

Performance Leaders make sure that Business Athletes and key stakeholders also see and celebrate success. Publicizing and recognizing results has the double benefit of boosting the morale of people and keeping them motivated (because of the publicity). It is also particularly important in tough times to recognize small wins because that builds an optimism about the future.

Reflection: What are the rituals of success that you have within your organization? Are you building these into the culture or is everyone too busy?

Create a language of complexity, not softness

The nature and language of conversations about business results and processes has shifted and needs to move further.

We are no longer in a finite game of fixed boundaries and roles, limited and relatively predictable competition, clear rules and minimal change. In those conditions, you could afford to leave performance conversations to the reporting cycle and to only those aspects that could be measured.

However, you are now a Performance Leader in an infinite game in which competition and cooperation coexist, boundaries are fuzzy at best and results are affected by many economic, social, political, technological and environmental variables.

You must be able to go beyond the "hard" issues of short-term financial and operational measures to engage in, and influence, conversations about "soft" issues such as leadership, culture and relationships. I suggest you start by replacing "soft" with "complex" in the language of your program. There is nothing soft or easy about changing culture, demonstrating acts of leadership or articulating a vision that inspires people to join. These are complex issues and need to have equal priority with the old favorites of cost reduction and operational efficiency. How you name those issues, and how you manage them when the pressure is on, will largely determine the nature of the culture.

Even average leaders can keep costs down and drive operational efficiencies, but it takes a far broader range of skills and capabilities to create a Performance Culture, to lift morale and to boost service standards. These are the areas where Performance Leaders are devoting an increasing amount of time to generating and fostering performance conversations. When you use 360-degree feedback and similar instruments to measure the results of these efforts, you start to create a sustainable Performance Culture.

Coach the scoreboards

Your Performance Set-up incorporates scoreboards that should include elements of the balanced scorecard and/or triple bottom line.

Of course, having a scoreboard that gives equal space to financial, customer, organizational and environmental data does not mean that they are equally important or that they will be treated as such.

The aspects that you focus on through your probing, through the content of meeting agendas and through the rewards systems will largely determine what behavior happens.

Use balanced scorecards in particularly dynamic and varied environments but adjust these for different Performance Units. For example, manufacturing areas need more emphasis on mechanistic, cost-down measures than does the research division. This does not mean ignoring people and customer measures: rather the weightings towards the mechanistic should be greater in some areas and more towards the dynamic in others.

Use the power of the short-term goal

Success does not have to be four years away. Nothing motivates better than achieving short-term goals. They pull our attention to successes that breed confidence. With confidence and focus, there are few limits to what we can do.

Often in culture-change programs, we don't get to see the big change for a long time. When a company implements a program to lift customer service and shift from being a computer hardware seller to a provider of services, it happens over a lengthy period. To keep the focus and the faith, Performance Leaders define success in meaningful ways so that people see the improvements and stay in tune with the mission.

Recognize local wins

High-performance organizations are structured into lots of Performance Units, each of which has its own local terrain. This opens the way for local wins. As a Performance Leader, make sure that you recognize the local wins. Simple things such as winning a new account, fixing a production problem and speeding up response times give you the opportunity to publicly recognize the effort.

Don't let people get ahead of themselves

The value of knowing where you are going is great, but it is easy to live in the fantasy world of the future and lose sight of what needs to be done today.

The art of performance focus is to move from an understanding of the future to a focus on the present. In Olympic competition, the successful athlete is not the one who focuses on the gold medal but, rather, the one who is absorbed in the task and the actions that will lead them to bring out their best performance. This message is hammered into Olympic athletes because it is so easy for them to start visualizing themselves on the dais and to get distracted from what needs to be done. As Olympic champion rower Mike McKay told Australia's Olympic team in pre-Games briefings, you don't get the medals for just being there; you have to go through the whole process and earn them.[4]

RESULTS MUST BE ADAPTABLE TOO

We live between order and chaos. Even small changes in the environment, such as the loss of a staff member, finding a new client or holding a meeting, can precipitate major change. The goals that you set a few months ago met all the SMARTA criteria (specific, measurable, achievable, relevant, timed and agreed) but circumstances now cause you to change.

In a changeable world where adaptation is the key to survival and growth, there will be few times when you end up with exactly what you started out to achieve. In a perfectly ordered world, Achieve Results would be a mirror of Take Aim, but the global game is not a perfect world.

New opportunities show up and expected opportunities disappear, which is why Performance Leaders are not afraid to redefine success. This creates a paradox. Success means achieving goals but you may have to shift your commitment to a different goal if conditions change.

Do you see better opportunities emerging in your field? Have you committed to a new product, invested time and effort and then decided to go with the next big trend? Leaders can drive their staff mad with this sort of change. It takes time for people to accept an aim. When you change before people get the results they feel that they deserve, this can easily give rise to bitterness and resentment.

The answer to leading this change rests with the Performance Model that you have created. If you have coached your people to see value and power in adaptation, if they truly want to be part of an agile organization and they know the real performance conditions, then there is a good chance that they will change.

Olympic coaches know that the agility of people and their preparedness to adapt is one of the great tests of leadership. It implies that trust has been built, and that will hold you in good stead in tough conditions.

SUMMARY

High performers are results-focused but not obsessed with the win-at-all-costs mentality. Rather, your challenge is to build a more sophisticated and yet practical Performance Model that deals with sustainability, that rewards exceptional performance and acts quickly to lift people who struggle. By using your scoreboards, reinforcing the importance of the complex ("soft") issues and building an enduring results-focus, you develop a lean (but not mean) organization that is better equipped for the global game.

Creating A Performance Culture

It is appropriate to finish the Performance Model by focusing on Performance Culture.

This whole book is about culture: Performance Culture. It is about you creating, leading and living in a vibrant, high-performing organization that values performance, and creates the symbols, rituals and practices needed to sustain that culture.

Of course, culture is such a notoriously vague concept that is almost as difficult to define as it is to change. The uniqueness of culture is the genetic code or DNA that pervades everything that your organization does and that is why culture must be on the "front page" for every Performance Leader.

Philip Evans and Thomas Wurster argue that in a performance environment such as the global game, where traditional organizations and hierarchies are being deconstructed, "... there remain only two things that leaders, and only leaders, can do". These, they suggest, are to create culture and make big strategic movements.[1]

Leaders do change culture. For example, the architects of the Australian sports system generated a significant cultural change and, in turn, the Strategic Leaders and Performance Coaches of each of the sports programs shifted those units towards a high-performance culture.

Most successful corporations, such as Qantas, Dell, National Australia Bank and Intel, have re-shaped and continue to sharpen their cultures to meet the new demands of speed, scale and standards. Michael Dell, chairman and CEO of Dell Computer Corporation, uses the term "hypergrowth" to describe the challenges faced by his organization in the years when it achieved a 30% growth in sales and profit. The Dell success formula of direct customer relationships was built on culture. As Michael Dell explains, "the Direct Model would not have generated hypergrowth without our people's drive for excellence and the constant focus on innovation."[2]

An awareness of the importance of culture, and the leader's role in creating and shaping it, is one of the major differences between the traditional Boss and the Performance Leader. It is also one your greatest Performance Leadership challenges.

Does creating a Performance Culture have to be that difficult?

The question that I often debate with colleagues is whether culture change has to be the highly complicated "beast" that we find in so many human-resource and business school models. Having seen many examples of Performance Leaders who genuinely reshaped the culture of organizations, I concur with the words of Melvin Goodes of Warner-Lambert Company: "Enduring cultural change is created with practical tools such as measures, rewards, and carefully structured people practices."[3]

Indeed, culture change has to be practical and relevant to the people who are involved and it has to be easy for them (not you) to implement. The latter point is core to the issue. You cannot command that people perform in new ways. No matter how directive you are as a leader, it is still up to each individual how they service the customers, how they make decisions and how they interact with each other.

Your challenge is to use the total toolkit of the Performance Leader to be, as Peter Bijur, chairman and CEO of Texaco, suggests, "a mixture of coach, preacher, therapist, cheer leader and role model".[4] Through this approach, you can influence and change behavior in ways that suit the global game.

LIFE CYCLE: IS IT TIME FOR CHANGE?

The greatest opportunities for you to change the culture of an organization usually come in the first three to nine months after your appointment. "You are only ever a new CEO once" is an important piece of advice to any new chief executive. Having said that, the global game produces a lot of new, unusual events that can be harnessed by skilled Performance Leaders to build the case for the indisputable need for change.

If you are new to your leadership role, then take the bold steps at the earliest opportunity as you start to create a new Performance Model. If not, and you see a need to transform or just reshape the Performance Culture, look first at where in the life cycle (young, developed, mature) your program currently sits and then act accordingly.

Young and fresh

If your program is relatively young (or the part that you are leading is relatively young), then the shift in culture is more likely to happen quickly and effectively (unless recruitment has been done poorly). In new operations, people are on the learning curve and are expecting to learn and adapt.

To capitalize on the newness, open people's eyes to the real performance environment through involving them in business problems, data about the culture and customers' real perceptions.

Use guided action-learning projects to coach people to build their capabilities. As they gain understanding and commitment, you can involve them in building a better Performance Model using the stages that are outlined in this chapter and throughout the book.

Developed and settled

If your organization has been in existence for quite some time, and is relatively settled in its systems and people practices, then culture change is more likely to be achieved through specific activities such as:

- defining a new, or clearer, mission
- setting challenging and specific goals with deadlines

- using new scoreboards to measure things that address some of the assumptions and other cultural icons (for example, speed of response)
- building an obsession for feedback around the scoreboards
- introducing new people and technologies.

To change the culture in developed teams and organizations requires a "show me, don't tell me" approach, which makes scoreboards, feedback and a strong results-focus essential.

A powerful illustration of the "show me, don't tell me" approach is that taken by the RAH retrieval unit. During training and continuing education programs, doctors and other trainees are placed in a car wreck and then cut free. They experience what it is like to be trapped, while metal is torn apart right next to them. They get the "customer's view" and tell other colleagues (who are helping to rescue them) what it is like. As Dr Bill Griggs reports, they all describe it as being "very scary. You felt you couldn't see, you were strapped in, [with] crunching going on next to you and people chopping doors."[5]

Mature and declining

If your organization is highly mature and declining (as is often the case when a new leader takes over), then it is time to really:

- infuse new talent in leadership roles
- confront and challenge many of the operational myths and assumptions (for example, "only sales deals directly with customers", "this is a product-driven business", "innovation comes from R&D")
- destroy things that are not central, in order to create a sense of rebirth (for example, new structure, office layout, internal service arrangements)
- focus on a core value and specific measurable results.

The successful turnaround time for mature organizations tends to be measured in years, not months. So, while major turnarounds might be a seductive way to move, unless you can build a completely new program from scratch and not suffer the difficulties of destruction, the decision to turn the culture around completely is one not to be taken lightly. (Remember the indisputable need for change. If you've got that in everyone's head then you are on a potential winner!)

IMPLEMENTING THE PERFORMANCE MODEL

High-Performance Leadership is about practical, on-the-ground strategies that you can use to build and sustain a Performance Culture. The Performance Model gives you the framework or template, and the coaching practices of the Performance Leader are exactly those that are so important in engaging people in the possibilities of higher performance.

Accordingly, what follows is a step-by-step walk through the Performance Model, with clear explanations of the essential and the discretionary elements. These are explained in each of the seven aspects of the model and the essential elements are then summarized at the end.

Remember the zone — aim for flow

You will recall that we developed the Performance Model by reviewing the major triggers to the performance zone and grouping them into seven elements. As you now reflect on how to generate a performance culture, keep in mind those things that trigger your zone in each of the seven elements. Chances are that they give a strong hint of things that you can do as a Performance Leader to create the environment in which people are in the zone more often than not. And that is a Performance Culture!

TAKE AIM

Make sure that everyone knows what you mean by performance. Start with the common language. Define your terms. Use the 10.10 Model or the Everest-scape (Chapter 12) to explain it in ways that work for the people in your program.

Apply the discipline of the Clipboard Plan to every Performance Unit, no matter how small or short-lived. Even in the toughest of situations, it is essential that you coach every unit to define their own unique mission and to set and publish bold, aggressive goals. (Use a skilled facilitator if possible.)

Be obsessive and relentless about creating a direct line from Take Aim to Achieve Results. Make people accountable and excited about their goals so they will know whether they are winning. Success breeds success, even in chaotic, negative environments.

Publish your Clipboard Plans so that each unit leader can see how your area fits into the overall picture. Generate a culture in which people talk about performance and know what it means for every team/unit in which they perform.

Culture is about human values

It is possible to create high-performance programs without a focus on the human values and behaviors, such as trust, respect and teamwork, but these ultimately break down under extreme and prolonged pressure. When the mission and goals are lost or clouded in uncertainty, you need something to hold things together. For the SAS, the values and behaviors that perform this function are mutual respect; clear, common purpose; and detailed briefings.

The values that you and other leaders display through your actions under pressure are what will define the culture in the months and years ahead. Values extend beyond goals in their reach and power.

Above all else, the most important value that I have seen in pressure situations is trust. In high-trust organizations and teams, people have confidence in each other to do what is needed to create success and to minimize setbacks.

Margaret Hansford, CEO of FPA Health, led a significant cultural transformation and describes a key implementation issue as having "staff who feel they're treated fairly ... [with] trust and procedural transparency and consistency".[6]

It is too late to generate trust when the pressure is on. You do it earlier through demonstrating your competency in building the foundations of performance (Clipboards, common language), respectfully involving people in determining the direction (their unique mission and goals) and maintaining dialogue.

When you create meaningful, shared values, define a compelling mission and generate focus through clear goals, you move towards a Performance Culture. Equally, if you ignore the importance of values and fail to create a Take Aim for each Performance Unit,

FIGURE 18.1 How leaders build trust

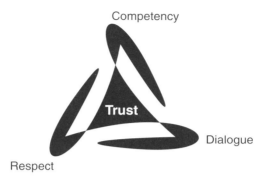

Competency

Trust

Dialogue

Respect

you limit the chances of a creating such a culture.

Be alert to opportunities to demonstrate the values, and reinforce them when you see the behaviors in others. Equally, when you see breaches, confront them because these are the coachable moments.

Essential elements

Of course, everything is important but you can't make everything world class (and don't need to). Performance Leaders have to make a choice when building their Performance Model to make particular elements a real high-performance feature. Figure 18.2 highlights three essential elements that Performance Leaders should make a high-performance feature in the Take Aim part of their Performance Model. These are: mission, goals and shared human values.

FIGURE 18.2 The essential Take Aim elements in the Performance Model

Essential elements	How to implement	Impact on Performance Culture
Mission	Coach every unit to define its unique mission	Sense of purpose ensures each unit adds value
Goals	Ensure that Clipboard Plans record specific, challenging and published goals for every unit	Creates a performance focus, gives direction and energy
Shared human values	Engage your people in dialogue about the essential shared values	Creates certainty and enhances agility

SCAN: KNOW THE CONDITIONS

Make sure that your people understand the conditions of the global game and how they can make a difference for their customers, owners or community. This is essential so they can make informed decisions in their daily work, and recognize the need for continual adaptation and shaping.

When you direct people's attention outwards and away from themselves and their immediate environment, you actually decrease resistance to change, and create a greater sense of "we", rather than "me". For example, when manufacturing teams get closer to the customer, they understand why sales staff say that speed is important to meeting customers' demands and beating a competitor. Through a combination of direct experience and information (for example, of measures covering delivery in full, on time and to specification), people get a much better perspective on the world in which they are performing.

Performance Cultures accept that adaptation is a part of self-preservation, whereas non-performance cultures typically resist change and try to preserve themselves in their current state. This is a dangerous strategy but, unfortunately, one that too many opportunistic politicians capitalize on for their own benefit.

FIGURE 18.3 Two key differences in culture

Performance Culture	Non-performance culture
"We"	"Me"
Change to survive and prosper	Avoid change for self-preservation

When Roger Bannister ran the first sub-four-minute mile, he started a virtual flood of runners who emulated his feat. The so-called Bannister effect can be used to foster Performance Cultures. Just as runners saw what was possible from Bannister's effort, so you can take your Business Athletes to a new level by showing how organizations in other industries are breaking through barriers that are still a part of your culture.

Prepared for all conditions

You can get by without scanning in the short-term, but in changeable conditions you need all hands on deck to navigate through the storms that characterize the global game.

As we discussed in Chapter 13, the Sydney-to-Hobart Yacht Race tragedy highlighted the need to prepare for extreme conditions; to anticipate changes in conditions, to respond quickly and correctly to them and to communicate these changes to others.

Do your Scan coaching on the job by exposing people to data on customers, competitors and markets, implementing short-term SWOTs, and getting them actively involved in scouting for important information. And be careful not to fall into the typical Boss pattern and turn your team into passive spectators by not actively engaging in scanning.

An essential element in this part of the Performance Model is highlighted in Figure 18.4.

FIGURE 18.4 Essential Scan: Know the Conditions element in the Performance Model

Essential element	How to implement	Impact on Performance Culture
Scanning process	Use regular SWOT reports, allocate scanning responsibilities to all team members	Anticipate changes in conditions, rapid response and increased potential to shape the environment

Performance Set-up

Of the eight elements of Performance Set-up covered in Chapter 14, the two most essential are Design for Fitness and Scoreboards. While each of the other elements needs attention, most Performance Leaders focus primarily on getting the right design and scoreboards.

Can you pass the "instant team" test?

While there are many different organization designs, the key is to create a design that fits the demands of the task. In most cases, this is a design based on teamwork as the organizing principle.

Terms such as "flocking", "atomized" and "modular" all describe the characteristic of forming small groups or teams to tackle issues. An excellent example of this is the Olympic swimming team in which swimmers are selected for relays just hours before the event. This is a great test of the Performance Culture that has been created and is a strength of the Australian team, in which the swimmers run their own meetings, don't have an individual captain and work to a collective mission.

As former Australian champion Nicole Stevenson reports, "The relays are a big part of it; our relays are selected with only 24-hours' notice, so you go very quickly from swimming just for yourself, with everyone else sitting in the stands, to swimming for three other people in a relay. Suddenly, you're an instant team and you have to gel, have to make sure that you're working successfully as a group."[7]

By creating a Performance Model that everyone understands and by building trust in that model and each other, you are also working towards getting people to gel.

Use the One-on-One Agreement with teams/units

The One-on-One Agreement described in Chapter 11 offers an ideal process in team-oriented environments where you also want individual accountability.

- Begin by presenting your direction in a clear and succinct manner. Highlight what is important to you in terms of vision, values and priorities, state your expectations of the team and give a brief overview of your commitment to the team.
- Have the team members work either collectively or, if it's a large team, in sub-groups, to reflect on your comments and to consider what the implications are for them.
- When they've spent sufficient time considering those implications, have them identify, from a team point of view, what is important to them, their expectations of you and their commitment.
- Ask each individual to present to the team and to you what is important to them, their expectations and commitment.

One of the great advantages of this process is that it gives you a chance to check that the mission is clearly understood, to ensure that people see the part that they can play and to gauge their commitment. The Agreement is also useful when establishing the fundamentals between strategic alliance partners.

Which scoreboards reflect the main game?

You have many choices to make in the scoreboards that you use. Some are mandatory, such as financial indicators, while others depend on the nature of your operations and the culture that you want to create. The table below highlights some of the issues with scoreboards that contain financial, operational, people and customer data. Select the scoreboards that best suit the style of culture that you are seeking and then actively coach around the data, providing specific feedback to your people.

FIGURE 18.5 Scoreboard options and impact on culture

Score-board element	Characteristics	Positive impact on culture	Potential concerns
Financial	Clear, specific measures of items such as profitability, margin, return on assets, cost of sale	Clear results-focus, less ambiguity than with other measures, relevant to owners and executive	Can create excessive short-term focus, which is negative in longer term
Operat-ional	Data on operations processes such as yield, speed of response, work in progress	Better understanding of the business; more accurate decisions	Can become overly focused on process and not responsive
People	Quantitative and qualitative data such as staff turnover, climate/morale, leadership and teamwork	Brings HR issues to leaders' attention: can be used to measure performance of leader and team	Not given same weight as other data: can become "feel-good" instead of performance-focused
Customer	Varied quality ranging from survey, direct data (e.g. complaints) and anecdotal	Focuses people outwards, links to the "real world", breaks down resistance to change	Inaccurate data; not used to coach people or to increase understanding; sometimes is negative i.e. complaints

Essential elements

The following table highlights two essential Performance Set-up elements that are part of creating a Performance Culture. Other elements should be included at your discretion.

FIGURE 18.6 Essential Performance Set-up elements in the Performance Model

Essential elements	How to implement	Impact on Performance Culture
Designed for Fitness	Design for agility; modular; create teamwork as an organizing principle by using tools such as Clipboard Plans and Fast Teams	Agility, people enjoy working in fast teams, fit for purpose
Scoreboards	Establish financial and other scoreboards: coach actively around the data	Creates a performance focus and a culture of feedback, shows success

MINDSET/CULTURE

One of my enduring memories of the 1988 Seoul Olympics was the stark difference between the way that the leading athletes in individual sports prepared for competition and the methods of those in the majority of team sports. In both mindset and behavior, the individual athletes were more professional and better prepared for the challenges of the ultimate global sporting contest. It seemed that the athletes and coaches in individual sports had evolved to a higher psychological level, leaving the team players and their coaches some years behind.

This experience made me curious about three things. What was the nature of these differences? What conditions/forces had led to the differences? How had the athletes and their coaches evolved to this higher level?

From discussions with colleagues and coaches and from my own observations, a profile started to emerge that described two distinct cultures. In the individual sports, there was a "culture of the athlete", while in the team sports there existed a less-rigorous "culture of the player". The following table highlights some of the characteristics of these two cultures and gives an insight into the key differences.

FIGURE 18.7 Differences in culture: player/athlete

Culture of the player	Culture of the athlete
Individual performance is concealed	Individual accountability — there's nowhere to hide
Autocratic coaching style — "tell" leadership	Multiple coaches with athlete
Gross performance measures — results, score and basic performance measures	Precise performance measures
Predictable training routines, team structures and roles	Constantly challenging the set-up — flexibility and agility in roles and structure
Prepares mainly for technical (sporting) skills and some physical training	Holistic preparation — technical, physical, psychological
Complacency about standards — slow improvement, usually sparked by competitors	Relentless improvement — always seeking breakthroughs
Play inside unwritten rules — assumptions	Push boundaries/rules — challenge and discard assumptions

On closer investigation there seemed to be three interlinked reasons for the differences in culture:

- You can't hide in an individual sport. The time, distance or height is a performance fact and one that can be easily benchmarked against others.
- Only one person wins an individual gold medal and that means that the level of competition amongst individual athletes was much higher than within teams (*and* more nations competed in many of those events).
- Coaches of athletes wanted an edge so they brought in the sports scientists and technologists with their heart-rate monitors, psychological-skills training, biomechanical assessment (video analysis of technique) and advanced equipment design (e.g. cycles, carbon-fiber paddles). Coaches of "the players" relied on their own experiences, intuition and some very basic strategies and statistics.

Over the next two Olympiads (Barcelona and Atlanta), the Performance Leaders of the leading teams embraced the "culture of the athlete" by focusing on accountability of individuals for their performance as an athlete within a team. Soon the heart-rate monitors, video analysis, benchmarking against competitors and innovative strategies and tactics re-shaped the rules of the game. Add to that the inflow of money to the professional and Olympic sports and you have the perfect incubator for world-class performance.

At the Sydney Olympics there was little difference between the cultures of individual and team sports, and clearly both had adopted the culture of the athlete.

Have you got athletes or players?

As we now shift our attention to the business game of the 21st century, take a few moments to reflect on the following two questions. Are you a player or an athlete? Does your business have a "culture of the athlete"?

When facilitating High Performance Leadership Programmes, I use expanded versions of Figure 18.7 to encourage Performance Leaders and teams to challenge themselves and to shape their thinking about practices that can generate a Performance Culture. During the review of progress from "player" to "athlete", Performance Leaders often spot opportunities to make performance breakthroughs.

To create a winning culture, give responsibility

When sporting teams rely too heavily on a champion player, you very quickly notice a drop in the initiative and motivation of the rest of the group. Players rely on the person to make the big plays.

Most importantly, players lose a connection between what they do and the results. They have not been given responsibility for being a part of the result and this diminishes leadership and performance. In a highly competitive environment this is a dangerous practice and one that separates the "player culture" from the "athlete culture".

Look for every way possible to give your Business Athletes responsibility that is clearly connected to the overall result. At the very senior level, this also means making sure that you do not put too much weight on the sales function over manufacturing, or front office over back office, or supply over corporate services. When you put yourself into a situation where some roles are seen as more important than others, you diminish the chances of success.

Essential element

The following table highlights the essential Mindset/Culture element that is part of creating a Performance Culture. Include others at your discretion.

FIGURE 18.8 Essential Mindset/Culture element in the Performance Model

Essential elements	How to implement	Impact on Performance Culture
Performance Leadership	Performance Leaders implement a Performance Model using the skills of Strategic Leadership, Performance Coaching and Development Coaching	Creates the common language and Performance Model needed

PERFORM

In the organization of today it is easy to get lost in activity, and to mistake all that action for a Performance Culture. The top field and court sports teams, the best surgery teams, the best cockpit teams all have one thing in common: high performance through efficient activity. Reflect for a moment: is the most frenetic person in your office really the highest performer? The best performers maintain that sense of active calmness, doing the most important things really well.

Execution: Under pressure, the basics beat the special

Early in my time in the performance psychology field I learned that the high performers usually don't do really special things:

they execute the basics reliably under all conditions. "Basics" beat "special" time and time again. High performers, as exemplified in Stuart Ellis's accounts of the SAS, are precise in their preparation and execution. They do the right things at the right time. Performance Cultures emphasize getting the basics and timing right, and they therefore drill the basics so that strategy execution becomes a distinctive feature of their culture.

It might sound boring, but only those things that are learned to the level of reflex are really reliable under pressure. Neil Flett, of Rogen International and coach to the team that pitched for and won the bid for the 2000 Olympic Games, sums up the strategy of the winners: "The winning pitch team goes further than any other and focuses on the smallest details, fine-tuning again until it is as good as it can be in the time available."[8]

Performance Leaders build a competitive advantage around executing strategy by devising a winning strategy, communicating that strategy and leading the execution.

Keep the performance themes at front of mind

Make sure that everyone on your team knows which actions are most important by connecting your performance themes to day-to-day actions.

For example, the Australian Olympic women's basketball team (the Opals) identified assertiveness as a core performance theme.[9] The coach and athletes believed that it was particularly important to be strong and physical in international competition. The themes were decided by the team, owned by the team and used constantly to make decisions, such as how to react when a player was hit unfairly by an opponent. The performance themes defined the culture for the Opals.

Teams/units, divisions and total organizations perform better when their attention and actions are driven by one or more unifying performance themes, such as Philips Australia's theme to be a "a truly solutions-driven company".[10]

Your performance themes give a point of focus and you can use them to shape the culture by bringing your vision to life, guiding the process of organization change and defining your leadership models and behaviors.

Reflection: What are the performance themes that will define your culture?

Foster a culture of speed

Organizational cultures have more impact on the speed of response than any technology. When Performance Leaders and all members of their program are passionate and committed to responsiveness, agility and rapid execution, they design and run a Performance Model that captures the best opportunities and they re-group quickly when mishaps occur.

For example, if you genuinely want a more agile and responsive culture, then it begins with your commitment to building that model. Tools and practices such as Clipboard Plans, Scoreboards, feedback and miniature presentations must be coached into the program. This requires working in partnership with your people to find the best approaches.

Coach your teams and individuals to make 80/20 judgments by developing competency in risk management, showing confidence in people's judgment and driving out the potentially deadly paralysis-by-analysis. And be mindful that pushing people to make 80/20 judgments instills accountability and often leads to better decisions because people know that what they decide is going to be implemented immediately.

Designed for the zone

People are more likely to enter their zone when they do things that are stimulating and enjoyable. That means putting them in that zone on the edge of chaos, where the challenge of the performance and their own perceived abilities are in line.

Performance Leaders stretch people to that edge and bring out their best, while Bosses act and argue for the comfort of the status quo. This creates a totally different culture because Bosses then punish those who go over the edge, while Performance Leaders expect some setbacks.

The compelling argument again falls on the side of Performance Leaders/Coaches who work with people to create the Performance Culture, rather than of Bosses who restrict it.

Reflection: Are ideas about job redesign coming from your staff on a very regular basis, or is it time to probe, challenge and question? Maybe start with your own job because a big key performance indicator for Performance Leaders is performance ideas originating from the teams that are implemented and save or earn dollars. How's your Scoreboard looking?

Build in some fun

Be wary that your Performance Culture does not become one of those super-serious, narrow cultures where only performance matters. Equally important is enjoyment.

Louise Sauvage works with many emerging athletes who are learning to perform in national and international competition. She knows from personal experience that a Performance Culture is only sustainable when people want to be a part of it, and that means having what she simply calls a "happy environment".[11] That positive environment helps the athletes to do the hard work needed to capitalize on their talent and to work through the inevitable tough times.

If I were to walk around your organization, would it look like people were having fun or has it all become a bit serious? One of the strategies used by Australian teams at the Olympics was to hold entertainment evenings and barbecues at which athletes could unwind. The corporate equivalents are theme days (for example, where everyone wears beach clothes), pizza lunches and visits to cool places.

"Perform" is an essential part of the Performance Model but be careful you don't overdo it and turn it into a chore.

Use defensive situations to develop teamwork

Teamwork is an organizing principle in the High-Performance Leadership Model.

The Chicago Bulls and LA Lakers basketball coaching legend Phil Jackson talks about using defensive situations to build teamwork.[12]

You can apply the same principle by putting people in situations where they have no alternative but to work together to achieve a major imperative. This can be a real situation (a business crisis, for example) or one that you engineer, such as a potential disaster scenario. Crises build teamwork because they provide a:

- tight timeframe (deadline)
- very visible endgame (win or lose)
- lot of responsibility on individuals
- full-time focus by the key players.

The Fast Teams that are needed to execute the strategy and implement change can be developed through using "crisis situation" training in the same fashion as the SAS uses rigorous physical training to strengthen character and build performance toughness.

The following table highlights the essential Perform element that is part of creating a high-performance culture.

FIGURE 18.9   Essential Perform element in the Performance Model

Essential element	How to implement	Impact on Performance Culture
Strategy execution	Make fast strategy execution a performance theme, focus on a clearly understood mission, use Fast Teams, keep score of speed (e.g. responsiveness)	Generates a productive urgency, produces "wins" that build confidence

LEARN AND ADAPT

Performance Cultures cannot exist without learning and improvement. Conditions change too much for anyone to be able to map out the total project or activity from the beginning and then follow the bouncing ball without changing anything. Fast organizations such as Virgin and Cisco learn in the field and use the learning to lift for the future.

Your organization will be called upon to adapt and, at times, perhaps to evolve into a new form. Therefore, building a capability for learning and adaptation is arguably one of your most critical leadership roles. The adaptive intelligence of your organization might not be as measurable as the current cash flow but it is as important as any aspect of your Performance Model.

Create a culture of feedback

A primary goal of High-Performance Leadership is to create a culture of feedback, in which high-performance units hungrily seek information that guides them to improve their performance.

This means putting yourself in the middle of feedback loops, training managers in how to give and receive feedback, putting in the Performance Set-up needed to provide up-to-date information and relentlessly facilitating conversations about performance and adaptation.

You will know that you have that culture when your performance-management system becomes irrelevant because people and teams take personal responsibility for finding and acting on the feedback that they receive.

Perhaps you currently have a culture that finds feedback threatening. If so, make feedback your number-one performance theme and invest all the time and effort available. It will reap benefits many times over.

You will also gain personally as people grow in confidence from learning that feedback strengthens. This is a wonderful experience and clear evidence of the power of leaders to shape the culture of an organization.

In-the-game coaching

Coaches invest a lot of time helping athletes to make correct decisions. Ultimately, the success of an athlete is assured if the coach has embedded in them a way of making decisions that will work under pressure. This is no different from what Performance Leaders must do to create high-performance business programs.

You want your people to make the right decisions when faced with any of the hundreds of things that can happen in a business day. This requires a commitment to relentless debriefing of performance and a willingness to engage in performance conversations. Building the discipline of the debrief into informal day-to-day activities and into the formal performance cycles is one of the most powerful ways to shape the culture.

Porous and high performing

No matter what league you are playing in, if you want to be the champions of that league your Business Athletes have to get better, your Performance Leaders have to get better and every part of your system and process will have to get better as the environment around you changes. When organizations lose that hunger for improvement, they fall far off the championship pace and it is very hard to get back again.

Cultures that capture the essence of continuous improvement are porous and adaptively intelligent. Unlike the traditional hierarchy, there are interconnections and relationships that allow information to flow in all directions. Some of the best Performance Leadership strategies to open up organizations include large-group design sessions, detailed performance debriefing and using the coachable moments to instill new beliefs and attitudes.

High performers join high performers

Talented people will only join your outfit if you can provide them with personal and professional growth. This is essential for their careers and they also know that one of their most important triggers for reaching the zone is the sense that they are growing and developing. Performance Leaders who create a learning environment (that incorporates providing support) can push people right to the edge of their comfort zone and beyond, and they like it! Bosses push people out of their comfort zone (but don't support them) and sooner or later they leave because they feel that they're being used.

There is no doubt that when people are supported while they are being pushed out of their comfort zone, they genuinely exceed their own expectations for performance.

Identify people who want to grow and take responsibility for themselves and for the broader program. Spend time with these emerging leaders to coach, support and motivate them to fulfill their potential. Be mindful of times when they are stagnant or stifled in what they are doing, and when they're frustrated and unable to exert leadership. If Business Athletes find themselves not growing and developing, you are in danger of losing them. Make the time to work one-on-one with them to debrief their performance, to talk about their development and make sure they understand your unrelenting commitment to build them as Performance Leaders.

One of the hallmarks of great Performance Leaders is that they develop their people into being leaders/coaches of other programs. Do you have a track record of developing leaders?

Essential element

The following table highlights the essential Learn and Adapt element that is part of creating a Performance Culture.

FIGURE 18.10 Essential Learn and Adapt element in the Performance Model

Essential element	How to implement	Impact on Performance Culture
Feedback	Embed measures in the Performance Set-up and use techniques of debriefing and Development Coaching	Builds on strengths, captures learning, stimulates adaptation, improves results at all levels

ACHIEVE RESULTS

Creating a results-focus element is an essential ingredient in your Performance Model. High performers are unquestionably results-focused and they build this into the culture by setting and maintaining very high performance standards and linking consequences directly to performance.

Begin the results-focus at the Take Aim stage by creating a clear mission and goals for every unit and maintain that focus in every aspect of your Performance Model. For example, benchmark against others' results, measure outcomes and set meeting agendas that are focused on outcomes.

Constantly check that everyone can answer the question, "What does success mean?", and make sure that you know who is going to judge your success. Engage these people in performance conversations to agree expectations, and then manage those expectations.

Don't let yourself get into a situation where you are just hoping that your standards are the same as those who will judge your success. Know also that with multiple stakeholders it is unlikely that you can meet all their needs; hence, managing expectations is as important as delivering to those expectations.

While average cultures have fuzzy goals and linkages, in the Performance Culture every unit is connected to results (but without becoming narrowly obsessed with them). Instead, Performance Leaders reward processes that lead to results. They use balanced scoreboards to keep a breadth of focus on more than just short financial measures. They establish credibility through short-term results and create future success through investment in people, relationships and technologies.

Success breeds success

In successful organizations, people get used to winning. They expect to succeed and they know what needs to be done to achieve success. This creates a momentum that can be sensed immediately by every new person who joins the organization. Conversations are based on the expectation that the company is aiming for the summit, and there is a powerful confidence that this will be achieved.

Create the expectation of success by engineering and highlighting small wins that you reinforce and build on. When people see success, it causes them to lift. Start with small wins and you are on track to creating a culture in which success breeds more success.

High standards and consequences

The benchmarks that you use to measure and assess performance will tell a lot about the culture that you create. Performance Leaders are sensitive to not overstretching their people but also recognize that only a relentless focus on performance standards will deliver the results they want.

Reflect on your performance themes and make these the highest of standards. For example, if your theme is responsiveness to customers, then build high measures into your program around elements such as speed of response and customer satisfaction with that responsiveness.

Reward the exceptional performers with exceptional rewards. Recognize and reward your performers and move quickly to develop poor performers. Be aware that the way you deal with subpar performance will go a long way to determining the style of culture that you create.

Essential elements

The following table highlights the essential Achieve Results elements that are part of creating a Performance Culture.

FIGURE 18.11   Essential Achieve Results elements in the Performance Model

Essential elements	How to implement	Impact on Performance Culture
Results-focus	Set high standards, build evaluation processes in to all activities, and benchmark results	Challenges people to relate what they do to the return on investment: increases effectiveness and efficiency
Consequences	Reward exceptional performance, and act quickly on less-than-acceptable performance	Attracts and keeps exceptional performers and reduces the impact of poor performers on business performance

IMPLEMENTATION SUMMARY

During this chapter, we have looked at each of the seven elements of the Performance Model and at those aspects that are essential to your model. From experience of coaching Performance Leaders to build models in the Olympics, business and other settings, I believe that these essential elements should be considered as "not negotiable". They are summarized in Figure 18.12.

FIGURE 18.12 Summary of essential elements in the Performance Model

Essential elements	How to implement	Impact on Performance Culture
Mission	Coach every unit to define their unique mission	Sense of purpose, ensures each unit adds value
Goals	Ensure that Clipboard Plans record specific, challenging and published goals for every unit	Creates a performance focus, gives direction and energy
Shared Human Values	Engage your people in dialogue about the essential, shared values	Creates certainty and enhances agility
Scanning Process	Use regular SWOT reports; allocate scanning responsibilities to all team members	Anticipate changes in conditions, rapid response and increased potential to shape the environment
Designed for Fitness	Design for agility; modular; create teamwork as an organizing principle by using tools such as Clipboard Plans and Fast Teams	Agility, people enjoy working in Fast Teams, fit for purpose
Scoreboards	Establish financial and other scoreboards: coach actively around the data	Creates a performance focus and a culture of feedback; shows success
Performance Leadership	Performance Leaders implement a Performance Model using the skills of Strategic Leadership, Performance Coaching and Development Coaching	Creates the common language and Performance Model needed in a High-Performance Culture

FIGURE 18.12 (cont'd)

Essential elements	How to implement	Impact on Performance Culture
Strategy Execution	Make fast strategy execution a performance theme; focus on a clearly understood mission; use Fast Teams; keep score of speed (e.g. responsiveness)	Generates a productive urgency; produces "wins" that build confidence
Feedback	Embed measures in the Performance Set-up and use techniques of debriefing and Development Coaching	Builds on strengths, captures learning, stimulates adaptation, improves results at all levels
Results-focus	Set high standards, build evaluation processes into all activities, and benchmark results	Challenges people to relate what they do to the return on investment: increases effectiveness and efficiency
Consequences	Reward exceptional performance, and act quickly on less-than-acceptable performance	Attracts and keeps exceptional performers and reduces the impact of poor performers on business performance

There are many other aspects that you will want to build into your Performance Model and make a distinctive feature of your program. The approach I recommend is to decide on a small number of features (over and above the "not negotiables" or sub-sets of those) that you believe to be essential to performance in your field. For example, in the SAS it is detailed briefings; in medical retrieval, it is co-ordination; and in the Olympic program, it is world-class benchmarking.

Get the "not-negotiables" in place and then add to other elements as you create a vibrant Performance Model for creating, leading and living in a high-performance world.

AFTERWORD

As this book draws to a close, it is time to reflect one final time on the fundamental principles that underpin High-Performance Leadership.

We began in Section One with the global game, its rapid changes in speed, scale and standards and the need for a practical Performance Leadership strategy to apply across an organization. With this in mind, we used the Australian sports system as a model to identify high-performance principles, which were then checked against practices in other high-performance programs, including businesses, special military forces, medical retrieval and an Everest expedition.

What emerged were three common elements: a recognition of the importance of Performance Leadership as a source of competitive or performance advantage; the importance of personal performance skills (the Business Athlete); and, finally, the nature of the Performance Model that is employed in each of these environments.

Throughout the book, I have tried to link these three elements together and to bring them to life through the many examples of people and organizations who are creating, leading and living in a high-performance world.

As we close, my hope is that you gain strength from the practices of the Business Athlete and use the skills of Performance Leadership to create and sustain your own high-performance program. Ideally, others in your program will share your passion for performance and for creating a Performance Culture that attracts people who come together and genuinely make a difference.

As you apply the principles of *High-Performance Leadership*, keep in mind that all of the tools, techniques and models rest with you and how you bring them to life. On this note, I think it is appropriate to finish with the words of Mahatma Gandhi:

"We must be the changes we want to see in the world."

Endnotes

CHAPTER 1

1   Bach, Richard, *Illusions: The Adventures of a Reluctant Messiah*, Dell Publishing Co, 1994.
2   Gates, Bill, *Business at the Speed of Thought*, Penguin, 1999.
3   In PricewaterhouseCoopers (PwC) Consulting Executive Survey 2002.
4   In an interview with the author, April 2002.
5   Covey, Stephen, *Principle Centred Leadership*, Fireside, 1992.
6   Kotter, John, *Leading Change*, Harvard Business School Publishing, 1996.
7   Senge, P., *The Fifth Discipline*, Doubleday, 1990.
8   Evans, P. & Wurster, T., *Harvard Business Review*, November/December, 1999.
9   Barker, Joel, *Paradigms*, The Business Library, 1992.
10 In "Value from the Center" from *Wisdom of the CEO* by Dauphinais, G.W., Means, G. & Price, C., PricewaterhouseCoopers, 2000, p.35.
11 Chistensen, Clayton, *The Innovator's Dilemma*, Harvard Business Press, 1997.
12 *Wisdom of the CEO*, op. cit., p.228.
13 Breton, Thierry, in "Marketing Reshaped by Technology" from *Wisdom of the CEO*, p.263.
14 Ruettgers, Michael, in "Disrupt or Be Disrupted" from *Wisdom of the CEO*, p.232.
15 Carse, James, *Finite and Infinite Games*, Penguin, 1987.
16 In PwC Consulting Executive Survey 2002.
17 Faludi, Susan, *Stiffed: The Betrayal of the American Man*, Harper Perennial, 2000.
18 Mitchell, Susan, *The Australian*, September 10, 1999, p.13.

CHAPTER 2

1   In PricewaterhouseCoopers (PwC) Consulting Executive Survey 2002.
2   Ibid.
3   Coates, John, *"2000 Australian Olympic Team Handbook and Media Guide"*, News Limited in association with Harper Collins Publishers, 2000, p.3.
4   In PwC Executive Survey 2002.
5   Dauphinais G.W., Means G. & Price, C., *Wisdom of the CEO*, PricewaterhouseCoopers, 2000, p.100.
6   Kelley, Tom, *The Art of Innovation*, Currency Doubleday, 2001, p.31.
7   McCall, M., Lombardo, M. & Morrison, A., *The Lessons of Experience*, Lexington, MA: Lexington Books, 1988.
8   Gordon, Harry, *"2000 Australian Olympic Team Handbook and Media Guide"*, op. cit., p.22.

9   Argus, Don, "Focusing Leadership Through Core Values", in *Straight from the CEO*, Dauphinais G.W. & Price C., PricewaterhouseCoopers, Nicholas Brealey Publishing, 1998, p.202.

10   Katzenbach, J., & Smith, D., *The Wisdom of Teams*, Harvard Business School Press, 1993.

11   In an interview with the author, March 2002.

12   In an interview with the author, April 2002.

13   Coates, op.cit.

14   In an interview with the author, March 2002.

15   Ibid.

CHAPTER 3

1   Kauffman, Stuart, *At Home in the Universe*, Oxford University Press, 1995.

2   Csikszentmihalyi, Mihaly, *Flow: The Psychology of Happiness*, Rider, 1992.

3   Unestahl, Lars Eric, *Integrated Mental Training*, SISU forlag., Stockholm, 1997.

4   In an interview with the author, March 2002.

5   Csikszentmihalyi, op.cit.

6   Bennis, Warren, "Behavior OnLine: Conversations with some of our contributors", www.behavior.net, 1997.

7   Fritz, Robert, *Creating*, Fawcett Columbine Books, 1991.

8   In an interview with the author, March 2002.

CHAPTER 4

1   Branson, Richard, *Losing my Virginity*, Random House, 1998, p.14.

2   Handy, Charles, *Beyond Certainty*, Arrow Books, 1996, p.17.

3   Green, Nick, *Winning Attitudes*, Hardie Grant Books, Australian Olympic Committee 2000, p.131.

4   Elliott, Herb, *Winning Attitudes*, op. cit., p.5.

5   Kiyoaski, Robert, *The Cashflow Quadrant*, Techpress Inc., 1998.

6   *The Next Lap*, Government of Singapore, Times Editions, 1991, p.57.

7   Thompson, Daley, in Gelman S. (Ed), *Official Olympic Souvenir Program; Games of the XXIIIrd Olympiad Los Angeles 1984*, Australian Consolidated Press, Sydney, 1984, p.71.

8   Hayhurst, Jim Snr., *The Right Mountain*, John Wiley & Sons, 1996, p.166.

9   In an interview with the author, March 2002.

10   Covey Stephen, *Seven Habits of Highly Effective People*, The Business Library, 1989.

11   In an interview with the author, March 2002.

12   In an interview with the author, March 2002.

13   "Focused in a Fuzzy World", by Al Ries and Jack Trout, in *Rethinking The Future*, Rowan Gibson (Ed), Nicholas Brealey Publishing, 1997, p.194.

14   In an interview with the author, April 2002.

CHAPTER 5

1   In an interview with the author, April 2002.

2   In PricewaterhouseCoopers (PwC) Consulting Executive Survey 2002.

3   From "Banking is 90 Percent Action, 10 Percent Strategy", in *Wisdom of the CEO*, Dauphinais G.W., Means, G, & Price, C,, PricewaterhouseCoopers, 2000, p.47.

4   In an interview with the author, March 2002.

5   In an interview with the author, April 2002.

6   In PwC Consulting Executive Survey 2002.

7   McGrath, John, *You Don't Have To Be Born Brilliant*, Hodder Books, 2000, p.17.

8   Garai, Hugh, *Managing Information, Working Smarter, Not Harder*, Gower, 1997.

CHAPTER 6

1   Handy, Charles, *Beyond Certainty*, Arrow Books, 1996, p.28.

2   Sellars, Peter, in *The Director's Voice*, Arthur Bartow (Ed,) Theatre Communications Group, 1988, p.276.

3   Biddulph, Steven, *Raising Boys*, Finch Publishing, 1998, p.62.

4   In Air Canada *Flightline*, March/April 1999.

5   In *Winning Attitudes*, Hardie Grant Books, 2000, p.9.

6   In PwC Consulting Executive Survey 2002.

CHAPTER 7

1   In discussions with the author, April 2002.

2   Markson, Max, *Show Me the Money*, Penguin Books Australia Ltd, 2000.

3   Ries, Al & Ries, Laura, *22 Immutable Laws of Branding*, Harper Business, 1998, p.28.

4   Wing, R.L., *The Art of Strategy, A New Translation of Sun Tzu's Classic, The Art of War*, Aquarian Press, 1988, p.55.

5   Peters, Tom, *The Tom Peters Seminar*, MacMillan, 1994.

6   In an interview with the author, April 2002.

CHAPTER 8

1   In an interview with the author, April 2002.
2   Quoted in PricewaterhouseCoopers Consulting Executive Survey 2002.
3   Rich, J. & Orr, L., *Networking Games*, Peacock Publications, 2001, p.19.

CHAPTER 9

1   In *The Leadership Advantage: Organizing For Complexity*, Butterworth-Heinemann, 1996.
2   In PwC Consulting Executive Survey 2002.
3   Ibid.
4   *CFO, Architect of the Corporation's Future*, PricewaterhouseCoopers Financial and Cost Management Team, John Wiley & Sons, 1997.

CHAPTER 10

1   In PricewaterhouseCoopers (PwC) Consulting Executive Survey 2002.
2   In an interview with the author, April 2002.
3   In PwC Consulting Executive Survey 2002.
4   Gerber, Michael, *The E-Myth Manager: Why Management Doesn't Work — and What to do About it*, Harperbusiness, 1999.
5   In an interview with the author, April 2002.
6   In PwC Consulting Executive Survey 2002.
7   In an interview with the author, May 2002.
8   In PwC Consulting Executive Survey 2002.
9   Gilley, J.W., "Career Development as a Partnership", in *Personnel Administrator* 33, no. 4, (1988), pp.62–68.
10 In an interview with the author, March 2002.
11 Bolleteri, Nick, *Bolleteri's Tennis Handbook*, Human Kinetics, 2001, p.280.
12 In PwC Consulting Executive Survey 2002.

CHAPTER 11

1   Battram, Arthur, *Navigating Complexity*, The Industrial Society, 1998, p.59.
2   In an interview with the author, March 2002.
3   In PricewaterhouseCoopers (PwC) Consulting Executive Survey 2002.
4   In an interview with the author, March 2002.
5   Peters, Tom, *The Pursuit of Wow*, Vintage Books, 1994.
6   Covey, Stephen, *Principle — Centred Leadership*, Fireside-Simon & Schuster, 1990, p.217.
7   In PwC Consulting Executive Summary 2002.
8   Courtenay, B., *The Power of One*, Ballantine Books, 1996.

Chapter 12

1   In PricewaterhouseCoopers (PwC) Consulting Executive Survey 2002.
2   In *Winning Attitudes*, op.cit, p.104.
3   NASA, in Strategic Plan 2000, www.nasa.gov
4   Australian Olympic Committee, excerpt from Team Handbook 2000 Olympic Games Sydney
5   Riley, Pat, *The Winner Within*, Berkley Business, 1993.
6   In PwC Consulting Executive Survey 2002.
7   Ibid.
8   Ibid.
9   Ibid.
10 Gilson, C., et al, *Peak Performance, Business lessons from the world's top sporting organizations*, HarperCollins, 2000, p.33.
11 Weisbord, Marvin and Janoff, Sandra, *Future Search: An action guide to finding common ground in organizations and communities*, Berrett-Koehler Publishers, 2000.
12 Benedict-Bunker, Barbara and Alban, Billy T., *Large Group Interventions: Engaging the whole system for rapid change*, Jossey-Bass, 1997.
13 Ibid.
14 Hillman, James, *Kinds of Power, An intelligent guide to its uses*, Currency DoubleDay, 1995.
15 Hemingway, Ernest, *The Old Man and the Sea*, Arrow Books, 1993, p.5.
16 In PwC Consulting Executive Survey 2002.
17 Bennis, Warren, (Ed) Preface to *Coach to Coach: Business Lessons from the Locker Room*, Pfeiffer Company, 1996.

Chapter 13

1   In PricewaterhouseCoopers (PwC) Consulting Executive Survey 2002.
2   From "The Energy of Leadership" in *Wisdom of the CEO*, PricewaterhouseCoopers, 2000, p.170.
3   In PwC Consulting Executive Survey 2002.
4   Purdy, C. and Koshnitsky, G., *Chess Made Easy*, Penguin Books, 1992.
5   Belbin, Meredith, *Management Teams: Why they succeed and fail*, Butterworth-Heinemann, Oxford, 1981.
6   In an interview with the author, April 2002.

Chapter 14

1   McNair, D.M., Lorr M. and Dropplemann, L.F., *Profile of Mood States*, San Diego Educational & Industrial Testing Service, 1971.
2   Larsen, Ralph, "Decentralisation is the crucible of growth", in *Wisdom of the CEO*, op. cit., p.153.

3   "The Day the Music Died", by Francis Gouillart, in *Journal of Business Strategy*, May 1995.

4   In an interview with the author, March 2002.

5   In an interview with the author, April 2002.

6   Charlesworth, Ric, *The Coach*, MacMillan, 2001, p.19.

7   Kern, Dr Tony, *Flight Discipline*, McGraw-Hill Professional Publishing, 1998.

8   Heinecke, William, *The Entrepreneur*, John Wiley & Sons, 2002, p.62.

9   In PWC Consulting Executive Survey 2002.

10   In an interview with the author, April 2002.

11   Ibid.

12   Gluyas, Richard, *Weekend Australian*, News Ltd, March 30–31, 2002, p.29.

13   Charlesworth, op. cit.

CHAPTER 15

1   In an interview with the author, April 2002.

2   In PwC Consulting Executive Survey 2002.

3   In an interview with the author, April 2002.

4   In an interview with the author, March 2002.

5   Handy, Charles, *The Age of Unreason*, Harvard Business School Press, 1998.

CHAPTER 16

1   Crichton, Michael, *Jurassic Park*, Arrow Books, 1991, p.60.

2   English, M. & Robertson, D., in *Make it Happen, but Fast*, PricewaterhouseCoopers, 1999, p.10.

3   Ibid., p.8.

4   Idei, Nobuyuki, "Teams on Fire: Sony's Innovation Culture" in *Wisdom of the CEO*, PricewaterhouseCoopers, 2000, p.292.

5   In PricewaterhouseCoopers (PwC) Consulting Executive Survey 2002.

6   In an interview with the author, April 2002.

7   In an interview with the author, April 2002.

8   In PwC Consulting Executive Survey 2002.

9   Ibid.

10   In an interview with the author, April 2002.

11   Weinstein, Krystyna, *Action Learning, A practical guide*, Gower, 2nd edition 1999.

12   In an interview with the author, 2002.

13   Gardner, Howard, *The Unschooled Mind*, Basic Books, 1991.

14   Gerber, Michael E., *The E-Myth*, Harper Business, 1986.

15   In *The Advertiser*, April 5, 2002, p.17.

16   In an interview with the author, April 2002.

CHAPTER 17

1   Quoted in "Children of the Revolution" by Rochelle Burbury, *The Australian Financial Review*, March 2002, p.30.

2   Roddick, Anita, *Body and Soul*, Vermilion, 1992, p.242.

3   In an interview with the author, March 2002.

4   Quoted in *Winning Attitudes*, Heads, I. and Armstrong, G. (Eds), Hardie Grant Books: Australian Olympic Committee, 2000, p.36.

CHAPTER 18

1   Evans, Philip, and Wuster, Thomas, *Blown to Bits*, Harvard Business School Press 2000, p.228.

2   In *Wisdom of the CEO*, PricewaterhouseCoopers, Wiley 2000, p.73.

3   Goodes, Melvin R., "Transforming the culture of the global enterprise … one employee at a time", in *Straight from the CEO*, Dauphinais, G.W. & Price, C. (Eds), Nicholas Brealey Publishing 1998, p.191.

4   Bijur, Peter I. "The Energy of leadership" in *Wisdom of the CEO*, op. cit., p.169.

5   In an interview with the author, March 2002.

6   In PricewaterhouseCoopers Consulting Executive Survey 2002.

7   Interviewed in *Winning Attitudes*, op. cit., p.100.

8   Flett, Neil, *Pitch Doctor: Presenting to win multi-million-dollar accounts*, Prentice Hall, 1996, p.70.

9   In *Winning Attitudes*, op. cit., p.106.

10 Veenelakas, Justus, in "Reinventing Philips DownUnder: Customers seek systems solutions, Not Black Boxes", in *Straight from the CEO*, op. cit., p.259.

11 In an interview with the author, April 2002.

12 Jackson, Phil, *Sacred Hoops: Spiritual Lessons of a Hardwood Warrior*, Hyperion, 1996.

Index

Confidence 43, 69, 84, 93, 172, 187, 203, 216–224, 228, 247, 249, 250, 252, 257, 360, 368, 380, 382, 383, 386, 389

Consequences 28, 80, 92, 93, 179, 185, 189, 190, 259, 296, 298, 309, 323, 340, 350, 351, 355, 357, 358, 385–387, 389

Covey, Steven 68

Csikszentmihalyi, Mihaly 43

Culture 13, 14, 17, 20, 21, 33, 44, 50, 74, 86, 131, 163, 166, 168–170, 185, 186, 188, 189, 195, 199, 205, 211, 216, 221, 223–225, 232, 233, 247, 248, 255, 261, 265, 269, 270, 280, 283, 284, 288, 290–292, 296, 301, 302, 304, 307, 308, 313, 321, 327, 329, 336–340, 346, 349, 352, 356, 357–361, 363–389, 391, 398, 399

Customer Relationships Management (CRM) 241

D

Dauphinais, W 26, 393, 394, 395, 399

Davis, Reg 256

Debriefing/performance debriefing 81, 87, 114, 115, 171, 189, 277, 332–335, 340, 383–385, 389

De Coubertin, Baron Pierre 61

Dell 127, 314, 330, 364

Dell, Michael 364

Designed for Fitness 285

Detmold Packaging 278

Development Coach 32, 33, 177, 178, 189–192, 195, 196, 199, 210, 318, 334, 358, 385, 389

Discipline 21, 22, 28, 52, 69, 71, 84, 85, 92, 103, 131, 146, 152, 186, 187, 190, 193, 197, 211, 223, 236, 242, 296, 304, 308, 309, 340, 341, 345, 367, 384, 393, 398

Disruptive technology 10, 307

Domingo, Placido 63

E

80/20 101, 102, 323, 380

Elite Sport Properties 128

Elliott, Herb 63, 257

Ellis, Stuart 302, 304, 335, 379

English Matt 329

Mental energy 53, 109, 110, 112, 113, 115, 117

English Matt 329

Evans, Philip 363

Everest 18, 20, 33, 48, 51, 74, 139, 176, 231, 236–239, 242–245, 251, 259, 261, 313, 320, 333, 367, 391

F

Facilitation 242, 272

Fast break 97, 98, 100

Fast teams 303, 320, 321, 375, 382, 388, 389

Feedback, Performance feedback 261, 341

Fitzgerald, Niall 9

Five-level design 289, 290

Fletcher, John 307

Flett, Neil 379

Flock 285, 286

Flow 41, 43, 44, 72, 104, 107, 116, 122, 147, 191, 258, 274, 284, 295, 353, 367, 383, 384, 394

Ford, Professor Bill 5, 180, 217, 338

Formula One 62, 105, 116, 168, 252, 310, 356

Freeman, Cathy 251

Fritz, Robert 49

G

Games, finite and infinite 329, 393

Gandhi, Mahatma 391

Garai, Hugh 103

Gardner, Howard 343

Garland, Shane 102, 184, 198

Gates, Bill 5, 132

Gerber, Michael 182, 344